司公德買莫

REGD. No 130695.

BOUSTEAD & Cº. LTD

TALES FROM THE SOUTH CHINA SEAS

What shall we tell you? Tales, marvellous tales
Of ships and stars and isles where good men rest.

J. L. Flecker, *The Golden Road to Samarkand*

TALES FROM THE SOUTH CHINA SEAS

IMAGES OF THE BRITISH
IN SOUTH-EAST ASIA
IN THE TWENTIETH CENTURY

EDITED BY

Charles Allen

In association with Michael Mason

INTRODUCTION BY SJOVALD CUNYNGHAM-BROWN

ANDRE DEUTSCH

BRITISH BROADCASTING CORPORATION

First published 1983 by
André Deutsch Limited
105 Great Russell Street London WC1
ISBN 0 233 97504 7

and the British Broadcasting Corporation
35 Marylebone High Street London W1
ISBN 0 563 20032 4

Typeset by Phoenix Photosetting Chatham
Printed in Great Britain by
Mackays of Chatham Ltd

CONTENTS

LIST OF ILLUSTRATIONS

The four sisters
Household servants
Rafting on the Bernam River

Other illustrations

Trade marks on dust-jacket, end-papers and elsewhere courtesy of
  J. W. Hooton, Esq. and Boustead PLC.
Photograph on dust-jacket (back) courtesy of Alan Morkill, Esq.
Stamps courtesy of Lt-Col. M. G. Allen
Letter of appointment courtesy of Guy Madoc, Esq.
Cartoons from *Straits Produce* courtesy of the Royal
  Commonwealth Society
Letter refusing permission to marry courtesy of a gentleman who
  wishes to remain anonymous
Letter giving permission to marry courtesy of Anthony Richards,
  Esq.

PREFACE

Tales from the South China Seas is the final part of what might be
called an Imperial trilogy, one that began with *Plain Tales from the
Raj* and continued with *Tales from the Dark Continent*. Originally
commissioned by the Controller of Radio 4, and broadcast on BBC
Radio 4 as oral history documentaries, these three volumes contain
fragments from Britain's colonial past, mosaics shaped from the
spoken words of ordinary men and women who lived through the
last fifty years of the British Empire. So perhaps the word 'tales' is a
misnomer – and yet, as one contributor to the present volume
states, 'there was certainly a very great drama in the way we were
living when I first went out there'. This drama affected the lives of
many more British families than is generally supposed. 'So many
Englishmen gave their hearts and very often their health and their
lives,' declares that same contributor, adding 'It is a very great grief
to me that so much of this is not known to the young people of
today – and that a great deal of it has been forgotten.'

The first of these colonial mosaics took its inspiration from
Rudyard Kipling, whose *Plain Tales from the Hills* gave the world
its first inside view of Anglo-India and the British Raj. Michael
Mason's masterly radio programmes, first broadcast in 1975, and
the book that followed evoked that same ordered, complex society
in its last years – and perhaps in doing so showed that India's *koi
hais* and *memsahibs* were not quite the stuffed shirts and frivolous
creatures that popular opinion had made them out to be.

Tales from the Dark Continent carried the voices of the British in
Africa, concentrating on the District Officer, the often lonely
instrument of British colonial rule in the African bush. And here
again, a more sympathetic image of the real-life counterparts of
Edgar Wallace's fictional *Sanders of the River* seems to have
emerged.

Now *Tales from the South China Seas* – assembled from the
taped recollections of fifty men and women who spent the greater
part of their adult lives in one or other of the former British colonial
territories, settlements, protectorates and concessions that once ran
along the fringes of the South China Sea. Most of these 'survivors'
from Britain's colonial past went out in the 1920s and 1930s to such
places as the Straits Settlements of Penang and Province Wellesley,

Malacca, Singapore, Labuan, Christmas Island and the *Dindings* of Perak; the Federated Malay States of Perak, Selangor, Negri Sembilan and Pahang; the Unfederated Malay States of Kelantan, Trengganu, Kedah, Perlis and Johore; the Brooke family's Rajahdom of Sarawak; the British North Borneo Company's chartered territory of North Borneo; and, in passing, Shanghai, Canton and other less well-known treaty ports or concessions along the Chinese coast.

Here the central theme is no longer that of one supremely successful (in colonial terms) racial minority imposing itself upon a rather unsuccessful (again, speaking in colonial terms) majority – as in Africa and India – but of several races drawn to the same watery crossroads principally by the lure of trade; competing as rivals but co-existing more or less as equals. The central image is now a shifting one: of sea panoramas in place of great continental land-masses; of islands and archipelagos and casuarina-fringed sands backed by impenetrable rain forest. From Kipling and Edgar Wallace we have moved on to the uncertain, sea-girt world of Joseph Conrad and Somerset Maugham.

No writer echoes more exactly the cadences of the orient than Conrad the sailor, or wrote so well about the strange passion for trade that 'seemed to burn like a flame of love in the breasts of Dutch and English adventurers', driving them eastwards generation after generation to the Indies and beyond. But it was Somerset Maugham, using South-East Asia as a backdrop for his suburban melodramas and aided and abetted by Noel Coward, who gave us our public image of the British in the Far East as a fast, hard-drinking, socially and morally second-rate set ('A first-rate country for second-rate people'). In later years Maugham made some effort to set the record straight but the popular image undoubtedly persists. Perhaps this book will help to show what life was really like in the Malayan archipelago for the seafarers, traders, planters, tin-miners and government servants, and for their wives and children.

I have concentrated on the period between the wars, going back as far as living memory allows. My oldest contributor is Alan Morkill, born in 1890, who joined the Malayan Civil Service in 1913 and served in the newly-created Unfederated Malay State of Kelantan. He represents the last of the pioneer administrators of Malaya, being part of that first wave of Britons who helped establish British rule in the Malayan peninsula. By contrast, the youngest contributor was born almost forty years later, one of four daughters born to a rubber planter in the 1920s. Susan Whitley's childhood experiences, along with those of her three sisters, are recounted in Chapter 10, in the same form in which they were originally broadcast.

Such matters as upbringing and background, details of public administration and day-to-day routine are part of the common ground of the British colonial experience and have already been chronicled either in *Plain Tales from the Raj* or *Tales from the Dark Continent*. In this final volume I have focussed on what appear to me to be the unique features of British rule in South-East Asia – that curious (to modern sensibilities) relationship between the different races, the striking contrast between life in the big towns and life up-river in what was known as the *ulu,* the Sarawak of the White Rajahs, the planter's life and the sea captain's life on the little steamers that plied the archipelago – and, inescapably, that terrible Nemesis that we now see hanging over this most peaceful corner of the British Empire as the Thirties drew to a close.

It was here in the South China Seas that the disintegration of that Empire really began, with the fall of Hong Kong to the Japanese forces on Christmas Day 1941 and the surrender of 'Fortress Singapore' just six weeks later. These events and the traumatic years that followed affected directly and often cruelly the lives of all those who have contributed to this book. This was not only the last chapter of British rule in South-East Asia but also, for the great majority, the last chapter in their working lives. For this reason I have extended this last of three volumes of what is essentially social history to include at least a part of their experiences of the war years and a little of what followed in the years leading up to *Merdeka* (Independence).

This extension of the book's natural scope has been bought at the expense of all those others who so kindly allowed me to interview them for the BBC, both in Malaysia and in Britain – and including quite a number of persons who had lived for many years in China. I have drawn on only one of these China interviews: Captain Robert Williamson's account of four years as Ship's Master on the Upper Yangtse from 1921 to 1924; an experience so remarkable – indeed, so utterly Conradesque – that I have felt impelled to include at least a part of his story in Chapter 8. China – and the British in China – demands a book on its own, which my colleague Christopher Cook will be supplying.

Similarly, there were interviews with a number of Malaysians that I have not been able to include. Theirs is the other side of the story and one that (as with India and Africa) is still waiting to be told.

Tales from the South China Seas makes no attempt to confront the political issues of colonialism. It is a book first and foremost about a group of ordinary people placed in what many of us would regard as extraordinary places and times. As before, I have confined

myself simply to recording on tape and on paper something of the
tenor of their lives, placing them and their beliefs in the context of
the times in which they lived and worked. Within this framework I
have retained a colonial sense of geography and spelling, with a
glossary to explain the latter at the back of the book. Similarly, I
have referred to my witnesses in the text as they were known then;
brief details of their circumstances will be found in the appended
notes on contributors.

Whatever their backgrounds and experiences these witnesses all
exercised power in some form in South-East Asia and may be fairly
regarded as representatives of their age. Accordingly, I have not
always identified quotations when reporting widely-held views or
common experiences, and the spoken words of my contributors
have been assembled and edited as inter-related parts of a whole.
For ease of reading I have made very minor amendments and added
conjunctions, but wherever possible excerpts have been quoted as
they were spoken. I have also limited myself to expressing only
those views and opinions that were stated in the original recorded
material. For this and the way in which extracts have been selected
and assembled, the responsibility is entirely mine. The end result is
my own interpretation but I hope it can still claim to be a fair and
faithful reanimation of the spirit of an age and a generation that I
greatly respect.

Neither this reconstruction nor its companion radio series would
have been possible without the fullest co-operation, candour and
generosity of those who were good enough to let me interview them
for the BBC. A great many extended help to me in other ways,
allowing me access to their photographs and mementoes (some of
which are included in this book) and offering me advice and suggestions. I would especially like to thank Sjovald Cunyngham-Brown,
who not only looked after me on the lovely island of Penang but has
most generously written an 'insider's' *Introduction* to this book –
providing a very salutary counter-balance of direct personal experience to my own impressions of other people's experiences; also Tan
Sri Dato Mubin Sheppard, who opened many doors for me in
Selangor and Negri Sembilan and did his best to diminish my
ignorance of the Malaysian scene; Raja Toh Puan Teh Zaitun, who
performed the same kind offices in Malacca; Dato Haji Mohamed
Yusuf Bangs in Kota Bharu, who showed me what the 'real'
Malaya of pre-war years might have been like; Datuk John Baxter
in Sabah and many others who in one way or another helped to
make my brief field-trip through Malaysia a most memorable
experience. To all these contributors and friends, both in the UK
and in Malaysia, I offer my deepest appreciation and thanks,

together with the hope that they will find in this book something to justify and reward their kindness.

My thanks are also due to the following for their most valuable advice and assistance: Mrs J. André, Wendy Barnes, Mrs Alice Berry-Hart, John Behague, Mrs Kathleen Clark, W. J. V. Cook, John Falconer, Enid Fernandes, Lady Goode, Will Garforth, Jenny Hogg, J. W. Hooton, A. H. P. Humphrey, H. M. Ismail, Stephanie Jones, Ian Macdonald, Campbell Macmurray, John McLeod, Mrs Hedda Morrison, Carl Openshaw, Alan Reid, D. Simpson, C. D. Stempson, Mrs Penelope Stevens, Alasdair Thompson, Lorna Tokeley, Commander Michael Wall, E. G. Waller, Major Idris Williams, John Willoughby, the *Illustrated London News*, the School of Oriental and African Studies, the Royal Commonwealth Society, the Overseas Pensioners Association, Barlow and Son, the Boustead Group, the Inchcape Group, the Guthrie Corporation, Harrison and Crosfield, the Malaysian Airline System, Ocean Transport and Trading and (for her always impeccable typing) Mrs Alice Rockwell.

Lastly, my special thanks to two old and trusted friends; Faith Evans, who has worked closely with me as editor of all three *Tales,* and my associate editor and the producer of *Tales from the South China Seas,* Michael Mason. Although best-known for such radio epics as *The Long March of Everyman, Plain Tales from the Raj* and *The British Seafarer,* Michael Mason's producership has over the last two decades covered an extraordinary range of programmes, all distinguished by an immensely skilful and sensitive touch. It would be impossible to conclude this final preface of our 'tales' – ending, as it began, as a thoroughly happy partnership – without acknowledging in some small part the immense contribution to radio (and to oral history in particular) that he has made.

INTRODUCTION

SJOVALD CUNYNGHAM-BROWN

IN Malay a *rentis* is a straight cutting through the jungle from which the land and its vegetation can be seen and explored. One must admire the *rentis* that Charles Allen has cut through the tangled mass of facts – often contradictory, generally uncertain and always stealthily shifting – that represented life in the pre-war Far Eastern territories that had fallen at one time or another under the paramount influence of Britain. Such a *rentis* must by its very nature be narrow, or the whole panorama would become incomprehensible, and in this case success has been achieved by selecting a number of representative eye-witnesses. The result is the truest account I have yet come across of how 'good, honest, English people', as Somerset Maugham describes them, passed their working lives in that part of the world that lies around the South China Sea. Allen's good humour and patience, in all sorts of outlandish places, encouraged us – his raw material – to 'give more than we thought we had in us', and his book will go a long way towards 'setting the record straight' for future generations.

Tales from the South China Seas has given me the chance to relive and relish again the excitement of meeting for the first time the 'Flaming East' in all its gross materialism and its shabby and intricate grandeur, and to savour once again its overmastering allure. Many a giggle, too, keeps breaking through as I recall such episodes as Norman Cleaveland's hilarious bathroom misadventure (which reminds me of the girl who similarly mistook the bathroom *tong* or water jar for an actual bath, squeezed herself in and got stuck, so that she had to be most 'naked and ashamed'-ly broken out); or Nancy Madoc instructing her head houseboy to 'pee on this' and 'pee on that' instead of 'lock this' and 'lock that'; and the frightful scene (which I shall never live down) of the Magistrate on the Bench in Singapore blatantly committing an act of Indecent Exposure! Such and other follies enliven the book as they enlivened the pre-war days of the hardworking but indomitably light-hearted sons and daughters of Britain out East.

And over all, as one reads, there spans the enormous Asian sky; nostrils fill again with the renewed peaty, fruity reek of Asia and the heart once more throbs with excitement at being associated in the attempt to build, in this great 'involution' of the world, the first slender, tentative bridges of understanding and affection between the ancient races of the Far East and the Western peoples. We were lucky, because we were living amongst a most attractive population of many races in one of the most beautiful parts of the world; which is certainly one of the reasons why everybody loved the life and why our mutual relationships both before and after Independence have been so successful.

But there are other reasons. First of all, ever since the East India Company first made trade arrangements with the rulers and chiefs of Western Sumatra in 1658, right up to the moment of Malaya's Independence in 1957, Britain's motives throughout East Asia had been *commercial* ones. Her territorial ambitions were strictly limited. Whenever Parliament was reluctantly forced to protect its trade-routes by approving the acquisition of some small but strategically important island, cape or corner of foreign soil, it was in all cases with the consent of the local ruler. There are many instances, but one need only think of the Rulers of Johore in 1707 offering Singapore to Captain Hamilton – and the offer being politely declined for lack of supporting authority from the East India Company; or the Dutch East Indies, a vast Empire which had come into the control of Britain during the Napoleonic War, being quietly handed back to Holland once the war was over; or, most significantly of all, of Queen Victoria's far-sighted instructions to Disraeli in 1874 regarding the Malay States to 'bring on the peoples of these countries to the stage where they can govern themselves.'

This was one of the most remarkable statements imaginable at that period and was, so far as I know, the first time that Britain had ever so clearly defined its imperial responsibilities in South-East Asia. Indeed, it was still being impressed on us in 1929, when we were under training at the School of Oriental Studies at Finsbury Circus, that we were among those destined to 'bring on' the countries of the Malayan peninsula to self-government.

I arrived as part of the third wave of administrators. The first, from 1875, had been the 'pioneers'. After about 1900, when they retired, there came the 'consolidators', laying down the laws, making the roads, building the railways, starting the schools, hospitals, health services and every aspect of government. This great work was done largely by the second generation, and we who followed were no more than 'polishers', adding the final touches to the work that had already been so expertly planned and begun. In short, a mere three generations separated 1875 from 1957, the year in which Britain granted complete independence to the united and brilliantly prosperous new countries of Malaya and Singapore. Within that short span these two lands, together with Sabah and Sarawak (soon to join Malaya to form the present Federation of Malaysia) had been transformed from warring medieval states into the most peaceful and progressive democracies in South-East Asia. Such things cannot be achieved by domination, but only by the closest and most friendly of working relationships.

Looking back over forty-odd years to 1941 and the 'Madhatter's Tea Party' of our rout from peninsular Malaya by the Japanese, followed by the debacle of Singapore's surrender and all that followed from it, it is highly refreshing to find that this book does not necessarily agonize or produce for us a positive Grand Guignol of horrors. As it comes from the mouths of survivors, there is much resilient good humour – if at times accompanied by a toothless grin.

To my mind one of the best things we learned then was the depth of sympathy and good feeling on the part of all races of Malaysia and Singapore toward the Europeans in their time of appalling trouble. Their friendliness was something that one perhaps tended to take for granted in time of peace, but when all the chips were down their endless acts and gestures of kindness – often at the risk of their own very lives – supported and encouraged us over the years of slavery. They are the best evidence possible of the generosity and courageous spirit of the people of South-East Asia, as well as evidence that in winning their friendship the British people out East could not have done so badly.

If this book conveys these impressions to the reader's mind, as it does to mine, then it will have achieved its goal not only of entertaining but also of telling a true story.

George Town, Penang

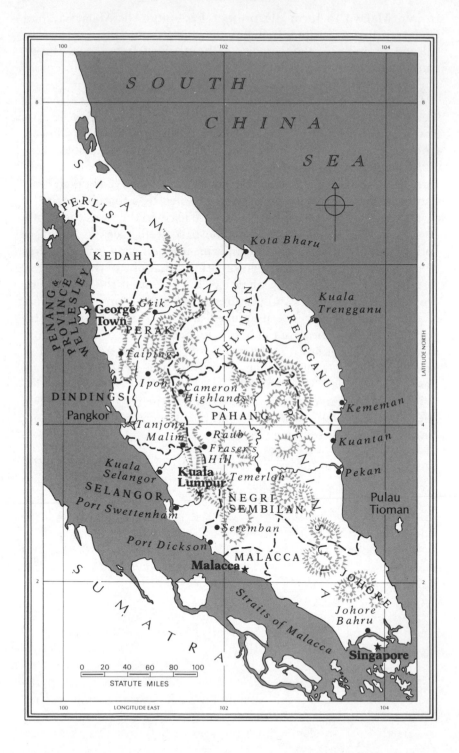

SOUTH

CHINA

SEA

S I A M

PERLIS

KEDAH

Kota Bharu

PENANG & PROVINCE WELLESLEY

George Town

Grik

PERAK

Kuala Trengganu

Taiping

KELANTAN

TRENGGANU

Ipoh

Cameron Highlands

DINDINGS

Pangkor

PAHANG

Kememan

Tanjong Malim

Raub

Fraser's Hill

Kuantan

Kuala Selangor

Kuala Lumpur

Temerloh

Pekan

SELANGOR

NEGRI SEMBILAN

Pulau Tioman

Port Swettenham

Seremban

Port Dickson

MALACCA

S U M A T R A

Malacca

JOHORE

Johore Bahru

Straits of Malacca

Singapore

LATITUDE NORTH

0 20 40 60 80 100

STATUTE MILES

THE FIRST SIGH
OF THE EAST

*Suddenly a puff of wind, a puff faint and tepid and
laden with strange odours of blossoms, of aromatic
wood, comes out of the still night – the first sigh of
the East on my face. That I can never forget. It was
impalpable and enslaving, like a charm, like a
whispered promise of mysterious delight.*

Joseph Conrad, *Youth*

To young Britons born in the early years of this century the East
was a mysterious and exotic place. Even in childhood its call was
sometimes irresistible. Bill Bangs, destined to become a rubber
planter and a Muslim, collected stamps as a boy and was always
drawn to the Federated Malay States' stamp which showed a leaping
tiger, telling himself, 'That's the country I want to go to.' As a child
of four or five, Anthony Richards had a retreat in the shrubbery of
his parents' country parsonage which he called 'Sarawak': 'I can
only suppose that the name was picked up from some newspaper
report that the Second Rajah had died. He died in 1917 and I dare
say that the papers contained quite a lot about Sarawak which I got
second-hand.' Twenty years later he would be embarking on the
Straits steamship *Rajah Vyner Brooke* at Singapore, bound for the
Sarawak Civil Service.

Other children were similarly imbued with romantic notions of
life in the East. Reared on a diet of Kipling, Derek Headley had
determined from an early age that India was to be the place for him,
while as a teenager Edward Tokeley found himself torn between
India and China: 'I had to make up my mind what I was going to do
and I was introduced to a lovely old man who was a retiring partner
in Bousteads in Malaya. I was sent out to dinner with him one night
and when he'd finished telling me about these gin-clear seas and

golden sands, and the waving casuarina trees, and the gorgeous, dusky girls with their *sarongs* and *kebayas*, I said, "Where is this place?"'

Then there were those with colonial connections in the family, who hoped when they grew up to follow in their fathers' or uncles' footsteps. John Forrester's father had captained tea clippers on the China run, Richard Broome's was a surgeon in the Indian Medical Service, Peter Lucy's uncle had been a ship's doctor before becoming a Medical Officer in Malaya: 'The ship called in at Singapore and they played cricket against Singapore Cricket Club. My uncle made a hundred and the Governor said, "You're the sort of man we want in the Malayan Service".'

What all these young men had in common was a British middle-class background. Like so many of their contemporaries in the Twenties and Thirties who were to take up careers in the Far East or South-East Asia, they came mostly from country homes and from the public schools, where 'the idea of service wasn't imposed on you but was intrinsic'. They found themselves subject to the traditions of their generation, which meant, in Guy Madoc's case, that his elder brother went into the armed services, 'while I, as the younger son, was expected to go overseas and make my fortune'. A career in the East, whether in government or business, offered a standard of living that could not always be guaranteed at home. And it seemed particularly attractive to those who, like Cecil Lee in 1933, had left school without any particular qualifications and without private means: 'If you wanted to be a lawyer or an accountant in those days you had to pay a premium. So the mercantile firms and the Asiatic Petroleum Company and the banks were an outlet for you. The fathers and friends of others used to say, "Go East, young man" – that was the sort of cry.'

A career in the East also offered an outlet for men like Bill Harrison, who had survived three years in the trenches in the Great War: 'I wanted to escape from offices, factories, streets of houses and the general hubbub of life in England. I was looking forward to another kind of adventure – to seeing foreign places, climbing mountains, sailing up rivers and exploring.' He had already qualified as a mining engineer before the war but with demobilization found 'millions of men of my age also looking for employment – so I was glad to have the first offer that came along'. Within a few months of the ending of the war he was prospecting for tin in the jungles of Malaya and Siam.

There were many others like Harrison for whom chance played the decisive role in shaping their futures. It was a casual encounter on a train that led John Theophilus to become a rubber planter:

I was going down to my parents in Hampshire and I had to change at Basingstoke Station, where I saw an extremely attractive young lady. When she got into the train I got into the same carriage. She couldn't run away because there was no corridor and in the course of the journey I got her name and address in Devonshire. And as soon as I got home I wrote to her, after which we used to meet in London quite frequently. After a few months she said, 'You're not getting very much pay here' – I was on thirty shillings a week. She had a lot of relations who were out in Malaya and so she spoke to one of them who arranged for me to have an interview with a rubber company, which I did in late '25.

Robert 'Perky' Perkins had a similarly fateful chance meeting:

In about Christmas 1928 I met the father of an old friend of mind and I said, 'Where's Archie?' – that was his son. 'Oh, Archie's gone out to Malaya.' And I thought of the Malay pirates with their little crinkly daggers. 'What's he doing there?' 'Rubber planting.' I thought of Archie walking along throwing seeds into the ground along set rows. 'He's having a wonderful time,' his father said. Well, I was going in for mining engineering at the time and I didn't like it much so I said, 'How did he get the job?' He says, 'You just go up to London. They're looking for new people.' So I went up to the address he gave me and a fortnight later there I was, on my way out to Malaya on the *Malwa*.

For Edward Banks, who in 1925 had just completed his degree at Oxford, it was a spur of the moment decision that decided his future: 'There were a number of my colleagues at a meeting wanting jobs and a professor said, "Well, they need a curator out in Rajah Brooke's museum in Sarawak. Does anybody want the job?" One of my colleagues said, "No, I don't want the job." And I said, "Well, I'll have it" – not knowing anything about it. I didn't even know where the place was.' In due course Banks was interviewed by the brother of the Rajah – 'a charming old gentleman' – and got the job.

The interview constituted the only real hurdle that the great majority of applicants for jobs overseas had to face. Whether for the government services or the business firms these interviews tended to follow the same pattern: 'They wanted athletic people and as long as you could play games and mix with people that was the sort of person they wanted.' But background and schooling were also important: 'There's no doubt at all that in those days they were only choosing people from public school backgrounds. They wanted

people who'd already experienced a degree of leadership through
being a praepositor in the school, from service in the Officer's
Training Corps and the like. And they certainly wanted people who
were accustomed to an open-air life.' Being good at games counted
for a lot more than academic ability: 'They asked the sort of questions which nowadays a lot of people sneer at. You ask a chap if he
plays games. If he does and he's got a reasonable academic record as
well, you're not going to go far wrong, because chaps who are good
at games are usually well-orientated overall.'

The larger rubber companies, in particular, took the sporting
ethic very seriously. In the years before the slump in 1929 two of
the biggest trading concerns in South-East Asia were Dunlops and
Guthries, and both companies took on players of international standard to play in their respective rugby teams. One, a former England
cap, started with Guthries but proved to be a better sportsman than
he was a rubber planter. 'He took to drink and was sacked,' recalls
John Theophilus, 'but he was such a good rugger player that Dunlops took him. Unfortunately, he still continued his habits so off he
went.' Theophilus himself has no doubts as to why his first job
interview with a Dunlops director went off so well: 'He asked me
one or two questions as to where I'd been born and what my parents
were and so on and then he said, "What's that tie you've got on?" I
said, "It's the Harlequin Rugby Club, sir." And he said, "You'll get
some rugger out there" – and that was my interview.'

Some of the larger Eastern trading houses, as well as the two
major banks – the Hongkong and Shanghai (the 'H&S' or the
'Honkers and Shankers') and the Chartered – were rather more
selective. The 'nicest' people were said to go to Bousteads and the
Asiatic Petroleum Company: 'We weren't snobbish about it but we
used to say without any doubt at all – and we never found anybody
in Malaya or Singapore who would disagree – that the chaps you
found in Bousteads and APC were the best of all.' Gerald Scott was
one of those who was soon to find that 'APC was a password to the
whole of the Far East. Wherever you went you just signed your
name and put APC after it. There was a certain arrogance. When
you were picked up on it you said, "But I'm APC".' Guthries, on
the other hand, was traditionally a Scots firm and most of its planters were Scots – who regarded their rivals in such firms as Bousteads as having 'not much topside and a lot of old school tie'.

Where academic ability did count was in the selection of administrators. Appointment to what were known as the 'Eastern
Cadetships' was by examination as well as interview and only open
to graduates. The Public Services Examination governed entry into
the Diplomatic and Home Civil Services, the Indian Civil Service

and the Eastern Cadetships, with selection based strictly on merit. As far as the overseas services were concerned there was an unofficial but clearly established hierarchy: 'The ICS was the supreme service, only the best people could get through. Then there were three Eastern Cadetships – Ceylon, Hong Kong and Malaya – and that was really the order of batting, with Malaya regarded as the least worthy of the three.'

Sjovald Cunyngham-Brown sat for the week-long exam in 1928 with the intention of entering the Consular Service. He passed high enough to enter – only to be told that there was a three-year waiting list:

> At the same time I learned that I could join the Indian Civil Service or the – to me – hitherto unknown services known as the Eastern Cadetships. My uncles and friends who had been or were in the Indian Services said: 'Don't join the ICS, old boy, because it'll be Indianized a considerable time before you're due for retirement.' I said, 'Well, what about the Eastern Cadetships?' Their eyes brightened at once. They said, 'Good God, if you're offered that, take it. The great island empires of the East. The Eastern archipelago, Malaya, half unexplored; a land of adventure: beautiful people, charming surroundings, tigers, elephants. And further east those wonderful islands; Bali, Sumatra, Java. All the riches of the East, loaded with romance and with things still worthwhile doing. Take it if you get the chance.'

Sitting the examination three years later William Goode found that he too was a victim of political change:

> There was only one vacancy for Ceylon and I wanted to go there because I had relatives who'd been in the Ceylon Service. When the results came out and we were called up for our medical interview, I remember complaining in a very loud voice that there was only one vacancy for Ceylon this year and some bloody black man had taken it, and a voice came from behind me and said, 'Yes, it's me, and what's worse, I come from Cambridge' – I being an Oxford man. It was a very nice man from Cambridge who later became very distinguished in the Ceylon Civil Service.

A generation earlier Alan Morkill had also been forced to settle for what he had at first regarded as second best, when he joined the Malayan Civil Service (MCS): 'The state of my knowledge about Malaya was absolutely nil. So I took my mother to Kew to find out what the climate was like. We went into the first greenhouse which was nice and cool, the next one was a little bit warmer but very nice and then finally we got into a place where the steam on our glasses made it difficult to see. But we saw a palm marked *Federated Malay States*. "Alan, you can't go to a country like that!" she said.'

There was widespread ignorance about conditions overseas. As John Baxter left the London offices of his future employer after a successful interview, he met an old school friend: 'He said, "Hullo John, what are you doing?" And I said, "I've just got a job in North Borneo." He said, "Where's that?" I said, "I'm going off to get a map to see."' There were others whose knowledge of South-East Asia came principally from the works of Somerset Maugham, notably a popular film from a play of his called 'The Letter', which was based on a notorious case of adultery and murder that took place in Kuala Lumpur in 1911.

But knowledge was less important than youthful enthusiasm. 'We were young men going off abroad, doing what we wanted to do,' was how John Davis remembers the mood at the time. 'We had no idea of what we were going to do – and I cannot honestly remember that worrying us in the very least.'

Davis was going out as a Police Probationer in the joint service of the Straits Settlements and the Federated Malay States, one of the few services that took on young men straight from school. The business concerns generally sent their employees out at twenty-one, when they were of an age to sign their own contracts. Until then they were taken on as 'Trainees for the East', going the rounds of the various departments and learning the business at the London end. Similarly, the newly-appointed Eastern Cadets were sent on half-pay to the School of Oriental Studies at Finsbury Circus for a six-month course, much of it taken up with learning Malay but with a smattering of colonial law and a rudimentary course on tropical health and hygiene thrown in. The instructors were usually former administrators, who 'filled us up with a great deal of romantic stuff about Malaya and the Malays'. The students were also subjected to a 'tone' test to see if they were suitable candidates for a department of the Malayan Civil Service known as the Chinese Protectorate. One of those who passed the test was Richard Broome:

> The Chinese language being tonal, it's useless unless you have a slightly musical ear. I did fairly well but a great friend deliberately cheated so as not to do well. He was quite prepared to do anything so as not to go into the Chinese Protectorate. It was in some ways a specialist department and it wasn't popular with those people who wished to be governors and things. People who were in the Protectorate were always thought to be mad anyway and I think it did rather affect one's career to a certain extent.

In commercial circles it was not thought necessary to learn Malay or Chinese. But one of those who took the trouble to learn something of the language before he went out was Bill Bangs: 'I got a Malay phrase book and a dictionary and I walked up and down the beach at Frinton learning these words and phrases by heart. Most of them I found were not used at all. I remember one of the things I learned was that champagne was called *simpkin* – and I don't think I needed that very much anyway.' However, his rudimentary Malay did prove to be surprisingly useful on the voyage out:

> When we got to Port Said it was so hot that the youngsters who were going out planting decided to take their mattresses up on the deck and sleep there. When we got up there the Lascars were closing the hatches and somebody asked them how long it was going to take. The answer was, 'No speak English. Can speak Malay.' And one of the phrases that I'd learned on the beach at Frinton-on-Sea was 'How long will it take to finish this?' And I remember shooting this out and after that everybody on the boat thought I was the finest Malay scholar possible.

But before the voyage could begin, other preparations for life out East had to be completed. Tropical kit had to be bought and contracts signed. Lists of required clothing were supplied, together with the names of recommended colonial outfitters, and friends and relatives with experience of the East came forward with such practical tips as to buy only the more formal articles of clothing in Britain and have the rest made up at half the cost by Chinese tailors and shoe-makers in such places as Singapore, where a white suit cost three dollars, a pair of shorts one dollar fifty cents and socks worked out at about a dollar for half-a-dozen: 'You didn't bother to darn them; when the holes came you just threw them away.' Shoes were equally cheap and made to measure: 'You went to your shoemaker and you put your foot down on a piece of paper. Then he drew round your foot and you got your shoes within three or four days. Made with English leather they cost three dollars.'

Alan Morkill's mother provided him with a 'green-lined umbrella, a special jacket with a protective strip for the spine and a steel-lined trunk which had been my aunt's in India, which we dug out from the stable where it was serving as a corn bin.' These umbrellas and spine pads – 'a thick felt pad that you had sewn into the back of your uniform with red cloth inside and khaki exterior' – and other items of protective wear, such as the Straits Settlements' *Sola Topee,* were regarded as essential prerequisites to good health in the tropics when Morkill joined the MCS in 1913. Twenty years later they were still to be found on all outfitters' lists.

Trevor Walker was one of those who bought a *topee* at Simon

Artz emporium in Port Said, only to find when he got to Kuala Lumpur in 1937 that scarcely anyone was wearing one. Edward Tokeley found that he only needed to wear his *topee* when 'fielding on the boundary at cricket', and although Sjovald Cunyngham-Brown wore his for several years, he found it increasingly cumbersome:

> There was a period from 1935 or so when it was generally regarded by all the newcomers as absolutely ridiculous to wear a *sola topee* or a spine pad but that we ought to lie naked in the sun and enjoy the gorgous, beautiful heat. This was all very well but anybody who did that, as I did, now gets skin cancer, and many of the people who had persistent sunstroke went mad or died. There was a great deal to be said for the old Civil Servants who used to shout at me, 'You'll be sorry for this one day, young fellow. You'll pay for it sooner or later.'

Some of the other items supplied by colonial outfitters seemed equally out of place. Soon after his arrival in Kuala Lumpur Walker noticed that one of his mess-mates wore undervests that were all curiously frayed at the bottom:

> I said to him, 'I understand that the laundry is pretty rough out here but that's a bit much.' He said, 'Oh no, it's nothing to do with the laundry. I had a list that must have been written in about 1900 because it included twelve pairs of long combinations which I duly bought. I wore them on the way out here and I wore them for the first month out here and in the end I got so fed up and so hot that I took a pair of scissors and cut them all in two.'

Guy Madoc and John Davis, both preparing to go out to Malaya as Police Probationers in 1931, were sent to Hawes in Farringdon Street where, 'amongst dusty surroundings, we were given beautiful white pipe-clayed *topees* and invited to indulge in something called "throw-away socks", which rather suggested that the moment you'd bought them and got sweaty feet, which wouldn't take long in the tropics, you just threw them away. So everything was bought in very considerable numbers.' They were also advised that it was compulsory for them to travel out on the P&O – 'a very high-class sort of shipping line' – and that they would require no less than eighteen stiff shirts – 'boiled shirts, we used to call them' – and thirty-six stiff collars.

Then there were the contracts or letters of appointment. Guy Madoc's was a very impressive document, informing him that he was to be 'elected' to an appointment to the Colonial Service at a salary of two hundred and fifty Malayan dollars a month, just under thirty pounds. There was also a small cost-of-living allowance – 'which was taken from us when we'd only been out for about three months'. The letter also set out various do's and don'ts: 'They were evidently very worried in case I got married in a hurry, because it said, "If you marry before reaching Malaya you will forfeit the appointment. And if you marry during your first tour of service, the government will not be liable to provide a passage for your wife, nor to issue you with married quarters or a marriage allowance".'

This starting salary was virtually the same for all the young men starting their careers and remained a fairly constant figure throughout the inter-war period. The major exception was the Malayan Civil Service, whose cadets received a starting salary of just under four hundred dollars and promise of a generous pension of a thousand pounds a year for life. Edward Tokeley's terms of service were typical for those joining the mercantile trading companies:

> We didn't have contracts in Bousteads; you had a letter of appointment which was backed by a gentleman's understanding. It said that I could expect my first home leave at the expiry of five years and before the end of my sixth year of service, subject to the exigencies of the service. And that I could expect one local leave holiday of three weeks during that time. There was nothing in the letter of appointment about marriage but it was made clear to you that in order to get the partners' approval to get married you had to earn a certain sum of money a month, which took about ten years' service to achieve.

Both in government and in business new recruits were left in no doubt that marriage before the end of the second tour of service was frowned upon, and that permission had always to be sought first. In Sarawak the Second Rajah had laid down that no officer was to marry before his second tour of five years was completed. The big banks were equally specific; their young men were required to sign an agreement by which they could ask for permission to marry only after they had completed eight years' overseas service. Insufficient income and the difficulty of providing married quarters were the stated reasons for this attitude, but at the back of it was the assumption that the new men were expected to spend their early years getting to know the country and their work.

Finally the time came for embarkation on one or other of the many passenger ships that plied between Tilbury or Southampton and the East: 'In those days it was another era, when all the great shipping lines – the P&O, which was rather posh, the Blue Funnel, the Glen Line, the BI and the Bibby Line – took British men,

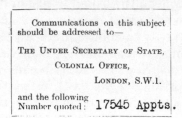

Communications on this subject
should be addressed to—

THE UNDER SECRETARY OF STATE,
    COLONIAL OFFICE,
        LONDON, S.W.1.

and the following
Number quoted: **17545 Appts**.

Downing Street,
August , 19̶3̶0.

Sir,

      I am directed by **Lord Passfield** to inform
you that, subject to your being passed by the
Consulting Physician to this Department as
physically fit for service, it is proposed to
select you for appointment to the Colonial Service
as a Police Probationer in the joint service of
the Straits Settlements and Federated Malay States,
with salary at the rate of $250 a month.   On
becoming a passed Probationer, with a minimum of
two years' service your salary will be increased
to $300 a month.   In view of the high cost of
living by which Malaya, like the United Kingdom
and other countries has been affected a temporary
allowance of 10 per cent of salary in the case of
unmarried officers and 20 per cent in the case of
married officers is at present also given.   You
will be provided with free (partly furnished)
                            quarters

G.C.MADOC, ESQ.

Letter of appointment, 1930. The temporary allowance referred
to was withdrawn within three months of the recipient arriving in Malaya.
The letter went on to warn that 'if you marry before reaching
Malaya you will forfeit the appointment'.

women and children backwards and forwards across the Empire.'

For all those sailing East for the first time the month-long voyage was to be a memorable experience. Cecil Lee boarded the *Patroclus,* a Blue Funnel liner, at Birkenhead: 'I'd never been beyond Brighton Pier and suddenly here I was living in comparative luxury on this ship which only had one class, not like the P&O. It was full of planters because they felt it was more free and easy than the P&O, which took out the Indian Army officers and the rather high civil servants and was said to be rather snobby.'

One of those travelling by P&O was Guy Madoc, who sailed from Tilbury Docks on a cold, grey December morning on the *Kashgar:*

> We young officers, ten of us, were pushed three to a cabin really designed for two. And so we sailed out with the usual rough weather down the Bay of Biscay and then round by Gibraltar. By that time, we ten policemen, going out to different branches of government service for the first time, had established ourselves right up in the eye of the fo'c's'le on the ship and when you looked right over the bows down to the forefoot of the vessel cleaving through the water, there were porpoises dashing backwards and forwards. It began to feel already that you were getting towards the tropics.

By tradition, the East began not at Suez but at the coaling port of Port Said:

> The orders therefore were that all portholes had to be closed, and your door must be kept carefully sealed, not only because of the coal dust, but because of the 'gippo' thieves who we were assured would come on in great numbers. Well, we young men all decided that we'd go ashore, and of course there were plenty of doubtful touts waiting on the quayside to take us around. One of us, I remember, even slipped a very small automatic pistol into his pocket, and was evidently prepared to defend himself to the death. Of course there were the gentlemen coming up under your elbow, offering you 'feelthy' pictures. But we were taken to an Arab mosque and we were taken to the famous Simon Artz, the great big store which lit its lights the moment the ship tied up alongside the dock. Most of us bought queer Arab burnous and other accoutrements, which were very useful later on in the voyage, when we had a fancy dress ball.

Cramped or not, travelling by P&O was done in considerable style, as Sjovald Cunyngham-Brown discovered on his first voyage out. During the daytime there was 'the fun of talking to friends, having pre-lunch drinks, a good lunch, happy afternoons playing deck tennis or splashing in the canvas pool that had been erected over the forehatch'. At mid-day there was the tote on the ship's daily run, followed by lunch and a siesta – a word that soon gave way in the newcomer's vocabulary to the curiously nautical 'lie-off', used throughout the Far East. Then there were more sports and outdoor entertainments until the evening when everybody, whether in First or Second Class, bathed and changed for dinner, wearing dinner-jackets as far as Port Said and thereafter 'the short white jacket, worn with black trousers, known as the bum-freezer, in which one went in to dinner in the tropics'.

There were two sittings for dinner and at first Cunyngham-Brown was annoyed to find that he had been put down for the second dinner:

> What I hadn't realized was that it was rather a good thing. The first service used to get hustled down to dinner pretty early, whereas the second service – mostly the senior officers, strangely enough – would stay around the bar for an hour-and-a-half until the bugle suddenly blew for the second service. You should realize that the P&O in those days was a very military establishment and the bugles rang at all hours, beautifully played. And the bugle for dinner, of course, resulted in our drinking our dry martinis as quick as we could and descending the large companion-way down into the very handsome dining-room with its great *punkahs* swinging, and all my friends in their mess-kits – Gurkhas, 11th Hussars, Indian civilians going back from furlough, whatever it might be – all of us laughing and chatting, getting to our appointed places and discussing the wines that we were to drink that evening.

Whether bound for Bombay, Colombo or beyond, the passengers were more or less of the same background. In consequence, a convivial and club-like atmosphere prevailed on board: 'Our little shipload became more and more intimately fond of each other. We became fast friends, some of which have remained to this day.' Sailing out on the P&O steamship *Carthage,* Edward Tokeley was astonished to find how 'the more seasoned of the Easterners looked after the newcomer. For meals I found myself sitting at a table with three generals, one of whom was going out to be GOC Singapore, and another to do the same job in India. But they looked after me very kindly.' On board the *Patroclus,* however, Cecil Lee found himself seated at the Chief Engineer's table:

> The stewards were Chinese and I remember one day how one came up to me and said: 'Your name Lee? My name Lee, too. Chinese.' I thought this rather funny and I told the story at the Chief Engineer's table and he growled at me: 'You should have kicked his arse!' That was rather the attitude, as I noticed later when we reached Penang from the way some of the officers set about the Tamils swarming on board as stevedores.

After dinner there was dancing, with the ship's band regaling the dancers with the tunes of Cole Porter and Ivor Novello. Those who did not wish to dance could play bridge – 'some women, who seemed very hard cases, played bridge from morning till night, as far as I can remember' – or retire to the bar and enjoy the novel experience of signing for drinks with *chits* which were then presented for payment weekly, on 'Black Monday'. Cecil Lee soon found that his small stock of money was being quickly exhausted: 'I was rather afraid of being thought "*chit*-shy" and not signing for my round but I had to draw in my horns.' Others who were on half-pay found themselves running up bar bills that could not be settled until the ship reached Penang or Singapore, where they began to draw their full salary.

Shipboard romance flourished: 'Aboard ship there is a very lovely feeling of freedom, of happiness, of quickly getting to know each other. And of course all the lovely young girls coming out East were the attraction of all the officers – and ourselves.' There were daughters going out to join their parents, fiancées coming out as brides-to-be and wives following their husbands after an extended leave: 'When we went on to the boat deck to have our cigarettes or cigars after dinner we'd select our partners for the evening and promise ourselves that, in the intervals between the dances, we'd come up on deck to have that beautiful fresh air of the Bay of Bengal blowing in our faces – whilst we underwent fierce flirtations on the boat deck.'

Like many of the youngsters on board, Cecil Lee felt himself to be 'too green and shy and callow' to make the most of the situation:

> I used to look with astonishment and wonderment at some of these chaps who'd been out before and knew the ropes. I remember one particular planter, always immaculately dressed, wonderful at all games, doing quite a strong line with a very attractive French wife who was on her way to Saigon. Strangely enough, I followed the career of this man who was a prominent cricketer in Malaya and I heard later that when the Japanese

overran us he got away to Java but when he discovered he was going to be taken prisoner he calmly shot himself. This seemed to be all at a piece with his character as I recall it. The life that he knew was gone and so he shot himself.

So the weeks passed – hot, listless days and 'cool, velvety nights spent gazing out over the limitless ocean', as the ship 'rolled gently over the Indian Ocean in starlight and phosphorescence'. There was often a coaling halt at Aden – where Edward Tokeley went ashore: 'I looked at the barren rock and said, "Cor, I do hope that Penang isn't like this." A little while later we landed at Colombo and I looked at this island of green and I thought, "Please, let Penang be as lovely as this. Even if it's half as lovely I shall be happy."'

One morning, as Sjovald Cunyngham-Brown remembers, a little cluster of trees appeared over the horizon. The voyage that had seemed 'as if it might go on for ever' was coming to an end:

Brilliant sunshine, blue sea, a huge Asian sky of clouds – because Asia has skies that no other place in the world has got; higher, more grandiose, more flamboyant – and clustering under it this little block of land: South-East Asia. The very beginning of the great romantic East, the island empires of which I dreamed. All my friends left the bar and came to the starboard side of the ship as this little dot of land called Pulau Wey – a tiny island at the tip of Sumatra – hove up into sight, with a great sea pounding on its beach, brilliant in the sunshine under bending palm trees. Gorgeous bathing, as I discovered later. We watched it and drank our Singapore gin-slings – or Singapore pink-gins – as it slid into the horizion behind us. Now we were east; this was the beginning.

Soon afterwards his ship made its landfall at Penang Island, the first of the British Straits Settlements: 'We watched it coming up in the early morning light. A big mound of land, a great whale lying there basking in the sea as we crept up toward it and went in between it and the mainland of Malaya. A beautiful land with high mountains, three thousand feet high, gorgeous little bays, cliffs and jungle. All under the keen light of morning and a strong wind from the northeast.'

Penang Island had already known a century and a half of trading and prosperity under the British. Rickshaws and hand-drawn carts filled the streets of George Town, and old-fashioned Chinese shops with red-tiled roofs and Chinese signs lined its bazaars. The most penetrating sounds were the cries of hawkers peddling their wares –

rice-cakes ('*nasi lemak!*'), green coconuts ('*ba-cha-cha!*' – with a pleasing inflection on the last syllable) or the large noodles known as 'pig's-guts cake' ('*chee-cheong-fan!*') – and the clip-clop of the wood clogs worn by Chinese women dressed in bright blue or white jackets and black trousers. On the outskirts of the town there were broad, tree-lined avenues dotted with elegant mansions, some dating back to the early days of the East India Company, others belonging to Chinese dollar millionaires, and shaded by flowering trees: 'the "trees of golden rain" called the *angsana,* the royal palms and the beautiful jacaranda that fell in blue drifts across the bougainvillaea'.

For the old Malay and China hands this was where South Asia ended and where the Far East began, for 'it was like coming home when you hit Penang'. And its appeal was not lost on newcomers. 'It was an enchanting place,' declares Cunyngham-Brown, 'and I was so happy to be there.' For Edward Tokeley, too, there was relief and delight as he became aware that Penang – where he was to be based for the next four years – appeared to be even more beautiful than Ceylon: 'It was completely unspoilt; it was paradise enow.'

As Bill Harrison's ship, the *Futala,* anchored off the wharf at George Town, a tropical storm broke overhead:

> We came up on deck early in the morning to be greeted by a terrific thunderstorm with the most vicious forked lightning I have ever seen, streaking across the sky, blue-white streaks of lightning from horizon to horizon and the most heavy downpour of tropical rain I've ever experienced. The rain hit the deck like two shilling pieces and bounced up as high as our knees, with a white haze of spray. You couldn't see through the rain it was so heavy. Finally, that blew across as it does with some of these Sumatras – storms that come across from Sumatra. The wind carried it away and up came the sun and we looked across to the mainland and there was a row of palm trees along part of the Butterworth shore and rubber plantations and, way in the distance, the Kedah peak, standing up like a sugar loaf.

The wharf itself was like a beehive, crowded with Chinese coolies and Tamils with their bullock carts, while piled up along the quay were stacks of hundredweight ingots of tin waiting to be shipped out, as well as canvas bales of SRS (Smoked Ribbed Sheets) rubber and copra. These 'scented the whole atmosphere with the sweet, nutty smell of drying coconut', mingling with the stink of the monsoon drains and the scent of cloves and pepper – 'that pungent, spicy odour so redolent of the Far East'.

The 'purple East' also began to exert its influence in other ways.

Unlike most other newcomers, Bill Harrison had travelled by way of India and then sailed from Madras to Penang on a 'coolie-ship', its decks crowded with immigrant Tamil labourers coming out under contract to work on the plantations, together with their wives and children:

> I remember on our arrival we were all trimming up for going ashore and one of the young lads with us – we were nearly all young fellows coming out to join our firms in Malaya – needed a haircut, so he called over a Tamil barber who was cropping the hair for the Indians on board. 'Give me a haircut as well,' he said. But when he got up out of the chair he'd been given a Hindu haircut and his head was shaved right across the top half and the back half was long. He did look a sight. All he needed was a couple of coloured spots on the centre of his forehead and he would have been a Hindu.

Sjovald Cunyngham-Brown was among those who would be leaving the ship at George Town in order to cross by ferry to the mainland or to catch the fast Straits Steamships' service to Port Swettenham and KL (Kuala Lumpur). When his ship finally came alongside the wharf a government representative came aboard to escort him and his fellow Eastern Cadets ashore:

> We all said, 'Good morning, sir.' To which he replied, 'Don't call me sir, for heaven's sake. I'm only eighteen months senior to yourselves.' I said, 'What are we going to wear?' 'Well, of course, wear your *tutup* jackets' – that is to say, the white cotton jacket that buttons up to the neck. That and white cotton trousers, black socks – which appeared to be *de rigueur* at that time – and black shoes. On our heads, naturally, were to be the *sola topees* and behind our backs the spine pad. Then, rejoicing, we went down the gangway.

Rickshaws, with their Chinese rickshaw-pullers, were waiting on the quay: 'We sat in them, rather hot and stifling in the morning sunshine, and John Hannington, in his rickshaw beside me, with sweat dripping off his nose and the tips of his ears and pouring down his face – as indeed it was off mine – said: "I suppose we're going to feel like this for the rest of our lives".' To Guy Madoc, however, the heat seemed 'glorious. It was nice to be slightly sweaty all day.'

As Cecil Lee left the ship he was overcome by homesickness, for 'it had been a wonderful voyage and suddenly I was saying goodbye to everyone and starting a new life'. There were no customs or immigration formalities to be observed and a rickshaw carried him straight to his firm's office, where he met the European staff:

> One of them – an awfully nice fellow – took me round and gave
> me lunch at the main hotel there, the 'E & O'. Then he left me to
> have a lie-off in the Penang Club. So I sat in this gaunt, high-
> ceilinged club with its great fans whirling round up above, lying
> in one of those long bamboo chairs with arms for your legs and a
> slot for your *stengah*. The Chinese 'boys' padded silently by and
> it was all quiet – except for raucous laughter coming occasionally
> from the bar and the cry of 'Boy!'

AGENTS OF TRADE

The seventeenth-century traders went there for pepper, because the passion for pepper seemed to burn like a flame of love in the breast of Dutch and English adventurers about the time of James the First. The bizarre obstinacy of that desire made them defy death in a thousand shapes; the unknown seas, the loathsome and strange diseases; wounds, captivity, hunger, pestilence, and despair. To us, their less tried successors, they appear magnified, not as agents of trade but as instruments of a recorded destiny, pushing out into the unknown in obedience to an inward voice, to an impulse beating in the blood, to a dream of the future.

Joseph Conrad, *Lord Jim*

Sacred to the memory of John Baird, Junior, son of the Hon. J. Baird, Master Attendant and Midshipman of the Wellesley East Indiaman, who arrived on this Island on 27 August 1800 and died the 6 September following aged 17 years and 6 months

Inscription on tombstone, Northern Road
Cemetery, George Town, Penang

UNDER the frangipani trees in Penang's oldest cemetery lies buried Francis Light, founder of the Settlement of Prince of Wales Island – later to become Penang. For Sjovald Cunyngham-Brown, still living for much of the year on the island, the cemetery has a special significance:

I never pass the cemetery without thinking of Francis Light in his completely neglected tomb. It's a melancholy place in a way. So many young people's graves are there, who died of malaria between the ages of eighteen and twenty-three; young cadets –

masses of them – girls in childbirth, all neglected these days. And among them Francis Light, who died of malaria like nearly everybody else on this island.

In British times a ceremony was held every year in the cemetery to mark the anniversary of the death of the settlement's founder on 21 October 1794. After *Merdeka* and the coming of independence to Malaysia the ceremony dwindled, until only two people were left to celebrate it: 'One was Henry Grummit, of long descent on this island, and the other was myself. We would come with a bottle of Cognac and discuss Francis Light, sitting on his very grave, and as the dusk came on we would get tipsier every minute!'

It was Francis Light, an independent 'country trader' newly commissioned by the British East India Company with the rank of captain, who in 1786 arrived with three ships off the island and began clearing the sandy headland on which George Town is built:

> The ground at that time was covered with a small hard coastal tree known as the *penaga,* which very soon blunted the axes that had been brought down from Calcutta, so the *Eliza* was sent down to Malacca to buy native *beliong,* as they're called – very small, hard iron axes from Dutch Malacca. She was away for about three weeks during which period, in order to keep the troops occupied and happy, Francis Light was in the habit of loading his guns on the *Prince Henry* and *Speedwell* and firing them off into the surrounding undergrowth of the island. He filled his cannon with small coinage of all descriptions – annas, pice, even an occasional rupee – and fired them off, and in the ensuing scramble for money more opening up of the headland was done than could possibly have been achieved in any other manner.

To all intents, this first scramble for money among the *penaga* trees of Penang Island marked the arrival of permanent British trading interests in the Malacca Straits. But long before the British, there had been Portuguese and Dutch traders, and before them other foreigners, all drawn by the lure of trade: 'From untold ages in the past South-East Asia has been the nodal point through which the trade of the world had to go. It has supplied the world with an essential commodity in the form of spice.'

The spice islands also provided humanity with one of its greatest mixing bowls:

> From the Marquesa Islands in the Pacific, right through South-East Asia and through Ceylon down to Madagascar in the shape of an enormous lozenge are the 'between the islands people', the

Nusantara in Sanscrit or the *Kun Lun* people, as they've been known to the Chinese since pre-Christian times. These people have on one side of their family a common origin in the Western Pacific, and although they formed only a tiny minority among the aboriginal tribes whom they encountered, they intermixed and the more primitive people naturally took on the characteristics of the more advanced ones.

Over the centuries other ingredients were added; waves of settlers from Northern India spreading east and south as far as Bali, to leave behind a Hindu culture, and then a second, sea-borne invasion from Southern India, bringing the new religion of Islam to Sumatra and Malaya, which thereafter became strongholds of Muslim teaching throughout South-East Asia:

Islam took a very rapid and permanent root in this part of the world because it hadn't got any very strong counter-religion to sweep back again over it – and of course this Islamization had the result of bringing in new traders from Southern Arabia, the 'Sinbad the Sailor' type of distant trading venture. And these people – Sheiks and Sayids, landed and slave-owning, wealthy and strong merchant princes – carved out land in this part of the world in the twelfth, thirteenth and fourteenth centuries, and their descendants form the present-day governing aristocracy of Malaya, Sumatra and Brunei.

The most powerful of these dynasties today is the Sultanate of Brunei, whose present ruler can trace a royal ancestry that goes back nearly a thousand years. Robert Nicholl, who spent many years in Sarawak as an educationalist, now works for the Sultan of Brunei as an historian and from this unique vantage point has examined the impact of Europeans on the established trading patterns of South-East Asia:

The South China Sea may be compared to the Mediterranean in the sense that it is the cradle of ancient and affluent civilizations. Not ancient in the sense of Egypt and China but ancient in the British sense. When Alfred was burning the cakes and being ravaged by the Danes, it is recorded that the Maharajah of Shrivijiya in Palembang each morning went out onto a balcony which overlooked a pond and into the pond he threw a brick of solid gold. It was a very successful arrangement of course, because when the Maharajah's successor took office he fished up all the thousands of bricks from the pond and started off with a healthy bank balance. Or, if we come a little further, to Henry VII's time, an observer at that time noted the children of the Chief Minister of

the Sultan of Malacca having a wonderful time building sand-
castles. The little tots greatly enjoyed themselves, but what was
interesting was that they weren't using sand, they were using
gold dust. So it wasn't without reason that the Indian travellers,
who were the first to explore South-East Asia, referred to it as the
Land of Gold and spoke of Sumatra, Borneo and Malaya as the
Islands of Gold. It was a very prosperous little world. It had a
great trade with China to the north and then to the west there
was the trade with India reaching far beyond to the Caliphate
and so ultimately to Europe. It was an area of peace and prosperity and great affluence.

Suddenly, into this stable world there came 'an eruption' in the
shape of the Portuguese, arriving not as ordinary traders but as a
hostile power intent on seizing the spice trade for themselves and
establishing a monopoly:

In 1498 Vasco de Gama was making his way along the East Coast
of Africa and at Melindi by some extraordinary chance he
encountered the greatest Arab navigator of his day, Ahmed Ibn
Majid, who guided him across to Calicut in India. Calicut was at
this time a great centre of the spice trade, which stretched from
the Moluccas in the east to Venice in the west. Now when you
talk of spices you're simply talking of curry powder and it's often
forgotten that the medieval Europeans were amongst the world's
greatest curry eaters. There was no means of feeding animals
during the winter except at great cost and therefore you killed off
all your fat animals in September and for the next six months or
more you lived on salted meat. Now the attractions of salted meat
pall and so the demand in Europe for anything that gave savour
to salted meat was very great indeed.

But before these spices could reach Europe they had to pass
through all sorts of customs barriers where levies, official and unofficial, had to be paid:

You bought your sack of pepper for five ducats in Calicut and by
the time it reached the Rialto in Venice it was sold for eighty
ducats – and pepper is the least valuable of the ingredients in
curry. Now when Vasco de Gama arrived in Calicut he loaded up
with spices and brought them straight back to Lisbon. No customs duties, no levies, no palms to be greased. The profits were
such that no man had ever seen them before! And there was an
immediate rush of the Portuguese out to India and beyond to
secure this profitable trade.

The Portuguese quickly became the super-power of the Indian

Ocean and in 1511 they captured the emporium of Malacca, which gave them control of the narrow straits between Sumatra and the Malayan mainland. But although they established a monopoly the effect on local trade was not as damaging as it might have been. It was the arrival of the Dutch in 1600 that finally brought devastation: 'The Dutch were not only powerful at sea, they were also hard-headed business men and the monopoly they fastened on the archipelago was one of iron efficiency. It really wrecked the trading pattern of the South China Sea. Native trade wasted away and by the time the British came on the scene the great ports that had been frequented by merchants from all over the East had sunk into decay and had become the nest of pirates.'

Groups of these 'pirates' helped to build up Malaya's still sparse population so that what was later to become the State of Selangor was 'largely peopled by Bugis immigrants, originally pirates, who came from the islands grouped to the south of Singapore. They settled mainly in *kampongs* along the coast and then penetrated gradually up the rivers. Similarly, the Negri Sembilan Malays came from Menangkabau in Sumatra, and they again were a sea-borne people who came in from outside and settled along the coast and gradually infiltrated up the rivers.'

The East Coast Malays had different origins. Many were immigrants from across the Gulf of Siam – but they too settled on the coast and then worked their way inland:

> These people came when the whole of the land was covered in absolutely impenetrable jungle so thick that when somebody wanted to visit what is now a tourist attraction seven miles outside Kuala Lumpur, he had to go there by elephant and it took him three days. Now the answer to this jungle for your ordinary immigrant was to settle either on a sea-shore or up a river, and there was a saying in the days when this Malay immigration was at its height, that a cat could walk from Port Swettenham down to Malacca without getting its feet wet, so thick on the ground were the houses along the beaches.

Compared with the Europeans, the impact of the Chinese on the Eastern archipelago was less traumatic and of far greater consequence in human terms. Living among a community that is still predominantly Chinese in origin, Sjovald Cunyngham-Brown has learned a great deal about them both as traders and as settlers:

> There have been coastal Chinese fishing communities in the archipelago from as far back as records go. But they became more numerous after the taking of Malacca by the Portuguese. Many

Chinese settled there and started the *Hokkien* communities in Malaya; soft-featured, Southern Chinese from Amoy. A preponderance of the Chinese in Penang are also of *Hokkien* descent, who came in as fishermen or cooks during the days of the East India Company.

Under Company and then (after 1867) under Crown rule the Chinese in Malacca and Penang prospered. They came to be known as the 'Queen's Chinese' and looked upon the Straits Settlements as 'practically a county of England. They were stoutly pro-Queen Victoria, strongly pro-British and sent their sons to England to be educated.'

In the middle of the nineteenth century a second wave of Chinese settlers began to arrive: the *Hakka* people, a 'notoriously stubborn race of hill-farmers' known throughout China as the 'stranger' people:

They came down to Malaya in enormous numbers as a result of the Taiping Rebellion in 1851–65. They were exiled officers' families from that rebellion, which gave General Gordon his name of 'Chinese' Gordon. He was called out as a very young man to help settle that affair and it took him ten years to get them all away. They went to Manila in the Philippines, to Surabaya and Batavia in the Dutch East Indies, and to Singapore in large numbers – and from Singapore they came on to Penang.

Those in Penang found themselves confronted with a highly organized community of *Hokkien* Chinese who knew not one word of their language and the two were antagonistic from the very beginning. The *Hakka* hated the *Hokkien* and the *Hokkien* were annoyed by these energetic, loud-voiced newcomers, so filled with initiative and push. Very soon they not only lived up at the top of the hill, where they opened farm lands, but they also came down into the town and began to bust up the settled *Hokkien* community.

Gang warfare between the *Hakka* and *Hokkien* secret societies more or less coincided with the discovery on the mainland of huge fields of tin ore. *Hokkien* prospectors had moved up the rivers into the Malayan jungle and were excavating open-caste tin-mines in such places as Kuala Lumpur, the 'muddy estuary' at the confluence of the Klang and Gombak rivers. They couldn't get up in large boats any further than the junction of the two rivers so they made a base there at what is now called Kuala Lumpur. The survival rate was very low in those early days, from jungle fevers and what not, but they just kept on bringing Chinese workmen in faster than they were dying and they finally moved the jungle back a bit and then things opened up. The Malays established forts at the mouth of the river where they could collect tribute on everything going in and everything coming out – and the Chinese paid the tribute and did the work. Then came warfare between rival gangs of Malays and Chinese and there was chaos.

The intervention of the *Hakka,* equally anxious to carve out spheres of influence on the mainland, further aggravated the situation: 'The upshot was that the Malay States under their native rulers began to take sides, one against the other. And so from about 1865 the entire Malay peninsula from north to south rapidly became a murderously dangerous blood bath – and something had to be done about it.'

By now the trading monopoly of the old East India Company had long since been broken by any number of rival syndicates of merchant adventurers based in Penang and the other two principal Straits Settlements, Malacca and Singapore. Typical of these East India merchants were such firms as Guthrie and Co. and Boustead and Co., both of which had their head offices in Singapore. The first had been founded by a Scotsman, Alexander Guthrie, only two years after Stamford Raffles had leased the island to Singapore from the Sultan of Johore in 1819. Bousteads was started six years later by a China trader, Edward Boustead; 'a far-sighted chap, because he and his partners bought some prize land sites and built splendid houses on them. He also started the first club in Singapore, the Billiards Club, and edited Singapore's only newspaper.' Like most of the other *hongs* or mercantile houses in Singapore, Guthries and Bousteads were in what was traditionally known as the 'jam and pickle' business, exporting what was available and importing whatever was needed.

These trading concerns found themselves inextricably involved in the disturbances on the mainland. In some cases they even took sides, supplying the combatants with 'unconventional items of mining equipment' in the form of brass cannon, rifles and ammunition. Partly at their behest and partly to keep open the Far Eastern trade routes, the British crown intervened. With the treaty of Pangkor, signed in 1874, peace was restored on the mainland – but at a price. The Sultan of Perak was required to accept at court a British officer whose advice was to be taken in all matters except those pertaining to Malay religion and custom. So began the direct involvement of the British Crown in the affairs of the Malay States, following the 'commercial *box-wallah* who'd gone in first and might have been in trouble if he hadn't been helped'. For here there was no question of

'Trade following the Flag': 'It was the flag that followed trade – often very reluctantly. Trade was the basis of the British endeavour in South-East Asia; trade and nothing but trade was at the bottom of the whole business.'

Nowhere was this reluctance to extend Britain's imperial domains more apparent that in the case of Borneo, where only the tiny island of Labuan was brought directly into the colonial fold, in order to provide a naval base against the pirates that infested the South China Sea. On the main island itself a large area in the north was leased in 1881 to a chartered company, the British North Borneo Company, to govern more or less as it pleased – just as the East India Company had earlier ruled India and the Straits Settlements. And further south there was the remarkable phenomenon of Sarawak, where it was said that 'the white man was held in higher regard that in any other British territory'. In 1841 the coastal strip of tropical jungle, inhabited mostly by tribal peoples, was handed over by the Rajah of Brunei to an English adventurer named James Brooke. When he died in 1868 he had already been succeeded by his nephew, Charles Brooke, who was known as the Second Rajah and was the true creator of Sarawak. Long after the Second Rajah's death in 1917 stories about him continued to be told in the longhouses of Borneo.

There was a very marked difference in the way that British North Borneo and Sarawak were governed. In the former, commercial considerations came first:

'Under the Chartered Company everything was far more simple. There weren't the rules and regulations that came with colonial government. The manager of a rubber estate was really more important than the government officer in his district. He was a law unto himself and the government really let him do more or less what he liked.' Thus when John Baxter first came to Sapong Rubber Estate, near Tenom, in 1924 he found it to be a 'very hard life' for European assistants like himself and for the estate's Javanese indented labour alike. His manager was a harsh disciplinarian of thirty years' standing in the country who was also responsible, as the local magistrate, for preserving law and order in the district. If any of the labour tried to run away he would send police after them and sentence them to be flogged as an example to the rest: 'Then in 1927 a Dutch Labour Inspector came to Sapong and for the whole day was interviewing people who had complained about the treatment they'd received. But they were frightened of speaking out on the estate, so that evening, when he was having his first beer back in Tenom, three dripping figures appeared. Despite the crocodiles, they had swum over the Padas river to put their case. That same night the Dutchman tried to cut his throat and had to be taken down to the coast.' Three months later a second Dutch Inspector came and this time succeeded in bringing charges: 'My manager was kicked out of the country and questions were asked about him in the House of Commons.'

In Sarawak, too, there were few of the rules and regulations of colonial administration. But here any attempt by outsiders to exploit either the country's natural resources or its people met with the strongest opposition:

> It was the policy of all the Rajahs, First, Second, and Third, not to develop the country. They would not have European companies in to plant rubber all over the place and mine it and work the timber. They wished that the local people should plant their own rubber gardens and work their own timber, or, if they wanted to work gold, to go and work it. They weren't wage-slaves; they were free to earn their own living. And this is a very important point in Brooke rule, because it was almost the only country where such a thing was done. The result was that nobody was rich and nobody was poor.

The one European company that was allowed to trade in Sarawak with any degree of freedom was the Borneo Company. It had earned this privileged position by coming to the rescue in 1857 when the little township of Kuching was attacked by Chinese and the Rajah was forced to flee down-river. It was the timely arrival of the Borneo Company's steamer, the *Sir James Brooke,* with the head of the company temporarily appointed 'acting Rajah', that had saved the day. This same company went on to win for itself a rather special place in popular history when a few years later its manager, acting on behalf of the King of Siam, engaged as a governess to his Court the widow of an Indian Army major, Anna Leonowens.

But the great boost that turned the more far-sighted of the trading companies into powerful managing agency houses was the advent of rubber. The discovery that the shallow but well-drained alluvial soil between Malaya's central mountain range and its western seaboard could grow better quality rubber than anywhere else in the world, led to an explosion of planting and trading that was to dramatically alter both the landscape and the economy of the country. And with the plantations came not only hundreds of young Englishmen and Scotsmen in search of profit and adventure, but also a vast force of unskilled labour in the person of the humble coolie. Tens of thousands came in junks across the South China Sea – and hundreds of thousands from India, mostly Tamils from the south. So the last waves of migration began, and by the end of the

nineteenth century the social, political and economic patterns for
the next fifty years had been more or less fixed throughout the
archipelago. It became a region where 'four separate communities
divided by race, religion and culture lived together – generally in
harmony but on the whole keeping themselves to themselves'.

On the peninsula the other eight Malay states followed Perak's
example: some became Federated States – the FMS – with a British
Resident and a British administrative system, while others hung on
to a greater degree of independence as Unfederated Malay States –
the UMS – where a British Adviser might advise the Sultan but
whose powers were otherwise strictly limited: 'These states each
had their own history, their own people and their own rulers, and
were almost foreigners to each other. They hardly mixed and
thought of themselves as being Perak Malays or Selangor Malays or
whatever it was.' There was 'no such nonsense as democracy and
egalitarianism and all that. The Malays accepted that the Sultans
were the rulers, and the lack of politics was one of the country's
great charms.'

Nevertheless, it was impressed upon young officers when they
first went out that, beyond the confines of the Straits Settlements,
Malaya was not to be thought of as a colony: 'It was a protectorate
of Britain and we had to behave with very great respect towards the
Malay rulers, who were all very dignified men indeed and carried
their dignity well.' Before any European official could take up an
appointment within an Unfederated Malay State his name had to be
submitted to the Sultan in Council for his approval. A special
courtly form of Malay had also to be used when writing to the ruler
or when speaking to him: 'There was a formula you used. If you
addressed the Rajah you addressed the dust below the feet of his
exalted highness and so on.'

When Bill Bangs first came to Kelantan State in 1933 the ruler
was Sultan Ishmail, who had been crowned in 1920. Even when it
came to dealing with the British, his authority was considerable:

He got his own way in many things but according to the Treaty
he was supposed to take the advice of the British Adviser in
anything except *adat*, which was Malay custom and religion.
However, I can remember on one occasion his sister, the *Tungku
Merani,* was very angry because the Posts and Telegraphs had
cut down some of her rubber branches which were interfering
with the telephone line. She called the Posts and Telegraphs'
man up to tick him off over this, and he rather stupidly lost his
temper and used the word '*mu*' to her instead of saying '*tungku*';
'*mu*' is a very low 'you' used only to labourers. He was also in

charge of Customs and he accused her of getting a lot of goods for her house in without paying duty on them. She was very, very angry and went and complained to her brother, the Sultan, and the Sultan called the British Adviser and this man, who was very senior in government service, was out of Kelantan on the next mail train.

The government officers who occupied these upper tiers of the civil administration in Malaya came from the ranks of the Malayan Civil Service. When Cunyngham-Brown joined in 1929 there were approximately three hundred such officers administering an area about the size of England and Wales – 'a small body with the greatest *esprit de corps,* with a vocation and dedication to our job – and that was one of the main and most endearing features of the MCS to anybody who belonged to it.'

Although the age of the pioneer administrators had ended long before the Great War, one or two survivors were still in evidence in the 1920s. In his first weeks in Malaya as an Eastern Cadet in 1928 Mervyn Sheppard was out in his district supervising the collection of rent:

We were carrying on the very simple, slow-moving process of collecting fifty cents or a dollar when suddenly down the road we heard a motor-car approaching – and there weren't any motor-cars in Malaya in those days. Then there was a screech of brakes and the car stopped, and down stepped a very tall figure with a rather pronounced stoop, dressed in a white uniform with a high collar – which was known in those days as a *tutup* – and long white trousers and wearing a *topee*. The village headman, who was with me, immediately recognized him and, taking absolutely no notice of me or anything else, hurried down the path and held out his hand in greeting. Then, in the Malay way, they just touched hands and exchanged the Arabic greeting: 'Salaam alaikum; peace be with you', and the answer, 'Wa alaikum salaam; to you be peace'. Then the tall figure started to speak, and he spoke for at least five minutes, in Malay and in the Pahang *patois,* of which I didn't understand a word. But everybody else was engrossed, enthralled by what he was saying. Then at the end of his brief address he turned round, got back into his car and was driven away.

This unexpected visitor was Sir Hugh Clifford, High Commissioner for the Malay States, who forty years earlier had come to Pahang as its first British Agent.

A rather more curious relic of the early days of British administration in Malaya also existed in the person of Captain Hubert Berkeley, the 'uncrowned king of Upper Perak', who was usually to be found dressed in full Malayan costume, consisting of *sarong, baju* and *songkok*, in the remote jungle district of Grik, close to the Siamese border. Stories about *tuan* Berkeley were part of the folk-lore of Perak:

> One day he was going out on an elephant ride, which he used to do very regularly. As he got up on his elephant and was about to go, the Court Clerk came running to him and said, 'Sir, you've got cases in court today.' Berkeley turned round and said, 'Blast it,' and then asked how many cases there were. The Court Clerk said, 'Twenty-five sir.' 'What are they?' said Berkeley. 'Minor offences, sir.' 'Have you read the charges?' 'Yes sir. They all plead guilty.' 'All right. Odd numbers discharged, even numbers fined five dollars.' Then he turned round and rode away.

Berkeley apparently preferred his own summary justice to the precepts laid down in the Indian Criminal Code and followed by British magistrates in Malaya. When a dispute over a boundary came before him he adjourned the court and summoned the litigants and all their witnesses to follow him to the site in question. Here he formed the disputants into two teams and held a tug-of-war contest using rotan creepers from the jungle, awarding the land to the winning team. Tales of Berkeley and his eccentricities also circulated widely among the European population on the peninsula:

> Berkeley was quite a good host, but he had a double-barrelled lavatory. And he seemed to think that it was part of being a good host to join his guests there. People with rather more delicate sensitivity used to spend a lot of time saying, 'I think I'll just take a little stroll before breakfast,' and hope that they'd be able to get into the loo without their host being there. But they very rarely succeeded. He'd come up and say, 'Oh, fancy meeting you. How nice! I've brought a spare copy of *The Times* along in case you'd like to read it.' On the opposite wall of this double-barrelled thunderbox was pinned up a large photograph of the Chief Secretary to Government of that time, Sir Frank Swettenham. Berkeley said that looking at that horrible chap made him have better motions.

It was said that Berkeley had jumped ship in Penang and had then enlisted in the police before eventually joining the MCS. He was known to come from an aristocratic Roman Catholic family in Worcestershire and 'seemed to regard himself as a combination of an English squire and a Malay chief'. Several times a week he could be seen driving off to bathe at some nearby hot springs 'in an English landau and pair, with a postillion dressed in a red and white garment that corresponded to the Berkeley family livery'. Having built up for himself an extraordinary degree of independence in his district, Berkeley was able to resist all attempts to get rid of him:

> He very much disliked seeing senior officers from more civilized parts of the country coming up to inspect his district and criticizing it. And on one occasion when a very senior government official sent a telegram saying, 'Am coming up tomorrow on Inspection,' Berkeley sent a telegram back saying, 'No bridge at sixty-fourth mile.' And that thoroughly discouraged the British official. The fact was that the sixty-fourth mile ran through fine flat country with no river or bridge. But he managed to keep most visiting firemen out of his district in that way.

Alan Morkill had the unenviable task of relieving Hubert Berkeley when he finally retired in 1925 at the age of sixty-two – seven years past official retiring age:

> I was received by Berkeley who was dressed in Malay costume. I took over a herd of cattle, three elephants and three or four horses. He had about fifty cattle and he warned me to be very careful when it came to the annual return. 'In order to avoid trouble with the Auditor-General, you must never alter the return,' he said. 'Calves are born and plod their weary way till they become beef in the DO's compound – but they must still go down as calves.' He showed me round and when we came to the Court House he said, 'Here we dispense justice but not law.'

Above the bench were two fox masks.
  Morkill once encountered another sort of relic from the past when in temporary occupancy of an old bungalow:

> It was the fashionable time, about midnight, when I heard steps coming up the drive and I assumed it was the police inspector coming to report a murder or something. I went outside and the steps continued but I didn't see anybody. I called out but there was no answer, so I thought no more about it. Then Haines, who'd had the district before me, was staying with me one Christmas and he said, 'Oh, do you ever hear Abraham Hale's ghost?' Abraham Hale was an early DO who had died out there. I said, 'No. What happens?' He said, 'Oh, he walks up the drive and onto the porch and disappears.' Well, I put a whisky and soda out in case he took it – but he never did.

Only in one other corner of the South China Sea did individualism on the Berkeley scale continue to flourish after the Great War. When Edward Banks came to Sarawak to take up his post as Museum Curator he found himself in a country that was full of eccentrics and characters drawn from all over the world:

> The Rajah rather liked having these people who weren't stuffed shirts, as he used to say. There were men there who'd been cowboys in the west – they'd been to Alaska on the Kicking Horse Pass gold rush; there were men who'd been round the Horn in sailing ships, or on the Ashanti goldfields and to Johannesburg. And, of course, men from the services. There was an RAF seapilot, there was a magnificent man off a destroyer, who was unable to go home on leave because he was a bigamist. Then they had chaps from the China Customs and the Burmese teak forests. They were not qualified in any scholastic way. They were simply men who'd gone out into the world and made their way. And very often they were the younger sons who had left home – as I was – and who'd gone out in the world and eventually fetched up in Sarawak. They met the young Rajah who'd had a stern father and could appreciate this type of chap who didn't want to be pushed around very much: 'Good chap, but he had to be handled carefully.' And I don't think anyone handled them as the Rajah did.

The commercial world also had its survivors from an earlier age. An outstanding figure in rubber circles was Sir Eric Macfadyen, who continued to act as what was known as a visiting agent for such companies as Harrison and Crosfield long after his planting days were over. 'I remember standing with him on the top of a hill from where you could see the upper reaches of the Klang river,' recalls Cecil Lee. 'And he said, "I used to come up here in a small boat to collect timber for my bridges." He was a small man who wore an eyeglass. I think he'd been run over by a gun-carriage in the Boer War and one eye tended to sink in a bit and so he wore an eye-glass. But he was a strong, humorous character with great foresight.'

Another pioneer planter was Henri Fauconnier, author of *The Soul of Malaya*. Bill Bangs met him during his first weeks with the Anglo-French company Socfin:

> I was put on Rantau Panjang Estate where Henri Fauconnier was the manager. Unfortunately, he was just retiring, but I do like to think that I worked under Fauconnier. And when he published *The Soul of Malaya* I must have read it twenty or thirty times. I became very keen on knowing more about Malaya and learning

the Malay language and trying to understand the Malays, and this was mostly due to Fauconnier's book. I remember in the book he said, 'No one will understand Malays unless they live with Malays and take the Malay religion,' which was one of the reasons why in 1928 I embraced Islam.

CONRAD'S EASTERN WORLD

Singapore docks at the turn of the century,
with Europeans disembarking and Chinese coolies loading coal.

Scenes from the Straits Settlements;
Beach Street in George Town, Penang, and the wharfside head offices
of the Borneo Company in Singapore.

The 'Pioneers'; British officials relaxing in their *sarongs* and *tutup*-jackets on Penang Hill, *c.* 1880 and Captain Hubert Berkeley, the 'uncrowned king of Upper Perak', seen with some of his horses and 'adopted daughters', 1926.

Above: The Resident of Labuan Island admires a crocodile, 1923. The rivers and tidal swamps of Borneo once teemed with these giant reptiles.

Left: DO and tiger: The Magistrate (Alan Morkill) was called out of court to shoot a tiger that had taken a Chinese smallholder's pig, Tampin *c.* 1924.

3

THE MEETING PLACE OF MANY RACES

Singapore is the meeting place of many races. The Malays, though natives of the soil, dwell uneasily in towns, and are few; and it is the Chinese, supple, alert, and industrious, who throng the streets; the dark-skinned Tamils walk on their silent, naked feet, as though they were but brief sojourners in a strange land . . . and the English in their topees and white ducks, speeding past in motorcars or at leisure in their rickshaws wear a nonchalant and careless air. The rulers of these teeming peoples take their authority with a smiling unconcern.

Somerset Maugham, *P&O*

IN the Twenties and Thirties the greater part of the small British community in the Malay archipelago was concentrated along the West Coast of the peninsula; on the rubber plantations in Lower Perak, Selangor, Negri Sembilan and Johore, and in Singapore and the capital of the FMS at Kuala Lumpur. Here the pre-war rubber boom had helped to lay down an efficient railway system and a network of rudimentary dirt roads that covered car drivers and passengers in red laterite dust and were, perhaps, more suited to bullock carts than to motor-cars:

> Motoring was in its infancy then in Malaya. We had roads but they were laid out along the contours of the hills and chiefly followed bullock tracks. The surveyors and the contractors got more mileage by going round the contours and using as many bends as they could, so you could make no speed. And there was jungle everywhere. You had a road into a rubber plantation or a road to a mine and where the rubber trees stopped the jungle

began – solid jungle, so thick that you couldn't see the sky above. If you spent any time in there you came out pale-faced.

Elsewhere in Malaya, and in Sarawak and Borneo, there was still no road system worth speaking of outside the towns and *kampongs*. Instead the rivers continued to provide the main lines of communication, with fleets of shallow-draught steamers and Malay *prahus* ferrying goods and passengers along the coast and inland.

Even the railways were no match for some of the steamers that plied the Straits of Malacca. The large ocean liners only called in at Penang and Singapore, so it was left to such shipping lines as Straits Steamships to handle local traffic. Passengers who disembarked at George Town could either cross by ferry to the mainland and catch the Malay Express which carried the night mail down to KL – or continue by sea on a local steamer. Straits Steamships ran more than fifty of these steamers – known as 'the little white fleet' on account of their white hulls and blue and white funnels – all shallow-draught vessels that ran with clockwork precision between nearly eighty ports in South-East Asia. But the pride of the fleet was the *Kedah*, which at twenty-one knots outran the Malay Express. First-Class passengers – 'Europeans always travelled First Class. It was a rule; you wouldn't sell a deck passage to a European before the war' – could board the *Kedah* in Penang in the evening and land at Port Swettenham – the port for the federal capital – at dawn. On Friday nights the *Kedah* also ran punters and racehorses up from Singapore in time for the Penang races the next day.

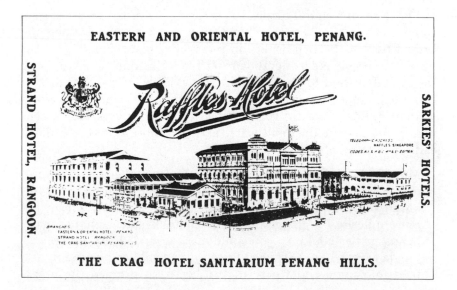

EASTERN AND ORIENTAL HOTEL, PENANG.

STRAND HOTEL, RANGOON.

SARKIES' HOTELS.

THE CRAG HOTEL SANITARIUM PENANG HILLS.

John Harrison was one of those who boarded the Malay Express after crossing over to the mainland from Penang Island on the ferry. Here he became aware for the first time of the manner in which the four principal races thrown together in the South-East Asian mixing-bowl co-existed while at the same time keeping each other at arm's length:

> We found that, without any orders or regulations, the First Class was used only by Europeans, the Second Class was mainly occupied by Chinese and the Third-Class compartments were occupied by Tamils. The races seemed to segregate in that manner, of their own accord. They didn't mix and they didn't mind not mixing. The Malays went according to their means. If they were of the ruling class they'd travel in the First Class. Otherwise, if they had the money they'd go in with the Chinese and take a table to themselves or if they were of the coolie class then they would go into the Third Class. But the working-class Malay never had any money in his pocket – unless he had come out of a pawn-shop.

The First-Class carriages had hard sleepers but in almost every other respect proved to be comfortable: 'They were kept nicely aired by little revolving fans in the corners of the carriage and the windows were screened in that flyproof screening you used to get in the old meat safes we used.' But with coal-burning engines even these turned out to be inadequate once the train had got underway: 'The railway company was buying soft coal from Rawang collieries down in Selangor and the smuts were coming in all along the way. So every time you got up from your seat you had to shake yourself to throw off the smuts.'

As the train crossed through Province Wellesley and Perak, Bill Harrison was able to enjoy a landscape of 'beautiful *padi*-fields with the most gorgeous pale-green young *padi*, where Malays with their *sarongs* tucked up round their loins were wading, planting the *padi* in the *sawa* – the wet *padi*-fields.' Interspersed between the fields were 'clumps of banana and coconut trees and little villages where the *padi*-planters lived in their palm-thatched houses'. But at Ipoh Harrison changed trains and travelled northwards into the wilder country of Siam – where the engine ran into a herd of bullocks, which left 'their entrails draped along the first carriages of the train'.

Travellers continuing on down the peninsula were woken at dawn as the train pulled into KL's railway station – a building belonging, as one newcomer heard it described, to the 'Late Marzipan' period. 'It wasn't in the least like any railway station we'd seen before. It was designed with domes and small spires and lots of oriental arched windows – and a hotel – all combined.' But this exotic unfamiliarity was offset by much that was familiar – which, to John Davis, at least, came as a tremendous relief: 'We arrived in the very cool of the morning, there was a mist around and a few chaps who'd come down to meet us were wearing ordinary blue, public school type blazers. They seemed to be our type completely and this I think raised our morale all round.' From the station he and the other Police Probationers were taken straight up to the police mess – 'known for some reason as the "Jam Factory"' – and given their rooms.

The station had its own hotel which, with the newly-opened *Majestic* and the *Empire,* made up the sum of Kuala Lumpur's European hotels. Cecil Lee's first night in KL was spent in the *Empire,* which he found to be 'rather a come-down from the purple East' as he had envisaged it:

> There was this rather scruffy room, embrowned mosquito net, thunderbox sanitation and a generally depressing ambience. I recall on the first night having to jump under my mosquito net to avoid a bunch of flying ants that came in through the window. I also remember leaning out in the cool of the night and there below me, under a large spreading rain tree, was a Chinese rickshaw puller, resting on the hafts of his rickshaw, utterly exhausted, because it was a killing business.

Singapore, too, had its modern hotels: notably, the slightly raffish Dutch hotel, the *Van Wijk,* 'the place of assignation' for European women of easy virtue – where 'you could get French, German, Dutch or Russian girls but not an English girl. If an English girl came out on the mail boat the CID sent her back on the next one. They wouldn't have it' – the old *Hotel de l'Europe,* regarded as *the* hotel in the inter-war period, and the *Raffles,* the hotel made famous by Somerset Maugham. The last was one of a chain of hotels that three enterprising Armenian brothers had built up in the East in the 1880s which included the *Strand* in Rangoon and the *Eastern and Oriental* in Penang. Arshak Sarkies, the youngest of the brothers, was sometimes to be seen waltzing round his own ballroom in the *E & O* with a whisky and soda balanced on his head. It was said of him that when the great slump came in the late 1920s dozens of planters and tin-miners who had run up large bills in his hotels had their accounts 'overlooked' on his orders – while others in even worse straits were provided with passages home to Britain.

However, arriving at the *Raffles* after journeying across the Pacific from America, Norman Cleaveland was shocked to see how 'extremely primitive' the hotel's plumbing was. It was his first introduction to the *jamban* and the 'Shanghai jar'. The first was no more than a simple commode, popularly known among Europeans out East as a 'thunderbox', while the 'Shanghai jar' – otherwise known as a *tong,* 'Suchow tub' or 'Siam jar' – was a 'huge ceramic receptacle from which you were supposed to ladle cold water to bathe yourself'. Like many a newly-arrived innocent, Cleaveland mistook the jar's purpose: 'I thought you were supposed to get *in* it so, much to the distress of the servants, I got in and bathed in the Shanghai jar. I thought it looked a little tight but it was kind of cosy.'

Primitive though it might have appeared, the Shanghai jar was a bathroom fixture that visitors quickly learned to appreciate. Due to evaporation through the porous clay, the water inside was always kept deliciously cold: 'One of the great delights in one's daily routine, morning and evening, was to douse oneself over with these lovely streams of cold water from a wooden scoop of large dimensions known in Malaya as a *gayong*. One would *gayong* the water over oneself with many a splash and shout and feel enormously better afterwards.' And in places where there was no refrigerator and no ice-box the Shanghai jar had another useful function: 'We used to put our beer in there.'

Another mistake that Cleaveland made was to turn up in Singapore improperly dressed in a straw hat:

It was an obsession that the people in Malaya had at that time that you had to wear what was called a *topee* to prevent the horrible effects of the sun on your head. When I arrived at the office I was promptly taken by the secretary out shopping to get proper headgear. There was only one *topee* we could find that would fit me, a heavy cork thing and most uncomfortable to wear, but I was constantly reminded that I should wear it, and whenever I showed up in my straw hat I was admonished – because the company had after all invested quite a bit of money in getting me out there and so they had good reason to look after their company's interests.

Bill Bangs was another newcomer who disembarked in Singapore – and he, too, was soon introduced to the Eastern way of doing things. He was met by the acting manager of the rubber estate on the mainland to which he was being sent and told that he would need some working clothes:

He took me to a tailor's shop in Singapore at ten o'clock in the morning where I was measured for six pairs of shorts, six shirts and four white drill suits. The acting manager said, 'When will they be ready?' And the man said, 'They can't be ready before two o'clock this afternoon.' So we did some more shopping else-where and had a very good lunch at the *Europa Hotel* and then we went to the tailor, where all my clothes were ready – and the tailor was apologizing that he hadn't been able to send them to the *dhobi*! At the end of the month I sent him a cheque, because in those days no Europeans ever carried any money; everything was signed for.

When his shopping was completed Bangs was taken by launch across the Johore Straits and then up a creek to his rubber estate.

However, for many newcomers their travels ended with their arrival in one of the three large towns – George Town, Singapore or the FMS capital, Kuala Lumpur. In KL the Eastern Cadets, as well as the Police Probationers, had their own mess. Officially designated the 'cadets' bungalow' but known to its occupants as the 'Bull's Head', it stood on a ridge overlooking the big parade ground and playing field known as the *padang,* which had originally been levelled for the police to drill on but soon became the central ground for the principal sporting activities of Kuala Lumpur.

Hanging about outside the cadets' bungalow when Mervyn Shep-pard first arrived were a number of Malays, Chinese and Indians, all hoping to pick up jobs as servants: 'Very often they'd been employed a number of times before, hadn't been successful and had been discarded. There were several cadets requiring a servant so I was more or less allotted a rather elderly Malay called Matt. He had at least two letters saying he'd been in previous service and had been satisfactory, so I took him on.'

The bungalow itself consisted of about a dozen single rooms opening onto a very large central dining room:

In our bedrooms we had no means of keeping cool and they were rather hot and mosquito-ridden, but over the dining-room there was a series of pleated fans called *punkahs* – not a Malay word but an Indian word which had been introduced from India. These hung from a wooden frame which was connected to the roof by struts. It had pleated blanks of cloth and a long rope which was pulled when required by a small boy, who was prob-ably the son or grandson of one of the staff. He might pull it with his finger or his toe, but he would go on pulling and letting go for as long as he was required to do so. And as long as he pulled the rope and let go the fans continued to flap and thereby caused a reasonable amount of movement of air.

While there were no formal lines of demarcation, both the police

and the cadets' messes in KL were sited in what amounted to a government officers' residential area west of the *padang* and overlooking the main town itself. Next door was the mercantile housing
area, where the larger companies and the banks had bungalows for
the senior and married staff and messes for the bachelors, concentrated mostly in the 'hilly area with its great albisia trees round the
Maxwell Road'. Between them these two areas constituted the
'European quarter' of Kuala Lumpur, leaving the Chinese in control of the town and the Malays on the outskirts. Thus, Harrison
and Crosfield had three staff houses up on Maxwell Road, named
Wycherley, Congreve and *Farquhar* 'after the naughty dramatists of
the Restoration Period', as well as a mess named *Sheridan:* 'Just
below it was the Hong Kong Bank house and opposite was a green,
grassy area which was a meeting place for a flock of Chinese *amahs*
with their little European charges, who played and gambolled
around while their *amahs* chatted amongst themselves like a sort of
Chinese club.'

The mess – sometimes referred to in Singapore and the other
Straits Settlements by the Anglo-Indian term *chummery* – provided
the means by which two or three bachelors could live together and
save expenses: 'We'd have one cook and one "boy" and one
gardener. All the food that came into the house was divided by
three and all the drink and expenses, and at the end of the month
you'd have to pay your third share of everything, which was very
small. I don't think it came to more than about a hundred and
twenty dollars all in.' But not all the companies provided a mess, in
which case 'you hunted round the various *chummeries* – maybe four
engineers or sales people or accountants or whatever there were of
that particular company – and you went and had dinner with them
and if you liked the sort of life they lived you became one of them'.
Gerald Scott was one of those who had to look for a mess when he first
came to join the Asiatic Petroleum Company in Singapore in 1938:

> I went out to dinner to three chaps in a *chummery* who had a
> vacancy and it was eating at eleven o'clock at night – which was
> fairly normal at that time in Singapore – and a lot of drink and so
> forth. It was a totally unintellectual, practical engineers' type of
> life and it wasn't my cup of tea. So I went off on my own and I
> quickly found another chap in the Shell Company who was an
> Oxford type, and we had something in common and so we went
> off to live in a Chinese palace which was quite magnificent. It
> was run by an extraordinary woman who was a hermaphrodite –
> although we didn't know it at the time – and whenever the moon
> was full this woman used to go absolutely berserk!

Rather more representative was the Harrison and Crosfield mess that Cecil Lee eventually moved into in KL:

It housed four of us – two Seniors and two Juniors – and we had two 'boys', a cook, a gardener or *kebun* and the Seniors had two *syces,* an Indian word for a groom for the horses which had been carried over with the advent of motor cars. The cook was said to have been with Sir Laurence Guillemard, a former governor, and one of his *pièces de resistance* was a pigeon pie. The idea was that when you cut the pie a pigeon flew out – and then he brought in the real one. Once, when we had some young girls round to dinner, one of the young topsies cut the crust and the poor little pigeon hopped out and misbehaved itself. The girl screamed and the whole thing was a bit of a flop.

The mess also had a large garden surrounded by jungle and full of such flowering exotics as Van de Joachim orchids, purple petria, yellow alamander, red poinsettias and white, fleshy fran-gipani. There were also jacaranda trees, bushes of blue plumbago and a pomelo tree, which had inedible fruit and was mainly used as missiles in some boisterous games. It was all very exotic and in some ways so attractive, but I missed the freshness of our home flowers and even the exotic scents seemed to have a harshness and a lack of the fragrance that I'd been used to at home.

Tending this garden was an old Malay *tukang kebun,* 'a retainer of twenty-seven years' service who had followed one *tuan* after another with exemplary patience and fidelity. In the morning you'd wake up and he'd be watering the plant pots or scything the grass, which seemed to be his main task. One master after another would pass through and some would take an interest in his work, but mostly he was left to his own devices.'

Away from the messes large numbers of servants were rarely to be found in individual households. Bachelors who set up house on their own generally managed to get by with a cook-boy 'who bought the food and cooked it for you' – possibly supported by his wife and a *tukang ayer* or water-carrier 'who did the washing and scrubbed the floors'. Even with increasing seniority and marriage it was unusual to find a European household with more than three or four personal servants.

As soon as the newcomers were established there were certain formalities to be observed, the first of which was the custom of call-ing. 'The business of calling and card-dropping, as in India, was still in vogue when I came out. It was probably declining,' Cecil Lee recalls, 'but I still remember being taken by my host, who was a government servant, to sign the book for the Chief Secretary and the Resident and the Chief Justice, which were kept in little boxes in the bottom of their gardens. And I remember being told that I and my colleague in the mess would not be invited to the house of a certain senior member of the firm unless we dropped cards.'

Before cards could be dropped they had first to be printed and then delivered personally at each bungalow. Artificial and old-fashioned as this ritual appeared to some, it was nevertheless based on good sense – as Edward Tokeley discovered when he joined Bousteads in George Town:

> This was a very important part of life in Malaya and Singapore in those days because the British community went out of its way to look after the new arrivals and see that everything was done to make them welcome and to bring them into that community. And in order to do that, you had to have some name cards printed. Then the mentor who met you gave you a list of senior people – married people of course – upon whom you had to drop these cards. We were supposed to do it in the evening time, and not be seen. All houses in those days had a little card box at the entrance to the drive, so you waffled around with your list with your mentor, who'd be driving you to show you where everybody lived, and you dropped a card in the proper boxes, and then it became obligatory upon those people on whom you dropped a card to invite you to their houses for a meal or a drink, so that within a very short space of time a newcomer became known and knew other people as well.

In a land where 'you were on the move the whole time' and where government servants particularly could expect to be moved from one posting to another about twenty times in the course of their careers, such customs may have made sense. But, increasingly, there were newcomers who saw such social conventions in a different light. 'When I arrived in Singapore I realized very quickly that I was living in the British colonial Raj and that there were certain rules to obey,' acknowledges Gerald Scott. 'I suppose at that age I was a bit bolshie and I wasn't going to cower down to any of these rules.' So Scott decided not to drop cards on anyone – 'for the simple reason that I realized from my colleagues out there that if you did you were absolutely done for. I didn't want to be under the discipline of the good wives of the British – and so I didn't call on them. I didn't drop cards on the Governor and I didn't drop cards on the Shell Company wives – quite wrongly, looking back.' In due course, he was forced to compromise: 'I got a girl-friend and her father, who was an important chap in the MCS, said, "You don't take my daughter out unless you have the courtesy as a visitor in a colony to call on the Governor." And of course when I was talked to by such an eminent creature, naturally this was the first thing I did – but I didn't do it on the Shell Company wives.'

After the proper introductions had been made the newcomer could then turn his attentions to joining the right clubs. Penang could boast the senior club in South-East Asia, the Penang Club, founded in 1858; an all-male preserve with a women's annexe attached known as the 'hen roost'. This was the *tuan besars'* (big masters') club, to which Juniors or *tuan kechils* (small masters) could not hope to gain admission – unless they happened to belong to the MCS. The club's presidents were mostly senior British businessmen but its membership included a number of leaders of the Asian community; Muslim Indian and Chinese business tycoons, as well as the Sultan of Kedah, who was automatically the patron of the club by virtue of the fact that his ancestor had leased the island to the British back in 1786.

For other Juniors in Penang, young mercantile assistants like Edward Tokeley, there was the Penang Cricket Club which, besides cricket, 'gave you absolutely everything you wanted – rugger, soccer, tennis, hockey. You also joined the Penang Swimming Club, which had a lovely swimming pool a few miles along the coast from the township.' The Swimming Club was 'strictly a European concern in those days, because no Chinese would think of swimming in the sea. Only the mad Englishmen would do that.'

Singapore and Kuala Lumpur had virtually the same set up, each with three major clubs that were 'for the Europeans and exclusive to the Europeans'. As a Junior in Singapore 'you could join the Tanglin Club and the Singapore Swimming Club, but you couldn't join the Singapore Club, which was the Seniors' club, where they all had their tiffin.' John Forrester's first visit to the Swimming Club had been as a young boy, when his ship had called at Singapore on its way back to England from China: 'It was in the sea and had nets all round it, but a shark got in and took one of the lady swimmers. This very brave man was on the raft that she'd just dived off and he dived on top of the shark and got her back to the raft, minus a leg. We were on the beach at the time and there was a terrible commotion. I remember being taken very quickly back to the ship.'

In KL there was the Golf Club, dominated by Scots, the Lake Club for the *tuan besars* and the more egalitarian Selangor Club for Juniors and Seniors alike. 'We would no more have dreamt of putting our names up for the Lake Club than flying,' asserts Trevor Walker, who joined Guthries in Kuala Lumpur in 1937. 'We should have been blackballed anyway. We joined the Selangor Club, which gave us our team games and the social outlet that we needed. There was dancing there with the daughters of senior men, but there weren't enough of them and we had to book them up about three weeks ahead.'

The Selangor Club – popularly known as the 'Spotted Dog' or simply the 'Dog' – was one of the great institutions of the East. From modest beginnings in 1884 in a wooden hut with an *atap* thatch roof on the northern side of the *padang*, it had grown into a rambling timbered complex of bungalows that housed two bars and a number of tiffin, card, billiards and reading rooms. The Dog was the scene of such high spots in KL's social calendar as the St George's Night Ball when, to the strains of *The Roast Beef of Olde England,* beefeaters from the Royal Society of St George carried dishes of roast beef onto a dance floor surrounded by enormous blocks of ice – with frozen roses inside. Perhaps its greatest moment was the occasion of the Prince of Wales' visit in 1922, when he was said to have greatly upset the senior *mems* by dancing all night with a particularly attractive Celanese Eurasian.

By the 1920s the bulk of the Dog's two thousand members were planters and others living outside Selangor State, for whom the club provided a second home where they 'could come in and have their lunch and sink into one of these great long chairs with leg rests and a hole in the side where you put your *stengah* – your whisky soda'. There were a number of conflicting stories as to why the club should have come to be known as the Spotted Dog. Some said it was because of its early policy of allowing Eurasians and Asians to join, others that it went back to KL's early days when the wife of the Superintendent of Police used to drive down to the club with two Dalmatians trotting under her carriage. Sjovald Cunyngham-Brown was given a possibly more authentic version, from an old friend of his named Harry Kindersley:

> He told me that his grandmother, the wife of the original Kindersley who planted a large estate not far from KL in 1885 or so, used to come up by dogcart from the estate very frequently and have a picnic with her young friends under a tree on the *padang*. Now under the dogcart were two Dalmatian dogs, and it became the habit of the young people having their picnic with this extremely attractive lady – as she was apparently – to say: 'Are you going down to the spotted dogs this morning?' And from that habitual picnic event there grew up the title 'Spotted Dog' for the club which was being built at that time.

The three European clubs were by no means the only ones in KL: 'The Chinese also had their own clubs – a well-known millionaires' club and a Chinese athletic association – and the Indians

had theirs, and so had the Malays and the Eurasians. As young men
we played cricket against them all – except the Chinese millionaires
– but they were as exclusive as our clubs were.' There was no
question of 'not wishing to mix with the other races', argues Trevor
Walker. 'That was just not true. But in the privacy of our clubs we
wished – and *they* wished – to follow our own way of life.'

However, if the races kept to their own clubs they did at least
meet on the playing field – as Alan Morkill experienced when he
was a District Officer in 1923 in Tampin:

> The wicket keeper was a Japanese photographer, the best bowler
> was a Sikh who took about a hundred yards' run and delivered a
> fearsome ball, and my Malay assistant magistrate had been at the
> Malay College and was a very good player. We had an Indian
> clerk from my office who was fielding at square leg and somebody
> hit a ball while he was watching a pretty girl go by on a bike,
> which hit him on the backside and knocked him flat. Our oppo-
> nents included a former captain of Eton who was a planter and
> another planter who had played for Hampshire, but by stone-
> walling we managed to make a draw of it.

Both in the towns and in the outlying districts organized sport
played a major part in the lives of the younger Europeans, because,
'when you weren't working, your life was playing games'. The year
was divided into two seasons 'not for climatic reasons, because there
wasn't an awful lot of difference between the months, but for sporting purposes'. Football and cricket were played from March
through to the end of August and then, for the next six months,
rugby football and hockey. Heat and humidity were ignored –
'although we used to sweat like hell, of course', and at the end of
every game 'you first of all wrung out your shirt and shorts and then
had a large glass of salt and water before getting down to more
serious drinking'. The only concession to the climate was that soccer
and rugger matches were five minutes shorter each half. 'When
one is young one can acclimatize very quickly and so the heat didn't
come into it,' Edward Tokeley maintains, 'although, if it was a particularly hot period and the ground became hard-baked, one did
appreciate the activity of the fire-brigade in hosing down the field a
bit beforehand – and in the Thirties they were kind enough to do
that.'

Sporting tournaments – notably the HMS Malaya cup for rugger
between the different states – as well as more local fixtures were
taken seriously but not to extremes. Norman Cleaveland found prevailing attitudes towards sport in marked contrast to those that he
had known in the United States. Although regarded as an 'inter-

loper' he was a good games-player and had even played some rugby football before coming to Malaya:

> I managed to get in the state side that won a couple of local championships and I found an extremely interesting contrast in the relaxed attitude that they had. In fact, I remember one important match in which we were severely criticized for questionable sportsmanship because we had been training and it was not considered proper to do that. I found that training generally consisted in not going on the field under the influence. But if you abstained from drinking and went to bed early and took exercise then you were violating the code.

However, this same social code ensured that in a small community 'the young bachelor was brought *into* the community'. Edward Tokeley in Penang found himself being asked out to dine two or three times a week. If the company was mixed, he was expected to wear a dinner jacket and a stiff collar, which was 'a bit of a bore – but not so much of a bore as it was on a dance night, because the collar that one wears with tails gets pretty limp if you're dancing in a temperature of eighty degrees, and so one had to change one's collar two or three times during the evening'. Yet, despite the discomfort, 'we managed to get through these evenings with the utmost ease and considerable pleasure'.

Some took the business of dressing for dinner very seriously, notably in KL a 'very pompous Chief Secretary with a very portly stomach, who dressed every night in a stiff shirt and black trousers and white mess jacket. All his shirts and stiff collars were sent back to the United Kingdom to be laundered – and every week a parcel used to come through from a laundry in Notting Hill Gate.' Bachelors dining on their own usually dressed much more informally. In Cecil Lee's mess it was the senior member who set the example:

> He was a bachelor and his ways were very fixed. Every night about six o'clock his car came chugging down and his *syce* took him off to the club, where he drank with his friends. He used to arrive back about seven-thirty and change into his *sarong* and *baju*, which was the Malayan equivalent of pyjamas, and then swallow a couple of whisky *pahits* and have his dinner and go to bed. We followed his custom of wearing a *sarong* and *baju* for dinner until a new member of the mess arrived who frowned upon it and regarded it as a sign of degeneracy, so then we always dressed for dinner.

To get to work Cecil Lee and his colleagues in the mess had only to jump into a rickshaw or simply 'walk across the green of the *padang* and past the government offices into Market Square, which housed the main European firms. It had tulip and jacaranda trees in little grass plots and in those days housed all the cars that were needed.' The Harrisons' office was 'an old-fashioned building with great bat-haunted Corinthian columns – and with an old *jaga*, a Sikh watchman, sitting out in front with his *charpoy* (bed). He was generally the man who lent most of the Asian staff money, which he used to collect from them when we paid them every month.'

The Guthries' head office was in Singapore but they also had a smart new office in KL in Java Street, with a *godown* or warehouse on its ground floor – 'harking back to the days when the shopkeepers lived over the shop with their goods down below them'. Bousteads, too, had its head office in Singapore but with a branch office in George Town; an imposing building facing the harbour with a *godown* below and offices above. Across the middle of the *godown* ran iron rails for loading and unloading ingots of tin. As well as tin the warehouse housed copra, which 'smelled a bit after the heat had been on it, encouraging little copra bugs that flew around in their hundreds and got in your hair'. Another feature of the Penang office was a monsoon drain in the road outside which 'got cleared when the tide was in but left a lot of evil-smelling mud when it went out. The smell of the mud with that of the copra and some of the other spices that were being held in the *godown* – these were the romantic smells of the East!'

Offices at this time were generally large open-plan areas 'with little horse-boxes where the Seniors sat'. All the executive staff were European. 'We all had telephones and like other young men we tended to be fairly noisy and light-hearted,' recalls Trevor Walker:

> Facing us in serried ranks were our subordinate staff; Indian and Chinese accounts clerks who knew much more about the work than I did and upon whom I was very dependent in my early period. But it was a feature that the subordinate staff worked in deathly silence and in deathly earnest until they went out to have a cigarette, which they were not allowed to smoke in the office itself, or have a cup of tea, which was served to them downstairs. These clerks were generally known as *keranis* – an Indian word that denotes clerk – and the office boys were generally Malays and were known as *peons,* which I think came from the Portuguese. In those days the more simple jobs were done by Malays, and the Indians and Chinese divided the rest of the work between them.

For the Juniors the working day began at eight-thirty with the Seniors arriving half an hour later. There was no air-conditioning until late in the 1930s; most offices had high ceilings from which hung electric fans, keeping the air circulating and at the same time 'disturbing all the papers on your desk'. Ties were worn but no coats, and only senior government servants and a few brokers still clung to the old-fashioned *tutup* jacket. 'We had jackets made of crash but we never wore them,' asserts Trevor Walker. 'You carried one over your arm and hung it up when you got to the office, and took it home in the evening without ever wearing it. So one was very free and easy in white trousers, a shirt and tie and rolled-up sleeves.' Prickly heat where one's arms rested on the desk was a common complaint but in other respects these were perfectly bearable working conditions for most Europeans, who found the climate monotonous rather than oppressive: 'You could walk across the *padang* to have your lunch and back again and, even with your coat on, you wouldn't be perspiring that much.'

Working out of doors was a different matter. Then the full force of the equatorial sun and the accompanying humidity became almost intolerable – as Edward Tokeley experienced whenever his duties took him out to the ships discharging coal opposite George Town:

> One had always to be properly dressed in a white drill suit and tie and standing on the iron decks of these ships at mid-day you could feel the heat coming up from the soles of your feet and down through the hair on your head. Then you did sweat – and the coal dust settled all over your nice white drill suit. I remember going back to my *tuan besar* and suggesting very politely that these suits should be a charge on the company. That produced no response that I welcomed at all.

Unlike the Dutch in their Eastern territories, who took long afternoon siestas and returned to work in the late afternoon, the British preferred to work through the day, leaving themselves an hour and a half for games and exercise before the short tropical twilight came on. It was also usual to work until one o'clock on Saturdays, with sport in the afternoon, which left them free on Sundays to enjoy a large curry lunch followed by a 'lie-off' in the afternoon. Attendance at church was not expected of anyone – but for those who did go there was one significant concession to local custom: 'you could even sign a *chit* for the collection'.

Between the leading mercantile houses there was also a distinct element of rivalry, 'dating back to the old days of the clippers, when Jardines sent their teas racing home to get them on the market before other people'. However, the 'sharp infighting' of the nineteenth century had long given way to a friendlier competitive spirit, partly because money had become scarcer in the 1920s and the slump had seriously weakened the market. Rivalry was also hard to keep up when one's competitors were also one's closest friends, for 'although we competed very hard with each other we all shared the same clubs and played rugger and cricket together and drank together. But at the same time you were very pleased if you could get a certain contract and the other chap couldn't.' It was also a fact that with the improvement of the shipping services and the telegraph a company's Eastern offices were no longer as independent from its board of directors in London as they had been in earlier times. Air-mail, however, only began to play an important role in the years immediately preceding the Second World War; companies and individuals alike were still heavily dependent on the weekly arrivals of the mail-boat, which arrived off Penang on the Thursday and left, homeward bound, on a Saturday afternoon: 'That was always a great day because you would pile on board and see your friends away who were going on leave. It also meant a certain activity beforehand in the office because the outgoing mail had to be completed in time to catch the ship.'

Juniors in the big companies were expected to toe the line. The borrowing of money was forbidden and the man who got into debt to a money-lender was regarded as beyond the pale. If his borrowing came to light he was usually bought out and packed off home. The firms were equally strict in enforcing the ban on marriage during the first tour of service. This proved to be the undoing of at least one Junior, who began his first contract in Ceylon while concealing from his employers his intention of getting married:

> I had assumed that I would work so diligently and they would be so impressed that they would waive the rules. However, the rules applied to a great many people and they weren't about to waive them for me – as it turned out when I got the sack and three months' pay, which made me richer than I had ever been before. I then found that I had to take the ship home within four weeks, otherwise a passage home would no longer be my entitlement and I would be thrown upon my own resources – which was not a very happy prospect in view of the fact that it was impossible for a Westerner to work in the ordinary sense in a colonial place. You either worked at the top or somewhere near it or not at all. Because of the social mores of the day nobody would consider taking me on. I stomped round all the offices I could think of, looking for another job, whereupon I found that the word had preceded me and every door was closed.

Europeans were expected to 'maintain the reputation of the white man' and to observe certain social standards: 'If a man "went native" he was frowned upon and ostracized. There was one man whom we called *Tuan Burong* – tuan bird – who went and lived native in the *kampong*, but nobody knew him and he never mixed with any of the other Europeans. That was the kind of attitude; the colours kept to themselves.' Inevitably, there were difficulties when it came to relations with the opposite sex. Guy Madoc remembers how when he first came to KL there was a 'considerable shortage of feminine company. As far as we could make out there were only two unattached young English women in the whole of that big town.' At

---

Hongkong & Shanghai Banking Corporation.

(INCORPORATED IN THE COLONY OF HONG KONG)
THE LIABILITY OF MEMBERS IS LIMITED TO THE EXTENT AND IN MANNER
PRESCRIBED BY ORDINANCE NO. 6 OF 1929 OF THE COLONY.

HEAD OFFICE
HONG KONG.   1.

16th January,

My dear M

    I have your letter of 30th December in which you ask my permission to get married in June after 8 years' Eastern service.

    In the normal way I would say Yes provided you can show me that you &/or your fiancée has enough private income to make up the difference between your present salary & what it would be on a 10 years service basis, and realise that your wife is not to be any extra expense to the Bank in the way of house allowance, passages etc.etc.until you have completed 10 years.

    But your proposition complicates matters somewhat, as you inform me that though you have been out 7½ years & are not in debt, you have no surplus to meet extra expenses which must & do come with marriage.

    Frankly, I do not think it is quite fair for any man to spend his total earnings in 7½ years & then ask a woman to join him in living on a salary which he has so far needed for himself alone during which time he has been housed by the Bank.

    That is the position as I see it, so I cannot very well say I approve of your proposal.

Letter from the Hongkong and Shanghai Bank's head office to the under-manager of one of the bank's many branches in the Malay Peninsula.

the same time, 'any relationship with a local native woman would have meant the sack'. This ban was most strictly applied in government circles but even among unofficial circles there was the same taboo. 'We weren't allowed to associate with Asian women,' declares Percy Bulbrook, at that time based in Singapore as a First Mate with Straits Steamships. 'When some poor lads broke the bonds they were just shot off home, with no redress whatsoever.' Bulbrook was one of those who married a Chinese girl:

> I said, to hell with them. This is my private life. You employ me, not my wife. But we had a hard fight to break this caste business down and that's what sent a lot of the young lads up the lines after prostitutes. It got so bad that about 1931 the Mothers' Union in the UK decided that the young fellows were all going astray out here, so out they came and made a few enquiries and went around. The brothels were down a place called Malay Street and of course the Governor ordered them all closed down, the lot of them. But the ladies of the street wouldn't be beat. They formed what the old stagers here called the 'rickshaw parade'. They used to get rickshaws from Johnson's Pier and come right up the Cathedral and Stanford Road. And we lads, of course, were all there ready – and off we went!

From the point of view of the more strait-laced Malay states, Singapore was regarded as a 'sort of Buenos Aires' of the East, a place where planters and others could take local leave and 'come down once in a blue moon to see the races and to beat it up'. But even in Kuala Lumpur there was Batu Road, lined with houses of ill-repute, the best-known of which was Mary's:

> One could go down to Mary's and pay for a young lady of one's choice, and, in due course, depart refreshed. But once some of the younger wives of a particular government department decided that to go down Batu Road and have a drink with old Mary, and a refreshing talk – heaven knows what they talked about – was the 'in' thing. And therefore the young and randy bachelor suddenly found himself faced with some lady whom he'd always supposed to be extremely respectable, and whom he had not expected to meet outside of the confines of the Selangor Club.

For those seeking more innocent pleasures there were the taxi dancers in places like the *Eastern Hotel*, where 'you could go and have a drink and have a dance by buying a book of tickets and giving the girl a ticket and dancing away'.

So, step by step, the Junior came to terms with Asia and its ways.

He learned to sprinkle his conversation with Anglo-Malay *argot;* to talk about *makan* for his food or meals, *barang* for his luggage or property, *gadji* for his pay, *chop* for his company's trade-mark. He learned to call out 'Boy!' with authority and to talk about 'coming round for *pahits'* rather than cocktails. He grew accustomed to a monotonous climate that remained damp and steamy throughout the year; with nights 'when you rolled around in a mosquito net and found it difficult to get a good night's sleep' and a rainy season in the winter when it did nothing but rain 'buckets and buckets'. He learned to consult the 'Birthday Book' or the Civil List, which listed the seniority, salary and date of birth of every official in the country and all his gazetted posts, and the equally invaluable *Straits and Malayan Directory,* which provided the equivalent details of commercial life – as well as offering information on everything from *'jinriksha* (rickshaw) fares within the municipal limits of Penang' to the 'payment of savings deposits belonging to lunatics'.

The newcomer also quickly learned to know his place, which in the British community was very largely decided 'by your work and for whom you worked'. In business circles this meant that a social barrier divided mercantile from trade. Europeans working in such large stores as John Little, Robinsons or Whiteaway and Laidlaws were held to be tradesmen and were expected to stick within their own social circles and clubs, as were a handful of other salaried workers such as the British or Eurasian engine-drivers, NCOs on attachment from the British Army and jockeys.

All the same, the British in South-East Asia never adopted the rigid hierarchical system of the British Raj in India. Commercial interests were still paramount, to the extent that 'whereas in India the *box-wallahs,* as they were called, took second place to the Indian Civil Service, in Malaya the heads of commerce were really the heads of the community'. And yet, when William Goode first arrived in Kuala Lumpur in 1931 he was perplexed to learn that he and his fellow Eastern Cadets had joined the 'heaven-born'. This was an Indian term associated with the highest Hindu caste and, by extension, the ICS in India and the MCS in Malaya: 'I suppose it was because we gave ourselves such superior airs, but it wasn't a title that I particularly enjoyed – nor, I think, was it meant to be complimentary.' However, the Malayan Civil Servant was rarely the remote and authoritarian figure that popular imagination sometimes made him out to be:

Generally speaking, the MCS officer was a mixer and did his best to get to know people of all communities. It was not at all common for a British officer to be aloof – and if he was he would be hurriedly put into the Treasury, perhaps, and kept there. There were certain jobs which were reserved, you might say, for people who didn't mix.

It was also a fact that the MCS provided the top layer of government, so that 'in the pecking order of the country they ranked above doctors and customs officers and policemen'. Its authority was inescapable, although it was less obvious in the towns than it was in the districts where, 'when you entered the club you went and said, "Good evening, sir", if the District Officer was there, rather as you did in the army. They weren't toffee-nosed about it but they did require that little bit of deference.'

If the civil servants occupied the top rung it was generally accepted that their closest rivals were the police, whose authority was greatly strengthened by the almost complete absence of military forces in British South-East Asia. It was also left to the police in Kuala Lumpur to provide a military note with its mess nights. Young Probationers like John Davis and Guy Madoc spent their first nine months in the country in the police depot, 'learning criminal law, learning the language, learning police regulations and, almost every morning of the week, square-bashing on the parade

She—You know darling, I shall never learn this beastly language—Do ask the Boy for some matches.
He—Matches, Boy.

Cartoon from *Straits Produce,* 1927, a satirical fortnightly which had been keeping Europeans in Singapore and Malaya amused since the 1880s.

ground'. But every evening at the mess they were required to dress in their 'pretty smart white uniforms', which on mess nights were exchanged for 'the full rig – what we called "tight-arse" trousers and a shell mess jacket, vulgarly known as a "bum-freezer"'. These mess nights invariably began as very solemn occasions:

> At the end of dinner the mess president would stand and say, 'Mr Vice, the King' – we did not say 'King-Emperor' in Malaya. Then Mr Vice would stand up and say, 'His Majesty the King'. After that came the second toast: 'Their Highnesses the Rulers' – by which we meant the ten sultans of the individual native states of the peninsula. After that, 'Gentlemen, you may smoke'. And then port – which most of us felt was just the wrong thing to drink in a hot sticky climate – and cigars.

After dinner the formal atmosphere continued until the senior officers departed – which was the signal for 'all sorts of high jinks'. Motor-cycles were brought up onto the veranda that ran right round the mess building and raced up and down, vulgar songs were sung and games like 'Are you there, Moriarty?' were played, where 'you would lie on the floor blindfolded and try and hit your opponent with a rolled-up magazine'. The police mess also had its own version of the naval gun drill competition seen at military tattoos:

> We had a gun which was made up entirely of wood with detachable wheels, just like a small field gun, into which a twelve-bore shotgun barrel had been cleverly inserted. You started at the back of the dining hall and you had to carry your piece of gun without touching the floor, so most of the time you were swinging from one beam of the roof to the next. At the end of it you clambered down into the port, at the front of the mess, where you quickly assembled your gun – whereupon a Malay from the armourer's staff handed you a blank twelve-bore cartridge. You shoved this up the breech and you fired it and with any luck you had beaten the other team. That was quite a favourite performance to put on when one of the sultans was invited to dine in the mess.

These essentially military rituals were being celebrated in a country that had no standing army – at least, not until 1933 when an experimental company of what was to become the Malay Regiment was formed. Even then, the expansion of this solitary 'native' regiment was very slow and only one full battalion had been formed by the time the Japanese invaded Malaya in 1941. One of its senior officers at the time of the invasion was Major George Wort, who had first come out East to Singapore as a young subaltern in the

Wiltshire Regiment in 1933: 'We were the only battalion on the island. In fact, the only other battalion in the whole of Malaya was the Burma Rifles, who were stationed in Taiping. Out at Changi there were also two barrack blocks built for gunners and occasionally we went out there on company training. Little was I to know that some years later I would find myself having to enjoy the lovely views of Changi under different circumstances.'

To make up for this military deficiency there were the Volunteers – either the FMS and Straits Settlements Volunteer Forces or the MVI (Malay Volunteer Infantry) which civilians from all the races were able to join as territorial soldiers – and which Britons were certainly expected to join. 'It was suggested to you that you joined,' asserts Edward Tokeley. 'It wasn't at all compulsory but the system and the social set up was such that you would have been uncomfortable if you hadn't – and I really can't remember anyone refusing.'

Run by officers and sergeants seconded from the British Army as staff instructors, these volunteer units provided opportunities for enjoyable and expense-free get-togethers that cut across many of the barriers of race and class: 'In many ways it was the best club of the lot.' Training was never taken too seriously; the units met once a week and on occasional weekends, and there was an annual camp with a fortnight spent under canvas. Once a year the Volunteers turned out in somewhat ragged ceremonial display on the local *padang* for the King's Birthday Parade.

Edward Tokeley joined the machine-gun section of the 3rd Battalion, Straits Settlements Volunteer Forces, Penang and Province Wellesley:

We had parades every Monday night and we had a superb Regimental Sergeant-Major from the Coldstream Guards who taught us how to march properly. He tore you to pieces when you were trying to mess around with the machine gun but called you 'Sir' if he saw you at any time in town. There were occasions when we had exercises over Penang Hill. A lot of them took place through the Chinese cemetery and I always suspected that they didn't bury their dead too far below the surface, because during the mid-day heat one could smell aromas of the East which were not quite as pleasant and romantic as they should have been. I also remember so vividly one exercise which was co-ordinated throughout the country by the GOC, Major-General Dobbie. When it was over he gave us a lecture – and I make no mistake in what he said then. He said, 'The enemy will be Japan and the Japanese will come down the mainland.'

4

MUSTER

*We were all standing round the bar. The Boy never
stopped pouring out whisky; bottles of soda-water
opened with a rhythmic hiss like ripples in the sand.
The talk was, of course, of rubber.*

Henri Fauconnier, *The Soul of Malaya*

THAT 'almost extinct tropical species', the British planter, was by
reputation 'whisky-swilling' and the sort of man 'who only married
barmaids'. His trade was said to be 'the highest paid form of unskilled labour'. Like most reputations, this was a little wide of the
mark.

Liquor was cheap and plentiful – 'a bottle of whisky in those days
was three dollars and gin one dollar, sixty cents' and few planters
would deny that as a group they did drink 'a tremendous amount'.
However, 'This drinking was not out of hand', argues Peter Lucy:

> It didn't do anybody any harm and it probably did us a lot of
> good. If we had a heavy night we had what's known as a prairie
> oyster for our early morning tea – raw eggs and Worcester sauce
> to settle the stomach – but at half past six we were out on the
> estate. The sun was hot by seven and by breakfast time the
> effects had all disappeared. At lunch time we certainly had such
> drinks as gin-slings, which in the hot climate didn't do us any
> harm, and in the evening we started drinking whisky and soda
> again, a lot of it – but always well diluted.

For some planters there was no question that 'without drink it
would have been difficult to carry on' – and, as far as John Baxter
was concerned, 'I don't think I could have stuck life without it'.

For men like Baxter, who began working on Sapong Estate deep
in the North Borneo jungle immediately after the First World War,

planting was a 'very hard life'. In such remote areas the average planter was a 'very rough type; the unpopular boy who was sent out because he couldn't get a job anywhere else – a very mixed crowd indeed.' One of the reasons why estates like Sapong had more than their quota of black sheep and remittance men – 'from families who sent them so much a month to keep them out of the country' – was the real danger to health. Baxter himself replaced a man who had died of malaria and 'there wasn't a case of a man *not* having malaria. I also had dysentery and scrub typhus, which very nearly killed me. I didn't sleep for a week and then it broke and luckily I lived. But in the early days there was continual malaria and sickness.'

A year was to pass before Baxter even got off the rubber estate and two years before he was able to visit the port of Jesselton, the headquarters of the North Borneo administration. It was a 'very narrow' existence, he recalls, with long working hours and little social life:

> You got up at four-thirty in the morning, roll call was at five-thirty by lamplight and you came back at ten-thirty for breakfast. You weighed in latex from eleven till one, came back and had a two-hour lie-off. Then you went to see your tappers working in the afternoon and went to the office at four, where on work-days you worked till six – and on Wednesdays and Sundays till five. You played tennis on the Wednesday and we had a little five-hole golf course where you played on the Sunday. We had two free days a month, four free days at Christmas and four days at *Hari Rayah,* the big Islamic holiday, because labour in those days was imported labour from Indonesia. There was no social life except that you went to the club every evening after six o'clock. I suppose at that time there were about eight members. We had a billiard table and you played billiards or you played bridge. Then you walked back to your house with your *tukang ayer* – your water-carrier – carrying a lamp. You were so fully employed that you were dead beat when you got back and you went to bed straight away.

Discipline on Sapong Estate was strictly enforced, following Dutch rather than British custom: 'If you were asked to the manager's house you had to take your hat off and stand outside. You always had to address him as "Sir" and he was a little king on his own. The assistants among themselves were very friendly but even there the senior assistant was on a superior stage and a junior assistant was a very unimportant man.' Dress was also more formal in those early days: 'You all wore the same – a *topee,* long trousers and *tutup* jacket with a collar. Khaki clothes in the morning and white in the afternoon.'

On the Malay peninsula working conditions were better and the quality of the planters themselves was higher. At the end of the First World War there were a great many officers on the labour market to choose from, some of whom, like Hugh Watts who spent a year after demobilization on a tropical agriculture course at Chelsea Polytechnic, were well qualified. In later years a firm like Guthries even made a point of looking for recruits with degrees in agriculture from the University of Aberdeen or with diplomas from the Edinburgh Botanical Gardens. However, technical skills were of no use to a planter who could not handle the estate's labour force: 'Literary gifts were not called for, nor any great expertise in the office side of the business. The great thing was that he had to be good at controlling labour.' And yet it was not a job that offered much security: 'The trouble with a planter's life really was that one never knew what was going to happen to the price of rubber. If the price of rubber was high, one got quite nice bonuses and the salary was quite good, but as soon as the price went down that was the end of the bonus and the directors quickly arranged for cuts in salary

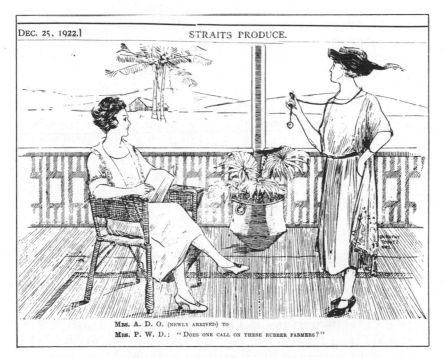

DEC. 25, 1922.]   STRAITS PRODUCE.

MRS. A. D. O. (NEWLY ARRIVED) TO
MRS. P. W. D.: "DOES ONE CALL ON THESE RUBBER FARMERS?"

'Mrs A. D. O.' refers to the wife of the Assistant District Officer,
'Mrs' P. W. D.' to the Public Works Department.
From *Straits Produce*, 1922

through their agents, and so a planter really never knew where he was.'

Handsome sums could indeed be earned as commission when the price of rubber was high. For every year that he worked the assistant received a number of shares that multiplied in number so that by the end of six or seven years of service he might have accumulated as many as two hundred shares, each paying a dividend on company profits. The only trouble was that there were few years of profit. Hugh Watts' first job, on Henrietta Estate in Kedah, lasted for a year before the rubber slump of 1921. The estate was put on a 'Care and Maintenance' footing and its three junior assistants were sent home. Then the price of rubber rose again and Watts returned – but at two-thirds of his original starting salary. Worse was to come with the great slump that began in 1929, when four out of every ten planters got the sack.

Yet for young men like John Theophilus and 'Perky' Perkins, both new recruits to Dunlops in the 1920s, life on a rubber estate on a starting salary of two hundred Malay dollars a month, rising by twenty-five dollars a year and with a bonus paid as commission from the fourth year onwards, still seemed an exciting prospect.

Perkins landed at Singapore and made his way to Bahow Estate by train: 'We stopped at a station and picked up another young chap who'd been out for a year or so and he told us all about planting and soon changed our ideas about it. He said, "Have you ever heard about muster?" I said, "No." "You've got to get up at half-past-five and take muster every morning, including Sundays."'

The ceremony of muster began every planter's day. After being roused before dawn 'by the sound of tom-toms' all assistants had to make their way in the dark to the coolie lines, where the labour force would be assembled in long columns that on some of the larger estates stretched for more than half a mile. Each estate had a number of Indian conductors or *kanganis* (overseers), as well as *mandors* (foremen) and *keranis* (clerks), so that assistants were required to do little more than be present:

The conductor does the actual calling out of names and the coolies answer if they're there. If they're not well they wait on one side and the dresser, who's fairly competent, will go and see if they're sick or pulling a line. Any labourer who's fairly ill is pushed off to the estate hospital or maybe the government hospital in the nearest town. The tappers have fixed tasks so they pick up their buckets and off they go. Then the weeders; they have to be told where to go and what to do. And then the factory workers; they know their job and where to go. And all this we used to do in the dark – with lamps, of course.

Bahow was one of Dunlops' larger estates, with several thousand acres under rubber and employing fifteen Europeans; one manager with an equal number of senior and junior assistants: 'Each senior was in charge of a division and he had a junior under him. The coolies were mostly Tamils from South India, thousands of them, so we had to learn Tamil. In fact, it was one of the conditions of your employment.' This meant sitting down with a copy of Wells' *Coolie Tamil* on the table at mealtimes and eventually taking the Incorporated Society of Planters' Tamil exam. Those who passed received a ten-dollar a month Tamil allowance; those who failed had to sit the exam again until they did pass – or risk dismissal.

Attendance at muster seven days a week was compulsory for all junior assistants – except when it rained. Soon after his arrival Perky Perkins and a fellow-assistant mistook the sound of water from overnight rain dripping off the trees around their bungalow for fresh rain and stayed in bed: 'But in fact there was muster that morning and later we were up on the mat in front of the manager. I remember him saying, "You've come out here to work. At least, I presume you've come out here to work." So we were gated for three weeks, which meant that we weren't allowed off the estate.'

At mid-morning there was the hearty breakfast that the planters called 'brunch' – 'usually porridge, eggs and bacon, toast and marmalade'. Then it was out to the field again to supervise the tappers and the weeders. Various systems of tapping the rubber trees were employed but the crucial point was to ensure that the trees were not 'wounded': 'We were allowed an inch of bark a month to cut. If you cut too deep the tree heals the wound and this intereferes with the renewal of the bark. But you must cut deep enough or you won't get the yield. The tappers start tapping the trees and putting down cups about half-past-five and at about half-past-ten they come round and collect the latex.' The latex had then to be weighed and checked for its dry rubber content – 'usually about three-and-a-half pounds of dry rubber to the gallon' – which was then recorded on the estate's check rolls. It was also necessary to see that the weeders kept the rubber trees free of undergrowth: 'When I first came out the custom was complete "clean weed", not a single blade of grass to be seen. Then people began to realize that the soil was being washed away. But I remember finding on my desk one morning a clump of grass which my senior assistant had found in my division.'

By two o'clock in the afternoon the day's work was finished and the assistants could do as they liked. After lunch and a lie-off they went down to the club which on larger estates was often part of the estate itself. Bahow planters' club had a fifty-acre golf course and tennis courts where the estate's assistants could work up a thirst

before repairing to the bar for their *stengahs,* gin *pahits* and beer –
although not everyone drank. 'We were very keen on sport in those
days,' avers Theophilus, 'so I and several of my friends never drank
during the week at all. We had a good beat-up on Saturday night
and Sunday and then stop. No smokes and no drink during the week –
and that went on for many years.'

Theophilus started as a junior assistant on Jindaram Estate, an
average sized plantation with twelve hundred acres under rubber.
His nearest club was the planters' club at Nilai, nine miles away and
with a membership of sixty. It held a Club Night every Thursday
when 'the local wives used to take it in turns to put up food for sup-
per' and members of other clubs in Negri Sembilan State would
drive over to play tennis or have a game of bridge. It was at this
level that social drinking could present problems, because 'the great
thing was that you sat in a circle of, say, ten people and each man
stood a round of ten drinks. Nobody wanted ten drinks but you had
to go on and do it; you couldn't jack out of that and live. And that is
where, undoubtedly, we did drink too much.'

On Saturdays Theophilus and his colleagues often went further
afield to the much larger Sungei Ujong Club in Seremban, the state
capital, which had been founded in 1886 and was reputed to have
'the longest bar in Asia'. This was disputed by the Shanghai Club
which claimed to have the longest *straight* bar in the East, whereas
the Sungei Ujong Club bar was oval-shaped. The club's patron was
the ruler of the state, the Yang De Pertuan Besar, a 'fine upstanding
old man with handlebar moustache' named Tuanku Muhammad,
who had a great sense of humour and was very popular among the
Europeans. He was in the habit of dropping in casually to play pool,
which he referred to as *main bola seribu* – 'the game of a thousand
balls' – but his patience was once sorely tried when a young Scots
planter, a newcomer to the club and unaware of his identity, hailed
him as *'Towkay'* (Chinese storeholder) and addressed him as *'Lu'*, a
familiar term used when speaking to inferiors.

Like other bars in the European clubs the Sungei Ujong Club bar
was to all intents an all-white and all-male preserve – although on
occasion it did have more unusual visitors. Coming in to Seremban
early one morning to attend a meeting, Theophilus found himself
alone at the bar: 'I ordered a beer and I had just taken a sip when I
suddenly felt something – hardly felt it – on both shoulders. I'd
already put the beer down and I looked round – straight into the
face of a live tiger! Luckily, I was still young then, otherwise I'd
have fallen off the stool with a heart attack.' The tiger turned out to
be a pet of a local planter and was named Blang: 'He used to take
pictures of Blang with empty Tiger Beer bottles and got quite a nice

bit of cash for it from the Malayan Breweries. He also gave curry
lunch parties on Sundays to which people came with *syces* to drive
their cars and when it was time to go home in the afternoon they'd
come out and call their *syces* but no one would answer; they'd all be
up the nearest trees because the tiger was walking round.'

The Sunday curry tiffin was a very popular social convention
among planters, given in turn by one or other of the managers or
senior assistants in the district. They were boisterous and cheerful
affairs where quantities of liquor were consumed before any lunch
was actually served. Perkins was present at one such tiffin where 'a
chap had invited a lot of people then had forgotten about it and
gone out himself to another curry tiffin. We all arrived and drank
everything he had in the house and then drove his chickens across
the lawn and shot them with his own rifle. Then we gave them to
the cook to make the curry.'

Outside working hours there was little contact with Asians on the
estate, other than with one's servants in the bungalow, although
Christmas, the Chinese New Year festivities at the end of January –
when fireworks and firecrackers were let off – and the Tamil festival
of Thaipusam soon afterwards, were occasions when fraternization
between the races did take place. All the same, the planter had 'a
very soft spot' for the men he called 'his *narlikis*' – the word being
Tamil for 'tomorrow', with the implication, as with the Spanish
manyana, that things would get done 'tomorrow' rather than at
once. And in the dark years that were to come the Tamil labourers
in their turn proved to be 'very faithful fellows', as many of their
former employers were to discover: 'In 1942 they were sent up in
droves by the Japanese to the railways in Siam where we were and it
was very touching to see how they met and greeted their old masters
– and even gave little presents and gifts to them.' Cecil Lee remembers one particular period as a prisoner of war when the Tamils and
the 'white coolies' worked side by side: 'We were carrying earth in
little baskets on our heads with them and dropping them on the line
to build an embankment. There we were, dressed exactly as they
were, in loin cloths and doing the same work, with the same mud on
our heads. We would gather together during the *yasume,* the rest
period, and yarn and smoke and exchange comments about the
funny little monkeys that were in charge of us. It was ironic really;
former masters and servants now comrades together in misfortune.'

But even at the best of times the planter's life had many drawbacks. On the smaller and more isolated estates it could be a very
lonely life indeed. When he was a District Officer in Tampin in the
1920s Alan Morkill had once to make enquiries into the case of a
planter who had killed himself: 'These wretched young men were

living alone in bungalows with rubber trees right up to the bungalow; all they heard was the crack, crack, crack as the nuts on the
rubber trees split and fell. When I went down to see what had happened to this man who had committed suicide I found six months'
letters which hadn't been opened.' Some years later Guy Madoc
had to face a rather similar situation in an outlying district when a
planter threatened suicide:

> One evening there was a hullabaloo back in the kitchen quarters
> and my cook came along with another Chinese whom I recog-
> nized as the cook of the neighbouring bachelor, whom I didn't
> know at all well. This cook was in an awful fluster and he said:
> 'My *tuan* has been drinking for the last two hours. He's got a pis-
> tol on the table in front of him and I'm afraid he's going to com-
> mit suicide.' I'd just come in all sweaty from a walk so I thought
> that the best thing was to pretend that I was passing his house
> and just looking in. So I went along and said, 'Hullo Snibbs, how
> are you getting on?' He said, 'Both my mistresses have dis-
> appeared, I'm afraid. They've gone off to become taxi dancers.
> I'm desperate' – and there was the pistol. I said, 'What's that for?'
> He said, 'I'll deal with that when I've had enough to drink.' So I
> said, 'Would you like to give me a drink?' He put out a certain brand
> of whisky and we started drinking. This was about six o'clock and I
> think it was about half-past-eight before I was able to grab the pistol
> from him. After that I didn't bother with him anymore; I told him,
> rather like my headmaster at school, to have a cold bath and forget
> it. But since then that particular brand of whisky has seemed to me
> to be an absolute abortion; I just cannot touch it.

The lack of European female company was, of course, even more
marked in planting circles than it was in the towns – and what few
mems there were near at hand were almost invariably married.
There was one well-known case of a young rubber assistant who, it
was said, fell 'violently' in love with the wife of the local District
Officer and who was so upset when the DO was transferred that he
drank a bottle of white ant poison. However, 'it was found out that
what would kill a white ant would not necessarily kill a European
and he recovered'.

One result of this lack of unattached white women was that the
strict taboos against consorting with Asian women were ignored. 'A
lot of planters kept women,' recalls Perky Perkins. 'They had
Siamese girls or Indian or Chinese and they used to help with the
bungalow.' These kept women were widely known as 'sleeping dictionaries' and were 'not seen around'; they usually remained at the
back of the bungalow when guests came to call. Japanese women

were also popular and, in North Borneo, tribal women from the interior. 'You took a local girl, as I did – a Kadazan girl who's now my wife,' declares John Baxter. 'It was not really respectable but it was done by everybody.' The only Asian women who did not find employment as mistresses were Malays. This unwritten ban was particularly strong in Johore State where 'you were never allowed to have a Malay girl. If you tried, the Sultan, Ibrahim, would see to it that you were thrown out of the state straight away.' Ironically, it was the Sultan himself who provoked what was probably Malaya's greatest public scandal since the notorious 'Letter' murder case in 1911, with his own efforts to consort with European women: 'At one time he was banned from Singapore in the evenings because if he saw a pretty girl he'd stop his car and take her off to Johore.' The scandal came to a head in 1938 when the Sultana – 'a doctor's wife he'd stolen from Singapore' – arrived at the door of the British commander of the Sultan's military forces in the middle of the night begging to be sent home to Scotland.

Isolated as they were on their estates, the planters enjoyed having visitors and always entertained in style. One such visitor to Jindaram Estate in the early 1920s was the writer Somerset Maugham. A newly-arrived assistant was deputed to give him a bed for the night and take him to muster in the morning: 'So Maugham arrived and they had a jolly good evening. There was plenty of booze and dinner and brandy afterwards and then they went to bed – but never woke up in the morning and missed muster.' Maugham apparently departed in a disagreeable frame of mind, having seen nothing of the working of the estate that he had come to see.

More frequent visitors to the rubber estates were the visiting agents and planting advisors, senior men from the agency houses who came to inspect and advise – as well as younger men from the estates departments of the same agencies whose job it was to handle the day-to-day business affairs of their rubber companies. As one of Guthries' estate agents, Trevor Walker felt it important 'to be on easy terms with the estate managers with whom I was otherwise just corresponding, so I used to visit their estates in my own time as often as I could. To start with they took a perverse delight in knocking one up at half-past-four so that one could go out with them to muster – to show the young man from the town how they lived – but once they had amused themselves I found that their life and routine was really the proper way to live in the tropics.' Many of the managers that he met in this way became his firm friends:

Some were daunting – they were much older men than I was, to start with – and I remember having a brush with a redoubtable

character who was in charge of our largest estate in Negri Sembilan, one Harry Thomas Piper, who looked rather like Aubrey
Smith in the old films. When I became his agent I had occasion
to write and pass on some criticisms of a shipment of rubber that
a certain firm of brokers had declared to be 'rusty, barky and
bubbly'. The phone rang early in the morning and this well-
known voice said, 'That you, Walker? You're a bloody liar and so
are the brokers.' I was not prepared to be spoken to like this,
even at the age of twenty-two, so I hung up – which infuriated
him. The phone rang again and he said, 'Were we cut off?' I said,
'No, you weren't. I hung up. Now what is it that you want?' –
after which we got on splendidly and never had another cross
word, because he was a very fine planter.

A manager's authority was considerable: 'The manager of any
rubber estate was very much king of the district and was respected
by everybody in the district.' The managing agency house deferred
to him and right up to the outbreak of the Second World War a
great deal of power was concentrated in his hands:

Due to lack of transport and communications a planter had to be
a bit of an engineer and a medical man as well as an agricultural-
ist. If anything went wrong with the machinery he had to put it
right on the spot and, just the same, if anybody got sick and it
wasn't easy to send him to hospital, he had to know something to
be able to treat him, even though each estate had its dresser. He
also had to collaborate with the District Officer. There was a bit
of a quarrel at one time because the Labour Department insisted
on certain things and managers thought they knew what was best
for their labour in the way of punishment, but on the whole the
managers of the rubber estates and the administrators got on well
together.

A manager's position was undoubtedly strengthened by the fact
that 'because one was an Englishman one didn't have any difficulty
in exerting one's authority; it was accepted straight away'. But
much depended on personality and between the wars many of the
older managers in Malaya were considered to be outstanding men.
Some of them 'weren't all that excellent from the agency's or the
company's point of view' but were still 'first-class men to lead a
community'. One such man was the planter C. B. Colson, whom
Cecil Lee got to know through his visits to his small estate when he
came to audit the books of his company, the New Crocodile Company:

He'd been a classical scholar at Cambridge, but some love affair
had sent him out East where he'd been recruited by Sir Eric

THE MALAY STATES

Orang puteh and elephants; Europeans fording a river in Perak State in style, 1927.

Mining in the *ulu;* the Commissioner of Lands (with *topee*) calls on
a woolfram miner in his *nipah* palm thatch hut in Ulu Dungan, Trengganu, 1924.

The 'highest paid form of unskilled labour';
rubber assistants supervise the sorting of strips of latex in bundles, FMS 1925.

Up the *ulu;* the wife of the Commissioner for Lands boards the Malay
prahu in which they toured the upper reaches of the Dungan River, Trengganu, 1924.

Fancy dress under the pull-*punkahs*;
a dance at the Tanjong Malim Planters' Club, *c.* 1922.

Out in the noon-day sun; planters and their *mems*
on a jungle picnic on the Bernam River, Perak, *c.* 1928.

Macfadyen to plant and he'd been the rest of his life on this little
estate. He was the only planter I knew who actually refused a rise
in salary because he said he wasn't worth it. The estate was only a
small one, he said, and couldn't afford it. But eventually Sir Eric
Macfadyen wrote out that he was to be paid the rise whatever he
said in the matter. He grew the most lovely roses which he got
every year from Australia and rather incongruously he used to
display them on his dinner table in Shipham paste pots. I have
memories of coming back from the Banting Club with him at
night after playing pool and drinking probably too much beer,
and sitting in his old open bungalow with the moon shining
through the coconut palm fronds and the Tamil gardener pad-
ding through and watering the lovely maidenhair ferns and pot
plants which surrounded the bungalow. Old 'Collie' would sip a
few more whisky *pahits* and I, gasping for food, would be waiting for the call for the old Indian cook, *'Makan!'* – which means
food. Then at dawn we used to arise and do a tour of the estates,
and come back to the most delicious and gargantuan breakfasts:
great piles of eggs and bacon and sausages and fried bread. I used
to dream about these breakfasts afterwards when I was a prisoner
of war in Siam.

Another well-known planter in Selangor was a 'tall, gangling fellow with a full prawn moustache' named H. V. Puckridge. Known
to everybody as 'Puck', he had won a DFC as a fighter pilot in the
First World War, was said to come from 'an old hunting family in
England' and blew a copper hunting horn 'on all possible occasions'. When Guy Madoc first knew him he owned a bull-nosed
Morris – 'but to make things difficult for the police he had the tail
taken off and another Morris radiator and bonnet put on at the back
– so that nobody knew whether he was coming or going'. Like the
great majority of planters, he was interned by the Japanese in 1941
but survived the war and was still planting in one of the loneliest
and most dangerous districts in the country throughout the
Malayan Emergency: 'He was given a small guard of special constables and he had them all trained so that every morning, shortly
after dawn, they were paraded in front of his office, the Union Jack
was raised and he blew reveille on his hunting horn.'

An even more unusual planter was Rupert Pease, a gifted
amateur artist who painted water-colours that 'evoked the very soul
of Malaya'. He ran his own small rubber estate of no more than
three or four hundred acres near Port Dickson. 'There was no
doubt whatsoever that he was a benevolent, honest, good man,'
declares Sjovald Cunyngham-Brown:

Everybody on that estate was devoted to Rupert. He had a blackboard upon which he wrote up every day the day's crop. Next to it was the current price of rubber. Next, the price of rubber per *kadi* and the price of rubber per pound. They saw it before their eyes: 'Total day's profit, so much. Those working it today were so and so. Divide that number into the other and each man's earnings for the day is that much – minus two days' wages for lazy me who didn't go out into the field but have had to do this sweat for you.' I'm simplifying a bit, but they all knew exactly what he was doing – and they all loved him devotedly.

Pease also was interned by the Japanese. He happened to be a diabetic and he took with him into prison enough insulin to last him for four years:

> But when he got in he discovered that there were several people also with diabetes who had not got enough. So he got a little committee together of all the diabetics and said, 'We will try to make the young survive.' Pease and a friend of his called Trevor Hughes, of the Malayan Civil Service, both gave all that they had and pooled it – and there were others, I believe. This did, in the event, entail the survival of the few who were diabetic in Changi during the war. Naturally, it also entailed the death of Trevor Hughes and Pease himself.

Even though it could hardly be compared with the terrible experiences of the war years, the depression and the slump just over a decade earlier also had a catastrophic effect on what had been till then an 'easy and very comfortable life' for most planters. When John Theophilus had first come out in 1925 the price of rubber had been about five shillings a pound: 'The next year it was down to about four shillings and from then on till the end of '29 it went down tremendously fast to about thirty cents a pound. In 1931 or '32 it went down to five cents, which was just over a penny. And it was from late '29 onwards that the planters were axed – about fifty per cent of them at that time – most of whom went home to England.'

Estates which in the early Twenties had been overstaffed with perhaps half-a-dozen assistants, were reduced to one manager and one assistant, while many of the smaller holdings were amalgamated with neighbouring estates. As the slump worsened some stopped tapping altogether and the salaries of remaining staff were further reduced. Quite a number of planters who had lost their jobs stayed on in the hope that circumstances would improve and in late 1930 the government stepped in to form a Special 'Service' Company of the FMS Volunteer Force, which was raised at Port Dickson specifically for unemployed planters and others in a similar plight. Among them was Hugh Watts. He found the training hard but in other respects 'life was very pleasant. There was plenty of company and we could swim or play tennis or go sailing.'

One of the lucky ones who kept his job was Peter Lucy, manager of the Slim River Estate on the northern borders of Seremban:

> I can remember receiving a letter from the agents saying that the company had no more money and the only way we could carry on was for us to sell our rubber to the local Chinese who would come and collect it at the factory. The wages of the labourers were to be paid out of the proceeds, and if there was anything over it would be the manager's salary. But for six months there was nothing over at all and so I had no salary whatsoever. There were other people in the district in a rather similar position and we simply got together and lived the best way we could, more or less off the jungle. We used to go shooting flying foxes, which had a rather strong meat but were not unpalatable and also mouse-deer, which provided a good meal. I remember giving a party once which was called a flying fox curry tiffin; this consisted of curried flying foxes and vegetables taken out of trees, which we had found in the jungle. We had no money to go to the club or anything of that kind so we just used to visit each other and enjoyed our life as best we could in those rather difficult circumstances.

Eventually the government was forced to take measures to stop the rubber industry from total collapse. A rubber restriction scheme was introduced and the price of rubber soon began to spiral upwards again. By 1933 most of the estates were able to resume tapping, but on a limited scale and without the large European staffs of the previous decade.

In August of that year Bill Bangs was appointed Manager of Kuala Pergau Estate in Kelantan, the most isolated and, in many ways, the most thoroughly Malay of the different Malay States. He was thirty years old: 'I think I was probably the youngest manager in Malaya and the reason was because the estate was very, very unhealthy and nobody wanted to take the job on.' Its last two managers had both caught blackwater fever; one had died and the other after recovering had refused to return to Kuala Pergau. The estate itself had been closed down for nearly four years, its Tamil and Javanese labour force had long since been paid off and it was sited a considerable distance up the Pergau river in what was known as the Ulu Pergau – 'the Malay word for anywhere up-river is *ulu*'.

At first the only way to get there was by walking in through the jungle and paddling downstream in a canoe on the return journey. Bangs found the estate completely run-down: 'Jungle had been allowed to grow up and no anti-malarial work had been done so there were considerable numbers of anopheles mosquitos around.' Within six months Bangs was himself seriously stricken with fever, which was assumed to be subtertian malaria but turned out to be tropical typhus. 'I became very ill indeed,' he recalls. 'At one time they came in and measured me for my coffin.' Once he had re-covered Bangs turned his attention to recruiting a suitable labour force. He had been surprised to find when he first came to Kelantan that although the population was ninety-five per cent Malay all sub-ordinate staff and labour on the railways, in the PWD and on the estates was Indian. He therefore decided to try to recruit a Malay labour force:

> All the planters in the district said I was quite mad: 'Malays were useless. Malays were lazy. There was no discipline' and so on. However, I took no notice and I got a hundred per cent Malay labour, with Malay clerks, Malay conductors and Malay *man-dors*. I did not have any other race on the estate and I found that if you treated them well and if you really liked them then the Malays liked you as well, and you could go very far. This paid off very well and Kuala Pergau was very successful. I also had the backing of the District Officer – he was the nearest European, forty-four miles away by river – who was very pleased when he heard that I was employing Malays.

At first there were problems of absenteeism which had to be over-come:

> They would ask for leave because a grandmother had died or a sister was ill or something like that – any excuse to get away. And I found the best way to deal with it was to recruit my labour from as far away as possible. If I took them from the *kampongs* close by they'd want to go back and see their mother or their grand-mother or somebody every other day. Then when it came to the big feast days like *Hari Raya* I always gave a big feast, killing a buffalo or a bullock, and had typical Malay shows; *wayang kulit* shadow plays, *mak yong* and *ronggeng* dances or *menora,* which is a Siamese show. I would arrange for these people to come and send boats down for them. I paid fifteen dollars a night and gave them their food.

Later Bangs bought a cine-camera and a projector, making Kuala Pergau probably the first estate in Malaya to have film shows for its labour. Charlie Chaplin films were always a great hit as well as Bangs' own films showing work on the estate.

Another problem with the labour force was improving standards of hygiene:

> I had a very good water supply from a waterfall in the hills and we just blocked up the waterfall and ran a pipe down and there was water for everyone. So it was quite easy to have modern sanitation, but the great difficulty was that the Malay labourer would go in and pull the chain and then do his business and leave. It was very difficult to make him understand that you pulled the plug afterwards not before. I also used to find a lot of human waste on the grass in front of the lines where the labourers lived. No one could ever find the culprit, so I found in the stores some old powder paint which was of no more use and took this out and started to sprinkle green and red and different colours on the grass in different places, and of course it wasn't long before one of the labourers came up and asked me what this was for. I said, 'I'll tell you if you promise not to tell anybody.' He said he wouldn't tell anybody, so I said, 'Well, the thing is this; I want to find out who is using this place as a lavatory and now whoever does use this place his behind will be one of these colours, and then I shall know immediately who it is – but *don't tell anybody.*' And from that day on there was no excreta found anywhere on the grass.

Few Europeans came up to Kuala Pergau apart from the Chief Medical Officer, who called once a month to inspect the labour force and to hunt for mosquito larvae in the surrounding ponds and streams. One other important guest who came to stay was the British Adviser in Kelantan, Captain Baker: 'I remember my "boy" coming into my room after I had had my bath and telling me that Captain Baker was outside and dressed in a dinner jacket. I hadn't thought about this and was merely putting on a white shirt, so I had to change hurriedly into a dinner jacket, which I had never worn in my bungalow, and pretend that I changed for dinner every night.' Another stickler for formality was the formidable Captain Anderson, who was Commissioner of Police in Kelantan for many years. Bangs used to go out on trips into the jungle with Malay friends and on one occasion, 'right up at the *ulu* of the Pergau river', met Captain Anderson camped outside the police station of a small village: 'He asked me to have dinner with him that night and I agreed and came along – and was rather surprised to find him fully dressed in a dinner jacket, because this was miles and miles away in the jungle. The drinks were all iced and I found out afterwards that he had prisoners from the jail in Kota Bharu running through the jungle with ice from the Cold Storage.'

Despite his isolation from other Europeans Bangs found it difficult to be lonely – 'because I surrounded myself with Malays. I don't think up the Pergau river there was ever a wedding without my advice being taken or without my being asked whether I could turn up for the wedding. I don't think there was a circumcision ceremony ever held without them contacting me first. I was mixed up with the Malays the whole time.' Bangs' 'boy' was also a Malay:

> When I first came out I joined the Selangor Golf Club in Kuala Lumpur, and I had a Malay caddie who was aged about fourteen. His father had just died and his mother asked me if I could give him a job, so he came into the bungalow and just pulled the *punkah* and then learnt to be a 'boy' and then learnt to cook. When I became a Muslim in 1928 I promised him that one day we would both go to Mecca and when I went on the *haj* to Mecca in 1954 he came with me. He retired after forty years' continuous service with me – except for the time when I was a guest of the Japanese.

5

THE SOUL OF MALAYA

As we crossed the first few hills, a new and unexpected Malaya was disclosed, and yet one that answered to the expectations of my heart.

Henri Fauconnier, *The Soul of Malaya*

THERE were really two Malayas. On the western side of the peninsula the developed Malaya that most Europeans knew, where the main activities lay and where most people lived and worked, with its large towns, its roads and railways, its unsightly tin-tailings and its thousands of square miles of rubber trees – 'quite beautiful when solitary but a very dull-looking thing in the mass when planted in neat symmetrical rows'. Then to the east, over the mountains and beyond, an altogether different Malaya, little developed and little visited by the majority of Europeans – 'in fact, to many people the thought of being moved across the mountain range to work in states like Kelantan and Trengganu or Pahang was very unacceptable indeed'.

But there were always Europeans who felt drawn to this undeveloped Malaya, even though the attraction was not easy to put into words. 'I find it difficult to describe,' acknowledged John Davis. 'I know I wanted the jungle and the East Coast. But there must have been others amongst our crowd for whom it was the last thing they wanted.' In their free time and at weekends Davis and Guy Madoc, along with other like-minded police cadets, began to venture out on their motor-cycles to see what the rest of Malaya outside Kuala Lumpur had to offer: 'When we got beyond the rubber estates and saw the wilderness of the jungle, that, I think, is really what got me – that first impression of the jungle as a mysterious and almost impenetrable place. I still remember so clearly John Davis and I getting off our motor-cycles and standing on the roadside and saying, "I wonder if we could get into this".' Later there came the moment when Madoc took his motor-cycle up to the central mountain range and saw what lay beyond:

> Hundreds of miles of jungle over rolling mountains, exciting torrents coming down through the jungle, and when the torrents levelled out into smooth river, green *padi*-fields and little Malay *kampongs*, dotted around in the shade of fruit trees and coconut trees. It was all that I had imagined of a rural Malaya.

There was at that time only one road across the mountains to the East Coast and one railway line, running north to Kota Bharu. To cover the two hundred and fifty miles of laterite road from KL to Kelantan it took the best part of a day of hard driving, along 'a thin streak of red winding its way through heavy jungle for mile after mile'. Those without private transport could go with the mail car on its daily run or – if they were European – sit up front in the 'seat of privilege' alongside the driver in a local 'mosquito' bus. But there was also a third way to get to the East Coast: 'The easy way and the best way was to go by night train to Singapore and then up by sea in a small coastal steamer.'

This sea journey took three or four days, with the ships passing through clusters of islands lying off the coast, each with its own legends. The largest was Pulau Tioman, 'lying exactly like a sleeping dragon', about which a story was told of 'a princess who came voyaging south and fell in love with a dragon and settled down there – which is entirely understandable if you come across Pulau Tioman in the early dawn'. Another 'most glorious' sight were the brightly-painted boats of the Malay fishing-fleets, 'going out in the morning with the rising sun coming up over the sea, the Malay fishermen wearing their kilted *sarongs* in striking colours – yellow and black, green and black, blue and black – and sailing back in the afternoon, a whole fleet of sails in the sunlight'.

One of those who travelled by sea when he first came to Kuantan in 1931 was Bill Goode:

> We took three days, calling at various little ports on the way up, along a very lovely coconut-fringed coast with sandy beaches and these little river mouths where the ship went in and usually anchored in mid-stream and people came off – until eventually early one morning we went across the sand-bar into the Kuantan river, with coconut palms on either side. There was not much sign of life but there was a little jetty against which the ship was tied up and on the jetty were two Europeans in white shorts and

white pith helmets. I was hoping they had come to meet me and indeed one was the District Officer, Huggins, who met me and took me to the rest house.

On the East Coast – as in Sarawak and North Borneo – the rivers were all-important: 'The Malays came in from the sea and the only way they could move up into the country was along the rivers'. And because of the dense tropical jungle they continued to be 'the high

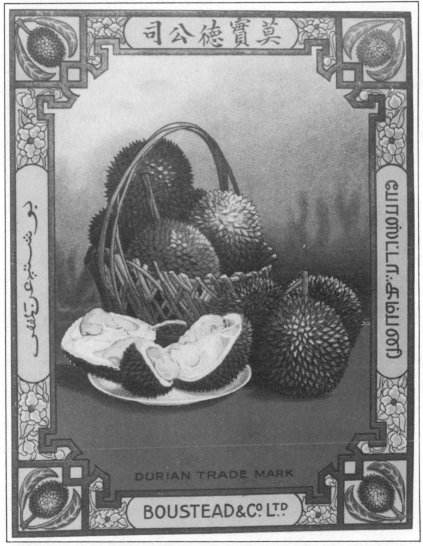

The notorious durian fruit that was said by its
admirers to taste of a mixture of 'rather rotten onions and strawberries
and cream'. From a company trade mark.

roads along which people travelled and on the edge of which people lived'. On their opaque, coffee-coloured waters could be seen 'small, overloaded boats – just about sinking by the look of them – full of women and children and men with their wide hats to keep the sun off', and at their banks 'women washing clothes or perhaps bathing their babies, and children who would rush down to the water's edge waving madly and jumping into the river because they liked to catch the wash of the boats'. The water itself was also full of life:

> There were fish and creatures of every sort, particularly croco-diles – although it wasn't as easy as all that to see them, because they were nearly always deep under water. But they were known when they took an animal or a person and they were a real dan-ger. They had larders deep in the mud-banks under the water where they kept their prey until it became nicely weathered before they ate it. They were in every way repulsive, repellent creatures. Yet all the Malays and Dayaks – who were the cleanest of people – regularly bathed in the rivers by the houses.

Young cadets like Bill Goode who were posted to the East Coast could usually expect a warm welcome from the local European community. In Kuantan this consisted of 'the District Officer and his wife, a Customs Officer and his wife, a Public Works Officer and his wife, a young policeman and myself – as well as three or four European planters who were scattered around at varying distances from Kuantan'.

Eastern Cadets could also expect to receive advice and guidance from the District Officer – although it was not always forthcoming. Mervyn Sheppard was placed under a notoriously difficult DO: 'After my preliminary interviews in the Secretariat there was an interval of about forty-eight hours before we were told where we were to go. When I was told that I was to go to a place called Temerloh in Pahang the senior MCS officer in the cadet bungalow reacted fairly strongly and said it was "the arse of the earth"! "Smith is the District Officer," he added, "and the combination will be undiluted purgatory."' Having got to Temerloh – 'a little village by the side of the big Pahang river' – he was allotted a 'funereal' three-roomed bungalow, 'which was raised three feet off the ground because of floods and was very unattractive because it had been painted with a kind of black creosote as an antidote to white ants'. He was then taken across to the district office to meet the DO:

> He suffered from three disabilities, none of which he could be blamed for. First of all, he came from Aberdeen. Secondly, he'd served in the war and he'd suffered shell shock. And thirdly, he

was just recovering from malaria, which was extremely prevalent in Temerloh. He was just cold and dour, with a grim face and no smile. He didn't say 'welcome', or 'glad to see you' or anything like that. He merely said, 'Well, you've been sent to me to learn Malay and the rudiments of administration. You won't be able to do anything useful for me for some time to come but I hope you will get over the preliminary studies as soon as possible, so that you can be of some use to me.'

Sheppard and Goode learned their jobs by being thrown in at the deep end, but to help them there were Malay Deputy and Assistant District Officers, members of the Malay Administrative Service. 'I was really put in the charge of the Malay Assistant DO,' recalls Bill Goode:

His name was Batta Hussain and he was a local territorial chief; a man of very considerable personality whose eldest son – then a very small boy – was later to become Prime Minister of Malaysia. But it was Batta Hussain who really taught me my job. He took me to the magistrate's court, where I sat beside him and listened to him administering justice. Because the courts produced a complete array of all the local people and all the local languages, interpreters had to translate from Malay into English and English into Chinese or possibly into an Indian language, so I got to recognize the local people and of course at the same time I was learning something of court work.

The Malay Administrative Service provided a second tier of administrators under the MCS. Its officers were all educated Malays; most had been to the Malay College, which was run on English public-school lines, and they were all fluent English-speakers. They were members of the local 'European' club and were regarded as social equals by their MCS colleagues – 'we went to each other's houses and played badminton together and they were very friendly and relaxed and excellent companions'. Further support came from the office clerks – Indian, Chinese and Malay. 'They were the best people to teach you because they knew the routine,' declares Sheppard. 'I spent the first week of my time in Temerloh simply watching and making notes from each of the chief clerks in the three different divisions: the District Office, the Land Office and the Sub-Treasury.'

But the first priority for any junior officer was to learn the local language. To encourage him to speak Malay, Goode was sent out into the district:

One of my jobs was to go out and inspect work on making what were known as bridle paths – the beginning of communications other than by river – and I was given the job of inspecting the work and paying off those who had worked there. When I got to a rendezvous I would be met by the local *penghulu,* a sort of parish headman, who of course would speak nothing but Malay. We would talk as best we could and we'd look at the work and very often I'd have lunch in his house, so that I was gradually introduced to Malay habits and Malay people. Naturally I would eat the food that they produced, which would be rice and some form of curry – chicken or, more likely, fish – with local vegetables, and probably a cup of very sweet coffee to finish up with. Being Muslims, of course, there was no question of their having any alcohol in their houses; life was still comparatively simple in those days and untouched by the evils of civilization.

Once the local Malay dialect had been mastered it was possible to become more closely involved with local people and their day-to-day affairs. After training in Kuala Lumpur and spending several months on short attachments, Guy Madoc was sent out for the first time as the Officer in Charge of a Police District (OCPD) in a remote area east of the central mountain range in Negri Sembilan:

I can claim that I made great progress in Jelebu because my office orderly used to encourage me to go around with him and attend local celebrations in the villages. I went to quite a lot of Malay weddings where I had to chat with the guests. I would be told, for example, that provided I embraced the Islamic religion the person talking with me would present me with his daughter as a wife. I also learned bit by bit some of the local taboos. One that is common through most Asian countries is eating only with the right hand, because the left is concerned more with the intimacies of personal hygiene. Another one was that you must never walk behind a sitting man without first asking permission to do so, the reason being that you might have a hate on him and be preparing to stab him in the back. In the same way, if you draw a *kris* – the famous curved Malay dagger – immediately you draw it from its sheath you must touch the wall or something solid nearby, because the Malay believed that when a *kris* was drawn it had the immediate desire and intention of stabbing, so therefore you must permit it to stab something it couldn't harm. And, again, you never asked a favour direct in Malay society in those days. You always asked a third person and then the third person would pass your question on to the man you really wanted to talk to.

Madoc was a very keen bird-watcher and here, too, he learned a lot about Malay customs:

The Malays had some very peculiar beliefs about birds. There's one which is called the spurwing plover, that was said to lie on its back and cradle its eggs on its feet. I couldn't believe that one, although this particular bird laid its egg on the sand, which was tremendously hot, and I do know that the spurwing plover used to go into the river and wet its breast feathers and then sit over its eggs. Then there was another belief regarding the Malayan moorhen, which is almost exactly like our moorhen. They said that if you could put a moorhen's nest on your head, then you were crowned with invisibility – very useful, of course, for thieves, although I never actually saw a gentleman bent on thieving walking along the road wearing a nest on his head.

Another pursuit that helped to strengthen local ties was touring the district – not in the grand manner of their contemporaries in India, but in a more relaxed and simple style. When OCPD in Pekan, the seat of the Sultan of Pahang, John Davis did most of his touring by bicycle and on foot:

I tried to set up a tradition that the OCPD would go and visit every single one of his stations down the coast once every month or two months. It was boyscouting in a way but it gave us a great thrill and kept us out, and it also kept our outlying stations on their toes because they never knew when this daft OCPD of theirs was going to call on them.

Part of the tour usually involved walking through the jungle but most of the distance covered was along the beach, where bicycles could be used:

I'd probably take my orderly along with me, and one or two other police constables who were perhaps relieving stations down south, and we'd travel with about half a day's journey between police stations. The idea would be to arrive at a police station, hold an inspection there, taking a couple of hours, perhaps, and then settle down for the evening, probably having a Malayan meal with the local police and the inhabitants, chatting, wandering about, seeing points of interest. Then early next day we'd set off again down to the next station, and because it was a very remote area and there were no other Europeans around you really began to become friends. You were always the boss – that was one of the inevitable things – but you felt very close to them. In those days our uniform was still rather formal, with a Wolseley helmet and a Sam Browne belt, worn with a shirt and shorts and stockings. This was necessary because you were on duty and you had to be fairly smart if you were inspecting the men, but there was no formality in conversation when we were going along together and helping each other along. It was a very happy relationship.

Touring also provided an opportunity to do a bit of shooting for the pot. Madoc would go out in the evenings 'either in the *padi*-fields shooting snipe or on the jungle edges shooting green pigeon' – which would fly over 'almost with the precision of a time clock' at about ten-to-six.

Junior administrators and other officials also toured, not always using the same means of transport but with very much the same end results. Goode did much of his touring in a Malay *prahu*, 'a native boat with a straw mat covering in which I slept and cooked and had my being'. His evenings were often spent in the local headman's house, 'sitting for hours collecting all the local gossip. One was very close to the people. One felt that one belonged and they seemed to accept one as belonging to them.'

Along with a greater sense of belonging came a greater understanding of the Malay character: 'The Malays in these rather under-developed areas may have been people of limited wealth and unsophisticated living but they were extremely astute in judging character. If they accepted you as being the sort of person that they could admire and like, they gave you everything that you would want. But they were quick enough to reject the meretricious and the spurious.' It was often said of the Malay that he was easy-going but 'you had only to see a Malay at work in irrigated *padi*-plots, ploughing, planting-out or reaping – or go out to sea once with the Malay fishermen to appreciate that they were in no way lazy'. Nor were they obsequious when it came to dealing with Europeans or officials: 'You were treated as an equal and they would tell you face to face where you were making a mistake and getting it wrong.'

One of the additional advantages of living in these predominantly Malay areas was the survival of traditional Malay culture, particularly in the many forms of Malay entertainment, from kite-flying and top-spinning to dancing and simple theatrical performances. What Guy Madoc particularly enjoyed was the *wayang kulit*, the 'leather theatre' shadow play performed with delicately-trimmed puppets cut out of thin leather and then brightly painted:

It always surprised me so much that they bothered to paint these leather figures because all that appeared was a black silhouette on a screen. If you were sitting out in front all you could see was a white cloth, which might have been a table cloth, with a brilliant light behind it. But the real excitement was to be allowed to go in behind stage and see what was happening. In a very remote village in Kelantan I once sat behind for, I suppose, a couple of hours. In front of me there was the operator sitting cross-legged on the ground and above his head was a brilliant pressure lamp illuminating the cloth in front of him. Then at the foot of the cloth but invisible to the audience there was a great big juicy stem of a banana-plant – something about eight inches thick – and all his puppets. He probably had about forty ranged on either side of him as if they were in the wings of an ordinary theatre, and each was mounted on a short stick, pointed so that he could stab it into the banana plant when its cue came. Some of them had movable jaws so that they appeared to be talking, particularly the comedians, and some at least one movable arm, so that they could gesticulate. This man was working in a pool of sweat, because he was telling a folk-tale – originally from the Hindu *Ramayana* but very considerably modified over the years so as to suit Mohammedan tastes – loud enough for the people on the other side of the screen to hear it and all the time he was also operating his puppets; bringing one in, making it talk, possibly making another one punch it with his fist, then pushing it back into the wings and bringing more out. Sometimes at the end of a performance like that the operator, who must have been in a trance, just fell over in a dead faint and had to be brought round with a bucket of water.

There was also a darker side to the Malay character: 'One of the dreaded things which we had heard about through Somerset Maugham and other people was the Malay business of *amok* or "running amuck". The typical *amok* involved a gentleman in a completely mad state running down the village street with a dagger in each hand and stabbing everybody who got in his path.' As policemen, both Madoc and Davis had to deal with a number of *amok* cases in their careers: 'You couldn't just stand there with your revolver and shoot the man dead, so we all felt that if we came across an *amok* we were in for real trouble.' The great difficulty for them was that 'everybody expected you to do something and what on earth could you do? There was no question of your being in any danger – unless you took action. But they were always difficult to handle simply because everybody turned to you and you didn't know what to do and you were inevitably excited like the rest of the crowd.' Davis recalls how *amok* 'seemed to create a strange, throbbing, reddish sort of atmosphere around it, with a man working himself up from beginning to seem a little strange and abrupt and then a little bit more difficult and gradually working up and working up but never becoming actively furious until perhaps he makes a lunge and tries to kill somebody. But internally they're absolutely boiling – and this boiling seems to spread over into the crowd which always encircles them. Of course, if it's at dusk and there are fires lit it's particularly dramatic in the flickering light.'

Guy Madoc had to deal with two cases of *amok* within three months of each other. 'I remember the first one very vividly,' he declares:

> I dashed out in the car to the village where the man was and the corporal in charge of the local police station said, 'Well, he's up on the platform outside his house and he's got an axe in one hand and he's got a *parang,* a jungle knife, in the other. He hasn't actually injured anybody yet, but don't go anywhere near him. The moment you go within six feet of him, he's up on his feet screaming, and wielding his weapons.' So I went along and I said in Malay: 'How do you do? Nice day isn't it?' And after about ten minutes, he said, 'Come and sit on the platform with me.' So I said, 'Right.' And I got up and I sat on the platform with him, and he hadn't touched his axe and he hadn't touched his jungle knife and when I was close enough and thought that his attention was diverted, I just put my arms right round his body and his arms and held him tightly against me and the corporal came up and put the handcuffs on him and that was that. After that I didn't think that an *amok* really was such a terrible thing.

But Davis remembers one particularly 'lurid' case that left him 'horribly frightened', where a man had barricaded himself in a Malay hut, having already killed two people:

> It was in the night and there were literally hundreds of people and a large number of policemen surrounding the place when I arrived. They didn't know whether there was still anybody alive in the house so that to rush him might have meant the needless death of some other person. The only thing one could do was to gradually get closer and closer until two or three Sikh policemen and myself crashed in from various directions carrying hockey sticks. The hockey stick is a most wonderful weapon in all riots and anything like that because you can hit hard and you can hook a man who's making a slash at you. We rushed the man and we succeeded in overpowering him and brought him in. That was a bad case.

For most young government servants and policemen, life on the East Coast was rarely dull or lonely. 'It was only in the first six or seven weeks when it poured with rain every day and I was having such difficulty with the language and didn't know anybody that I did feel lonely,' Goode acknowledges. 'But once I got settled down

I was too busy and the house was always open day and night so that anybody could come and go at any time – and they nearly always were coming and going.'

As regards female company in the bungalow, the prevailing ethic among officials was a simple one – 'it simply wasn't something that one did'. Early officials like Clifford and Swettenham had approved of concubinage and disapproved of European wives, but in later years this policy was reversed. Goode recalls how he and other newly-arrived cadets were handed 'a rather pompous piece of paper' which was the notorious Secret Circular A, written by the Duke of Devonshire when Secretary of State for the Colonies in 1909, which 'laid down the law that cadets were not expected to live with local ladies and that if they did they'd get the sack – about which we all laughed. But I think we all observed self-restraint. I certainly was conscious – and I think they were – that, if you took a local girl into your house and into your bed, it made a fundamental alteration in your relationship with the rest of the people in your district.'

Guy Madoc was equally content with his lot in his isolated district of Jelebu – 'but then I was twenty-one and proud that I was in charge of a district of several hundred square miles'. There was no club house as such; instead Madoc and two or three other Europeans foregathered in the late afternoon in one of the rooms of the Jelebu rest-house – or played a round of golf on a 'tiny golf course which bounced from one side of a cleared valley to the other'. After the golf they 'sat on the veranda and possibly had a whisky and soda, and usually dispersed before sunset, which all through the year occurred at precisely the same hour, about half-past-six'.

An occasional visitor to the club was *Abang* Braddon – 'the "elder brother", to distinguish him from his younger brother *Adik* Braddon, who lived the other side of the pass' – a mine-owner who had been in Malaya 'since the year dot' and enjoyed talking about his early life:

If he had to go to Seremban, the state capital across the hills, he used to start about six o'clock in the evening in an old-fashioned bullock cart. In the back of the bullock cart he would put his chaise-longue, and a bottle of whisky and something to eat for the journey. His buffalo cart would travel all through the night, and next morning he'd wake up quite refreshed on the outskirts of Seremban. Abang Braddon also had a Chinese mistress and at that time the Chinese community seemed to disapprove very much of their women having any truck with the red-headed devils, and so she always had to be disguised as a man. She wore men's clothes and a cap, and when out in public view she would go through the motions of being the *syce,* the driver of his pony trap.

In the evenings Madoc would bring papers back to his bungalow to work on or write long letters to his parents. The bungalow was enormous – 'I just rattled around in it like a pea in a drum' – and like most old-fashioned bungalows it stood on stilts, 'for the very good reason that in a Malay *kampong* you could get tigers and panthers wandering around at night. And indeed my own bungalow had what was called a *kramat* tiger, which I was told carried the spirit or the soul of one of the former Undungs of Jelebu, a local chief. I saw its pug-marks but I never heard it moving round the bungalow at night.'

At the back of the bungalow, but at ground level, was the bathroom: 'You walked down concrete steps, three or four of them, onto the concrete floor, and there was a hole in the corner where the water could go out and a great earthenware receptacle, which some people called a Shanghai jar, others a Siam jar, full of cold water. You had to keep a wooden cover on your jar, otherwise it was a tremendous breeding place for mosquitoes.' Then at the front of the house there was the veranda:

> Now in these old-fashioned bungalows you lived on the veranda, which was probably big enough to have played a game of badminton in. It had no windows or walls – just a balustrade about three foot high and otherwise open to the elements. The only protection when the wind blew and the rain beat were the roller blinds, which were called *chicks,* and which your cook-boy was expected to lower when things became unpleasant.

These *chicks* were often lined with blue canvas cloth which cast 'a very attractive, bluish, subdued light that was extremely pleasant; it was such a relief to the eyes to come from the glare outside into the gentle blue-green lighting that suffused the bungalow'. In the evenings the *chicks* would be raised again so as to let in as much air as possible, 'although you also got the maximum number of bats, moths and flying cockroaches. And of course the smaller avifauna all concentrated on your lamp, because mostly we worked after dark with things called Aladdin lamps which shed a brilliant light and attracted every bug in the district, so about every hour the thing would go out in a cloud of smoke.'

As well as insects every bungalow had its colony of pale little lizards known as *chi-chak* – 'quite harmless and perfectly clean' – running up and down the walls and across ceilings. It was a Malay belief that the *chi-chak* would interject its voice whenever it heard a truth being uttered: 'When you and I are talking, for instance, suddenly a *chi-chak* will say "chi-chi, chi-chak". And then I would be able to say to you, "You see, the *chi-chak* agrees. It's true."'

There was also the bigger lizard known as the *gekko*: 'When the *gekko* starts his "choh, choh" the Malays like to sit quietly listening – and betting as to the number of calls he makes before he stops. Some people hold four fingers up, some perhaps nine and then if you get it right you scoop the pool.'

As night came on there would be other insect and animal noises: noisy crickets that would 'start just at sunset and had a most tremendous wild squeal – but fortunately never went on long into the night'; the 'late evening trumpet beetles that were as big as your thumb and made the most appalling noise, like a child's tin trumpet, that would go on and on until nine o'clock at night and then suddenly stop'; and sometimes, overheard from the veranda, the call of the *tock-tock* bird – another sound that appealed to the Malay gambling instinct – 'actually it was a nightjar but it really did go "tock-tock, tock-tock, tock-tock". You never knew how many times it would produce that "tock-tock" without stopping and at a party when the Malays who had driven their *tuans* over to some entertainment were all sitting outside on the mudguards of their cars, you'd hear them laying bets as to how many times the *tock-tock* bird was going to produce its call.'

Madoc's bungalow stood on the top of a hill, and from his veranda he could look out over the police barracks and across towards the mountains: 'One could see, I suppose, for a score of miles across those jungle-clad hills; sometimes they were bright green, sometimes they were almost blue, depending on the time of day and the amount of sunlight – or of storm, because the elements could be mighty boisterous at times.'

On the West Coast there was the wind called the Sumatra – 'just a sudden squall that blows up, but when it blows it blows like blazes and is very often accompanied by torrential rain. Then it was the duty of your servants at the back to come running and release all the ropes and let the *chicks* come down at a run.' On the East Coast there was the winter monsoon, which brought welcome variety to the climate and played a decisive role in the lives of its inhabitants. When Mervyn Sheppard first came to Kemaman in November 1932 the north-east monsoon was just about to break:

The fishermen were just having their last outings before they pulled their boats high up on the beach for the next three or four months, because once the monsoon started, general communications by sea were cut off and you gave up all attempts to travel about the district. The north-east monsoon was known in Malay as *musim tutup kuala* – closed river mouth. It was a period of stagnation. The river mouth, which was the way in and out of the country and had been for perhaps a thousand years, was shut and the only way that anybody could get about was on land. So that was the time when, if you wanted to move at all, you walked.

During the monsoon period only two ships continued to battle their way up and down the coast. One was an ancient Chinese vessel known as the *Hong Ho* and the other was one of several owned and captained by Danish sea captains, who were 'very much admired and sometimes loved because they had very close contacts with the local people, particularly the Chinese businessmen in the various ports or villages where they stopped. They tried very hard never to let them down, however bad the weather was.' The most beloved and admired of these Danish sea captains was Captain Mogensen, about whom many stories – both true and apocryphal – were told:

Perhaps one of his most famous adventures was when he brought his ship into Kemaman on New Year's Eve and invited the local Malay commissioner and the local Malay shipping agent and one or two Chinese shopkeepers to come on board for a drink and dinner. Before going down to dinner he said he was going to let off a ship's rocket to entertain his guests and also the public. So he let off his rocket and it was a very great success and the entire village of Kemaman turned out and stood along the edge of the wharf. It was such a success that the guests asked him to let off a second one, by which time every single man, woman and child in Kemaman had assembled on the edge of the wharf and there was a demand for a third. So he agreed to make it three; the third and the last before dinner. So the third rocket was fastened to an upright support on the ship and lit, but something had gone wrong and as it rose from the ship it turned at right angles and directed itself straight down the main street of Kemaman, dividing the public sharply to right and left. When it got to the first crossroads, there was a strong breeze from the sea which blew it off course and it entered the door of the leading general store, where it buried its nose in a large collection of bottles of beer, Guinness and other liquids. There was the roar of an explosion – and that was that. The captain realized that there was nothing he could do and so he hurriedly took his guests down to dinner. But the story of the rocket survived for at least a generation and more.

The weekly steamers from Singapore provided a vital link with the outside world. 'I often used to go out in the boats taking out the

dried fish and have a very welcome cold beer with the Danish captain,' recalls Bill Goode. 'They really kept some of us along the
coast sane, because every week they brought in some supplies and
human contact.' As well as supplying duty-free drinks the steamers
provided first-class meals, which could be arranged and booked in
advance. It was also common for the Chief Officers on board to
come to private arrangements with some of the European wives
along the coast who would give them lists of shopping to be done in
Singapore. But perhaps their greatest service was that they brought
in goods from the Cold Storage Depot in Singapore: 'real meat,
packed originally in ice – which by then had melted – and sawdust,
all of which had to be washed off', but which made a welcome
change from local goat and Chinese pork; imported apples from
New Zealand and such luxuries as Iceberg Butter, 'which came in a
tin from Singapore and in the heat you had to put it on with a paint
brush'.

The ships also kept the local Chinese stores stocked up with the
kind of food that appealed to European bachelors: 'The grocers'
shops in the most remote of places always kept champagne, tins of
caviar, tinned salmon and tinned asparagus and one or two other
things that in those days were looked upon as the height of luxury
even in England.' These luxuries helped to make up the 'orthodox
bachelor dinner', so that 'when you went to a bachelor's dinner
party you knew what you were going to get: tomato soup, cold
asparagus served with bottled salad dressing, very tough chicken
roast with mashed potatoes and tinned peas, and tinned fruit salad.
That was routine.'

Opportunities for escape from day-to-day routine were inevitably
more limited on the East Coast than elsewhere in Malaya, particularly during the winter months, when an invitation to join the British Adviser for Christmas might mean walking a hundred miles – as
was once the case for Mervyn Sheppard in Trengganu. But a fortnight's annual leave always made it possible to get away to Singapore or perhaps to one of the small hill-stations that were fast
becoming a feature of European life in Malaya in the inter-war
years: the largely official Fraser's Hill in the hills outside Kuala
Lumpur and the more egalitarian Cameron Highlands in the higher
mountains further north. But there were always a number who preferred to find escape by exploring the jungles that still covered more
than three-quarters of the peninsula: the great primary rain forests
of South-East Asia. 'I used to spend my weekend in the jungle,'
Guy Madoc remembers. 'I also used to spend my annual leaves in
the jungle and even after I was married I sometimes deserted my
wife and family and went off. And I came to love the jungle and also

the islands off the coast. I claim that I've been on every island off both coasts and on two occasions I sneaked over to visit some islands on the far side of the Straits of Malacca which had a special ornithological interest for me.'

Another young man who quickly came to terms with the Malayan jungle – and was later to put this familiarity to good effect – was John Davis: 'We wore gym shoes, no socks of any kind, with shorts and a shirt – and we would carry a jungle knife. This was rash because we got covered with leeches and ended up having jungle ulcers, so we learned to keep our legs covered. But this was the quality of the jungle; that you just walked into it at any time in absolute comfort and with no fear whatsoever.'

Like Davis, Sjovald Cunyngham-Brown soon realized that the jungle was far from being a dangerous place. However, it was not always easy to walk through:

> The Malayan jungle undergrowth is extremely thick and you have to cut your way through with a knife or else quietly work your way through. There are so many thorn bushes that will hold you back, one in particular known as the *nanti dahulu* or 'wait a bit' thorn, but apart from that the Malayan jungle is the kindest jungle in the world; great hardwood trees, about twenty-five or thirty feet apart, and a dense cover of foliage at two hundred and fifty to three hundred feet above your head. That's where the flowers are and where the birds and butterflies live, while down below in these dark, cool caverns there's very little life indeed.

There was plenty of wildlife but it was more often seen than heard: the '"whoop, whoop, whoop" of the monkey which the Malays call the *wa-wa*. It lived in the high jungle trees and usually performed at dawn'; the 'rattling of woodpeckers tapping on hollow trees' and the 'whoosh of the wingbeats of the great hornbills flying over the tops of the jungle canopy'. One bird call that Madoc learned to reproduce was the sound of the hornbill, known to Malays as the 'chop down your mother-in-law' bird:

> The call goes 'Roo, roo, roo – karoo, karoo – hah, hah, hah!' and the Malays say that the 'roo, roo, roo' is the sound of the axe biting into the pillars, the 'karoo' is when the house suddenly falls down, presumably with mother-in-law in it, and then you have the idiot laughter as he trails away into the jungle with his axe. One evening when we were prisoners of the Japanese in Changi prison, I was permitted by the authorities to go over and lecture on these birds in the women's camp, a very rare privilege, and I started this call in full bellow. The women thought it was marvellous but I had forgotten that I had a Japanese sentry standing

immediately behind me and he came up with his bayonet and said 'Harghh!' and I rather thought I was going to get a bayonet up my backside.

The birds of the jungle were 'always calling, whistling, mocking, but seldom seen' – and the animals were equally shy. Tigers were no exception – although Cunyngham-Brown did meet one face to face:

I was pursuing a path which I must have lost and then found again. It was about five o'clock in the afternoon and the light was filtering down more and more obliquely through the tops of the trees, with the occasional lazy moth beginning to float through the sunbeams, and it was all becoming a little eerie and creepy. I wondered, 'Shall I go on or shall I try and get back before dark?' And thinking these thoughts I jumped up onto a fallen tree trunk, with a great patch of sunlight on the far side of it. And as I jumped there was the most appalling 'Aaarghh' from the other side of the tree trunk and a full-grown tiger of enormous dimensions swung round and glared at me, baring its teeth and with its yellow eyes boring into me. I stood there, with my legs turned to water, quivering on top of this tree trunk and then suddenly with a snarl it jumped – not at me, thank God, but sideways into the jungle and I fell, a quivering heap, into the sand pit where it had been basking in the sunshine. We must have been the most frightened man and the most frightened tiger in South-East Asia.

The denseness of the jungle discouraged big-game hunting but there were those who went out on shooting expeditions. Derek Headley once took a boat up-river to Ulu Pahang to hunt the Malayan wild ox known as the *seladang*. His plan was to make contact with some of the aborigines of the peninsula known as the *Sakai* or *Orang Asli* – the 'original people' of Malaya, who were usually to be found a day's journey up-stream of the last Malay villages on the river: 'At the last Malay *kampong* we went ashore and drank from green coconuts with the headman, and he then went on with us up-river, where we contacted these *Orang Asli*. One of the younger ones came with us while we were stalking the *seladang* and both these men were tremendously brave and a great help in the hunt.' Seven years later the three met up again in extraordinary circumstances:

It was shortly after I dropped back into Malaya by parachute in 1944. We were moving off through the jungle very early in the morning – one of those mornings in Pahang where the night mist hung over the tops of the trees. We came to the banks of a rather cold, broad river. We could see the tops of the trees on the other side with the grey mist swirling around and we stood there on the bank not liking the idea of getting into this rather deep, cold water and saying 'Oh, go on, you go first.' Then suddenly round a bend in the river came a little bamboo raft, poled by an *Orang Asli* with a Malay in a white turban sitting at the stern – the same *Orang Asli* and the village headman with whom I'd gone shooting seven years earlier. They took one look at me and I took one look at them and they made that marvellous sign of greeting, putting both their palms together and raising them to their foreheads. It was really a very moving moment.

Living and working on the East Coast was for John Davis, as for many others, 'altogether delightful'. But for him this period of what some of his colleagues in Kuala Lumpur referred to as 'lotus eating', suddenly came to an abrupt and distressing end:

I was a very young policeman in those days, aged twenty-one, and a great deal too big for my boots, thinking that I stood for the law and that the letter of the law must be upheld. The Sultan of Pahang was a young man of about twenty-four, a fairly ebullient, perhaps slightly provocative sultan in those days, although later on he became a very fine man indeed. But I decided against the advice of my policemen that as I had information that the Sultan's wives were gambling in the *Istana* and as this was against the law, then the law must be upheld. So I duly raided the Sultan's *Istana* – God knows why – and brought several of his wives in and I was going to have them prosecuted. I soon got instructions from my chief not to worry too much about the prosecution and that was all I heard of it for some time. Then one day my boss phoned me up and said I'd been selected to go to China to learn Chinese and should leave in two months' time. 'For heaven's sake, why?' I asked. 'I'm deliriously happy in Pekan.' And he said, 'Well, you can't stay there. You will go raiding the Sultan's wives and the Sultan has asked the Governor whether you can be removed from the state.' I was so delighted with Pahang but I suddenly realized that if I was going from Pahang I had no other interests, so I said to him on the phone, 'Well, if I've got to leave Pahang let me go to China and be done with it.' And in fact this was the most wonderful decision I ever made, because the whole of the rest of my career derived from my going to China.

All government servants knew that their postings were of limited duration, since it was not the policy of the government to allow officials to remain in one place for too long. The longest tours rarely exceeded two years and were often far shorter. After seven months in Temerloh Mervyn Sheppard received orders to report for duty in Kuala Lumpur as Private Secretary to the Chief Secretary:

This was the first occasion that I experienced what was one of the saddest parts of a civil servant's life; the infrequent but nevertheless unavoidable farewells to people with whom one has worked and for whom one has tried very hard to be of service. The more you put your efforts, your feelings, your affections into a job and into the people of the place where you were working, the harder it was to part from them and the more distressing – almost heart-rending – the experience. As time went on I came to dread this ultimate, unavoidable parting which had to come, whatever job you were allotted to.

Bill Goode felt very much the same way when, after two-and-a-half years in Trengganu, the time came for him to take his first home leave:

As I passed through Singapore, I sought an interview with the then Colonial Secretary to ask him if he could possibly see his way to arranging that I should be posted back to Besut when I came back from leave, as I hadn't been there long enough to complete a lot of things that I'd had in mind to do. But he told me in no uncertain terms that the last thing he would agree to would be that I should return to my own mess in Besut. He thought that was a very bad thing. I was upset at the time, but he was absolutely right. It would have been quite wrong for me to go back.

6

THE LAND OF THE WHITE RAJAHS

England was very far away and when at long intervals they went back was increasingly strange to them; their real home, their intimate friends, were in the land in which the better part of their lives was spent.

Somerset Maugham, *Preface,*
The Complete Short Stories, Vol III

SHORTLY before the Japanese attack on Pearl Harbour, Robert Nicholl was walking on the upper deck of the Dutch liner, *The New Amsterdam,* 'somewhere East of Zanzibar' and on his way to the Middle East, when he fell into conversation with another officer: 'We started talking about British possessions in the Far East and he said to me, "You know, as the Colonial Office Auditor I have had experience of all the British possessions in the Far East and South-East Asia and the status of the white man is highest in the little state of Sarawak. There he is held in higher regard than in any other territory."' Nicholl had never heard of Sarawak and asked his companion where it was: 'He said, "Oh, it's a dreadfully jungly little place in Borneo. They had a marvellous ruler, an old man named Charles Brooke, the Second White Rajah. He ran that place extraordinarily well but he's dead now and his son rules, the Third Rajah, Charles Vyner Brooke."'

Sarawak in 1941 had just celebrated a century of Brooke rule under its three White Rajahs – yet it was still a land about which most Britons knew very little. When told by the Cambridge University Appointments Board in 1934 that Sarawak was recruiting graduates as administrative officers, Bob Snelus had to admit that he had never heard of the place. Peter Howes, training to become a missionary with the Society for the Propagation of the Gospel in 1937, mainly associated the country with the 'head-hunters of Borneo' and with 'a pop tune of the time called *Sarawaki*, which was played by a band whose leader had married one of the Rajah's daughters'. Indeed, it was probably in connection with these daughters that most people in the 1930s thought of Sarawak, if at all: 'Charles Vyner Brooke had no male heirs but he was blessed with three lovely and attractive daughters. The eldest, a very gracious lady, married Lord Inchcape. The second one married the famous Harry Roy, the band leader, and the third one married an amateur all-in-wrestler.' All this did nothing for the image of Sarawak: 'When Didi – as she was known – married the band leader she promptly became known in the British press as Princess Pearl, which was entirely false as her local title was the honorary one of *dayang,* which didn't mean princess or anything like it. And it did become a little irritating to be asked from time to time if Harry Roy was your Rajah.'

Rajah Charles Vyner Brooke himself was 'a very much respected and well-liked old gentleman' but also something of an enigma to his officers. Although he and his family lived comfortably rather than lavishly, there were those who regarded him as a bit of a playboy because, in contrast to his father who was 'not addicted to the comforts of life and a bit of a spartan', Vyner Brooke made social life in Kuching 'more lively and much more joyous, with more parties, more dancing, more trips on his yacht and Race Week twice a year, when all the outstation officers were invited down in turn and used to have a terrific time'. The Rajah could indeed be 'perfectly charming – but his personal dignity was as great as his personal charm. He was always the ruler and nobody ever dreamt of addressing him in a familiar way.' Yet when he gave orders it was never done in an authoritarian manner: 'He would talk to you quietly, chat and make a few suggestions and if you took the hint then he was delighted – and you were one of his finest officers. If, on the other hand, you thought you knew better and did something else, you were apt to end up in one of his furthest outstations.'

The fact was that the Rajah was an absolute monarch, controlling everything except foreign policy. He was the 'ruler of a country the size of England and Wales which was entirely his own. He had no connection whatever with Whitehall. The revenue was his own. He had his own stamps, his own money, his own flag. It was his to do with as he liked. He even had power of life and death over his own subjects.' Yet at the same time he had no military power to impose his will: 'He had to get his way by persuasion and by consultation with people whom he trusted and who trusted him. He was Rajah with the consent of the local population, notably the Malays, and he could not really do very much without consulting them and senior members of the other communities and of course his brother officers.' This close and informal consultation formed the basis of what was known as the 'Brooke tradition': 'The government of Sarawak was purely personal; from the Rajah downwards every government officer had to be accessible – and that's why Sarawak was unlike any other English colony. There was an intimacy between the government and the people. It was men, not a machine, and there was practically no bureaucracy at all. All you had was a handful of Europeans assisted by another group of native officers, and it was all personal government.'

The country was divided up into five divisions, each under the charge of a Resident who was, according to Bob Snelus, 'king in his own little country. The true king had almost nothing to do with the way the division was run. The Resident ran it on his own lines and those lines might differ from one division to another depending on the nature and the character of the individual Resident.' Supporting him in each division were a handful of District Officers, but because of the surrounding jungle and the lack of roads, both Resident and District Officers were very much on their own. The latter reported to him by letter every month and the Resident in turn reported by letter direct to the Rajah.

The relationship between rulers and ruled was a feudal one – based quite deliberately on 'the principle of the close relationship between the lord of the manor and his tenants' – and yet without a doubt it was an extraordinarily popular regime by any standards, which flourished because Sarawak was a colonial cul-de-sac, self-contained, self-financing and all but cut off from the outside world.

There was only one way to get to Sarawak from the outside world and that was by catching a steamer from Singapore, preferably one of the Straits Steamships' boats that called in regularly at Kuching. There was the cargo-ship *Circe,* which carried 'an equal tonnage of cargo and cockroaches', or the far smarter mail-steamer, the *Rajah Vyner Brooke,* which was 'kept spotless like a yacht' and sailed from Singapore every ten days. The journey across the South China Sea took two days and three nights, with the sailings geared to the tides, so that the ship could navigate the sand-bar at the mouth of the Sarawak river and then go on up on the flood tide to Kuching town, some twenty miles up-river.

'The approach was most striking,' recalls Bob Snelus:

You arrive at the coastline to find there's Santubong mountain rising three thousand feet directly out of the sea. Then you wind your way up between the *nipah* palms for miles and miles and it's all rather dreary, with an occasional little native habitation but mostly unbroken *nipah* palms, until you are a mile or so from Kuching. You round a bend in the river which then opens up before you and all on the left are lines of Chinese shop-houses known as the bazaar, terminating in the government building which in those days was known as the Court House. Then on the other side of the river, opposite the shop-houses, there's first of all an old fort, Fort Margherita, with the guns still poking through its portholes, which was erected in the days of the Dayak pirates who used to come up the Sarawak river in their huge war *prahus*, with the aim of pillaging the Chinese shops and any wealthy Malays who might be around.

As well as Fort Margherita, built in 1879, there were other forts in Sarawak, built in 'places where the Second Rajah was still having difficulty in keeping order among the Iban tribes who inhabited that part of the country. They were nearly all named after female members of the Rajah's family – his daughters or people that he had known: Fort Alice, Fort Sylvia, Fort Lily, and names like that.'

A hundred yards beyond Fort Margherita there was the *Istana,* the palace of the Rajah, a 'fine old colonial building' with broad lawns sloping down to the water's edge. It had a stone-crenellated keep at one end but its most striking feature was an enormous roof made up of *bilian* hardwood shingles and covering 'a very cool veranda and a very cool interior'.

The arrival of the mail-ship was signalled by the firing of a gun from the fort, when 'everybody who had business with the ship went down to the wharf'. The vessel then had to be turned around in the narrow river before tying up at the Straits Steamships' wharf, a risky manoeuvre that only the most skilled captains could perform: 'The way they turned was to go up so close to the *Istana* that the bow was overhanging the garden and then swing with the tide so that the stern came round.'

As well as announcing the arrival of the mail-ship the signal gun also served as a time-gun, a fact that Peter Howes was unaware of when he first arrived in the country:

I was put up in the Bishop's house where I slept like a top for my first night – to be woken up, to my astonishment, by a great explosion. I was on my feet in a moment. It was pitch dark. I thought I'd come out to a rebellion and I stood by the bed all set for a burst of firing and the frantic shouts of natives as they rushed up the hill to set the mission on fire. But after a minute or two nothing happened, so I put on a torch, to see what the time was. It was five o'clock – and nobody had bothered to tell me that the Brooke Government provided an alarm clock for the residents of Kuching in the form of a time-gun, which was fired from Fort Margherita, precisely at five o'clock each morning. Fort Margherita was on the bank of the river just opposite the Bishop's house and when the water was high the sound used to ricochet off the water, straight into the Bishop's veranda and it really felt as if the whole house was being shaken to pieces.

A second signal gun was fired every evening at eight o'clock: 'During the Rajah's time anybody, Dayak or Chinese or Malay, who liked to go and see the Rajah and put a case to him was at liberty to do so. They usually went across in the evening and if you were a Dayak you could drink the Rajah's gin and chew betelnuts and spit out of the window, and behave just as you behaved at home. But at eight o'clock the second time-gun was fired and this was the sign that the Rajah was about to have dinner and then all his visitors left.'

All new arrivals to Kuching were rowed across the river in a *sampan* to sign their names in the visitors' book kept at the bottom of the steps leading up to the *Istana*. They were not, however, expected to call on the Rajah himself. Anthony Richards' first opportunity to meet him came when the Rajah was rowed over in his state barge to the Court House to hear what were known as 'Requests' or petitions: 'He had just arrived across with the Sergeant-at-Arms carrying his yellow umbrella over him and he was carrying his spear, presented to him by the Sultan of Brunei, which was a long walking stick with a silver cap on the top. He simply nodded, saying "How do you do?" and "Welcome to Sarawak" and then left me to my mentors, which seemed at first to be a bit offhand.'

Kuching was then still very much a 'man's community' from the European point of view. When Edward Banks had first arrived in 1925 to take up his curator's post at the Sarawak Museum there were no more than three or four European women in the town and practically none at all outside Kuching. A decade later there were still only twenty white women in the capital – out of a total population of about a hundred Europeans – and life continued to be 'pretty austere. You went to the club and drank and there was no alternative. The club itself was a very old-fashioned place, dingy and dark with a lot of elderly gentlemen sitting about and where you spoke only when you were spoken to. But as a junior you never signed for a drink – if you did your seniors took it away and signed the *chit* themselves, partly because they didn't want you to get into debt and partly because a young man was expected to be seen and not heard.'

However, it was not customary for cadets and other new arrivals to stay long in Kuching. Within three weeks Peter Howes found himself posted to the mission station at Betong in the second division. To get there he had first to travel in one of the many Chinese launches that plied the rivers of Sarawak with their holds filled with provisions for the up-country bazaars and with enough room on the hatches for twenty or thirty passengers:

> These passengers were a very mixed crowd; you would have some quite sophisticated types who came from houses near to a bazaar and they would be in trousers and shirts. And then you would have others who came from way up-country, wearing nothing but a loin cloth. But everybody got on extremely well together. You chatted away and they chewed betelnuts and offered you their Dayak tobacco and as you went along there were opportunities to speak to all sorts of people too, because you stopped at fish-traps where you could buy fresh fish from the Malay fishermen. Or perhaps a log-jam would block the river and it would be necessary for the passengers to try to move one or two so that the whole log-jam gave way and let the boat through. And then the boat would put in at little bazaars perhaps ten or twenty miles apart.

At Betong mission Howes was welcomed by the priest in charge and introduced to the two other priests who made up the staff of the station: 'It was a happy place but we lived a very hard and almost monastic life.' White cassocks were worn throughout the day – 'you would never be able to afford the washing bill that this would entail today but in those days we employed a Chinese cook-cum-houseboy who also did the washing and he cost us seventeen dollars a month' – and *topees* whenever the missionaries ventured out of doors: 'We had a *topee* stand just near the door so that the moment you went outside into this dangerous, tropical sunlight you grabbed your *topee* and put it on – even if it was only for the few hundred yards between the mission house and the church.' At first his mornings were spent teaching English in the mission school and his afternoons learning Iban, the language of the tribal people in that part of Sarawak. Without Iban, Howes was told, he could be of little use to the community since the bulk of the mission's Christians were scattered over an area equal in size to an English county.

In Sarawak the Muslim Malays formed only a tiny minority and there was no ban on Christian missionary activities as there was in the Malay States. Indeed, many of the Anglican missions had been in existence since the days of the First Rajah, James Brooke, as well as a number of other churches, and in order to avoid conflict between the different denominations the country had been divided by the Rajah into various zones of influence:

Anglicans and Roman Catholics worked together in the first division and the Anglicans worked alone in the second division. The Roman Catholics and the Methodists had the third division and to this day if you go up the Rejang river all the churches on the left-hand side of the river are likely to be Methodist and all on the right Roman Catholic. The fourth division was given to the Anglicans and Roman Catholics and the fifth division was left empty and remained so until just before the war when a non-denominational mission based in Australia came there.

Within these divisions the various missions had their headquarters, where each priest was 'given two or three rivers and was responsible for the Christians along the length of those rivers'.

The administration divided up its divisions and districts on very similar lines – and here, too, newcomers were very quickly sent out to get to grips with the country and its people. Bob Snelus was sent to the headquarters of the third division at Sibu, where he found himself one of four European officers under the command of a Resident who was very much of the old school, a man who had known the 'wilder days' of the Second Rajah: 'He was a strong character – but strong in a cheerful way; very much the country squire type of chap, a Devonian, I think, and by no means an academic. He didn't expect others to write long-winded reports about their jobs and what they'd been doing but he kept his finger on the pulse of things and generally knew what was going on in all his districts, of which there were five in his division.' Although the Resident 'was not a tyrant to his subordinates by any means', Snelus quickly learned that he was expected to toe the line:

The most important thing in those days as far as the Resident was concerned was that one should appear at the local club no later than six o'clock in the evening to engage in games of indoor bowls. So in the course of that one naturally got a good sweat up and imbibed a good deal of alcoholic refreshment. The other point was that one was not allowed to leave the club by the Resident until at the earliest nine o'clock. It was often nine-thirty before I was able to get away, by which time one felt pretty worn out and one hadn't had one's evening meal. But despite that, early in the morning, at about five-fifteen, one had to be up and about because one of the duties of the new cadet was to turn out

CAPTAINS AND KINGS

Above: The Sultan of Trengganu opens the new Land Office, 1923.

Left: Attending the Sultan; the Sultan of Perak shaded by the yellow umbrella of royalty, Kuala Kangsar, *c.* 1933.

The 'Consolidators';
The British Adviser opens a new bridge in Trengganu State, 1935.

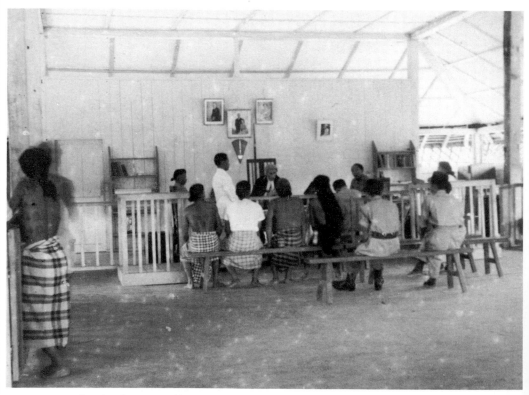

Justice in court; Ibans attending the court in Kapit, Sarawak, 1953.
In Rajah Brooke's time the scene would have been the same except for the pictures on the
wall and the presence of a local magistrate rather than a High Court judge.

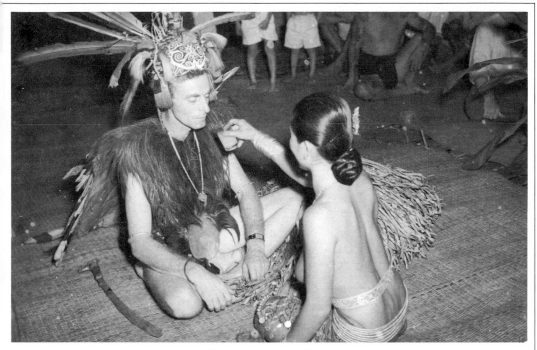

Entertaining the DO (Anthony Richards); traditional longhouse
hospitality in the Ulu Ai, Sarawak, 1950s.

Entertaining the children; the wife of the
Resident of the Fifth Division in a longhouse, Limbang, Sarawak, 1958.

Ibans hauling the Resident's boat up rapids on the Balui River, Sarawak, *c*. 1955.

the prisoners. I couldn't skip this early morning turnout because once or twice a week the Resident would turn up, too, on his pony, just to make sure you were there and on parade.

However, the Resident was not above letting his hair down when he was off-duty:

On one of my first Sundays in Sibu as a new boy I was invited to curry tiffin at the District Officer's house to meet the others. The curry tiffin didn't start till about three o'clock and we probably didn't rise from our chairs till after four o'clock, by which time everybody was rather jolly and I remember the Resident had a little bet with the doctor: there was one little Austin Five which the Resident was allowed to keep and run – it was the one car in Sibu in those days. There were no other cars in the whole third division, because there was only one road about seven miles long out to the golf course. The doctor and the Resident both reckoned they were good shots so they decided to take aim at the little Austin which was parked outside the bungalow. The Resident sent for his shotgun and the doctor had a revolver, and then they shot up the car until there was very little left of it; the tyres were all deflated, the windscreen was in smithereens, and when there was really no point in shooting at the body of the car any longer the Resident just swung his gun right round firing indiscriminately as he went, so that everybody was ducking and careering down the steps and hiding in ditches.

Snelus soon got down to learning the ropes as an outstation officer and, in the process, imbibing the Brooke philosophy. Perhaps its most important single element was that all government officers had to know their districts or their divisions intimately. This meant staying in the same place for some time:

You didn't want a man coming in and spending six months, or perhaps a year, as happened in Malaya. That would have been making nonsense of it all. Good gracious, no. He was expected to spend at least three years in that river basin, and get to know people. That was the key to the whole situation. He was on his own. He'd be days and days up-river and he had to make his own decisions. He couldn't take refuge behind some faceless bureaucracy; the most he could do would be to refer it to his Resident. And Residents weren't always easy to get at either, because there was also the Sarawak tradition of travel, which meant that all administrative officers were away from their offices for long periods each year. What happened if you wanted to contact your Resident when he himself was perhaps days up-river and completely out of reach? That meant you had to take the decision yourself, which was one of the reasons why the old Sarawak officers were men of forceful character.

Quite a number of these officers were the 'younger sons of landed gentry, a great many from the West Country because that was the Brookes' own background. They knew the sort of people they wanted – and they were just right for the job.' Until the mid-1930s few had qualifications or appropriate training. 'People who came out before then were apt to come out at the age of eighteen,' explains Anthony Richards, who was among the first of the graduate administrators:

> The list of incumbents of my office in Simanggang starts with two eighteen-year-olds in the 1850s when there were only two European officers at a time in that whole division. So these young men were faced with consultations with the locals, fighting off the various Dayaks, building a fort, protecting themselves and living somehow – with support from headquarters, but all by sea and very slow – at the age of eighteen. We in turn were not very much older than these people, just having a degree at twenty-three or twenty-four, and well before we were thirty we could be handing down sentences of two years' imprisonment, fines of a thousand dollars, several hundred pounds, and so on. And this without any specific training.

These long periods of service in distant outposts led almost inevitably to close identification with the people under their charge, particularly when the DOs were dealing not so much with the Malays or Chinese as with the indigenous tribal peoples of Sarawak, known to the Malays as 'Dayak' – the 'up-country' people. The largest of these tribal groups were the Sea Dayaks or Ibans who, with the Land Dayaks and the Melanaus, lived along the coastal belt and the rivers in the southern half of the country, while the Kayans, Kenyas and Kelabits occupied the highlands further to the west. To the British who knew them they were all equally 'nature's gentlemen – a hackneyed phrase, perhaps, but nevertheless apt, since they were hardworking, very courteous and very charming'. Anthony Richards spent most of his early years among the Ibans and came to regard them with great affection:

> They seemed to attract a great number of European officers, perhaps because they were so open and democratic. They had their leaders but they didn't have a class system. They would acknowledge status but their social behaviour cut right across and that was very impressive. When they came into a room, for

instance, there was no question of bowing or anything like that. They strode in as if they were making a stage entry, usually with a hand outstretched as one gentleman to another. Some were given to cadging, some to bragging and they got on your nerves sometimes but I found that having first associated with the Iban I stuck to the Iban, while other officers whose first contact was in the Baram river with the Kayans couldn't see anything in the Ibans at all. So we agreed that where your first love is, there you go and stay. You started by trying to get the hang of the Malays, the Chinese, the Ibans and all the rest and then you fell for one or the other.

The Ibans were also a very attractive people to look at:

Because of their poise and their immense natural dignity one was never at all conscious that they were in any way naked. The men wore their hair long, with a fringe at the front and knotted up into a sort of teapot handle at the back. They had copper-coloured skins with dark blue tattooing in the form of rosettes just inside their shoulders on the front and on their arms and legs and they wore long scarlet loin cloths which hung down at the back and front with long tasselled ends. They also wore black and silver arm and calf bracelets so that the general effect was of copper, black and red.

Many of the Iban men also carried tattoos on the backs of their hands and on their fingers, which showed not only that they had taken heads but also their exact number. Despite being vigorously suppressed by the Rajahs, in the early 1930s head-hunting had still not completely died out. One of Snelus' first duties as a cadet in Sibu was to go out after what was probably the last well-known band of rebel head-hunters in an effort to get them to surrender.

'Head-hunting is basically a fertility rite,' explains Robert Nicholl.

It was concerned with the fertility of crops and it was a religious rite. There were long prayers, and all sorts of ceremonies before the party set out. Off they went and back they came with the head which, as distinct from its owner, was always considered to be benevolent. It warded off evil spirits and it ensured the forth-coming harvest. The eyes were taken out and generally the lower jaw was taken off, and the rest of it was smoked and then hung up on a sort of circular frame in the roof. And that was the safest place in the whole longhouse, because no evil spirit would dare go near the heads, so when the guest came, he was given the place of honour under the heads.

However, with the Ibans the cult of head-hunting had developed far beyond a fertility cult:

It became an expression of valour. No young Iban could hope to win his girl unless he produced at least one head, and he would hope that his rival wouldn't come along with two. Head-hunting in this sense was obviously a menace to society. You could never have any stability if you had young men going about the country, whipping off the odd head here and there. That just wasn't the way you established any permanent order at all. So the Brookes were very effective in that they finally stamped it out completely. Even so, the ancient heads were kept because they were necessary for certain ceremonies and observances. But later, there were the odd Japanese heads to be seen hanging up. There was one that I noticed up in the Rejang river which actually had its spectacles on.

The women were just as striking in appearance and character as the men. They wore only 'a short black skirt which was very simply a short tube from waist to knee and held up by two or three canes' and confined themselves to tattoo marks on their wrists – 'usually signifying a change of name after recovery from illness'. Many of the younger women were extremely attractive and in general they were anything but reserved in their behaviour: 'One tends to think of women as second-class citizens in these communities but nothing would be more remote from the truth. They really had a say and a big say, too. They would sit round with everybody else and often played a very forceful part in the discussions. They were monogamous and their moral code was very rigorous indeed – but the young people could have lots of fun before they married.'

This relaxed attitude towards sexual matters had met with the approval of the Second Rajah, who believed that the presence of too many European women in Sarawak would prevent his officers from getting to know the country: 'It would have been perfectly ridiculous to have expected young men in those extraordinary circumstances to live a monastic existence and a promiscuous one would have been even worse, so the Second Rajah encouraged the adoption of one particular attractive girl as a housekeeper-mistress. This was so eminently sensible from every point of view that it became a pretty widespread habit.'

The practice of keeping what were known as *nyai* or 'housekeepers' continued right up to the last years of Brooke rule. 'Most of us had what were known as sleeping dictionaries,' Bob Snelus confirms. 'That expresses their purpose very well because they encouraged you and enabled you to learn the language and the dialect very much better and more colloquially than you could otherwise have done – and they satisfied the natural urge of many at the same time.' However, according to Anthony Richards, there was one disadvantage to learning the language in this way: 'For some reason the source of your knowledge was immediately evident the moment you opened your mouth, because the ladies have a distinct manner of speaking. One man that I knew quite well had learnt his Malay that way and it was quite obvious where it had come from – not that it mattered or that anybody minded.'

A detailed grasp of the language was essential to an understanding of a society bound up with all sorts of complex taboos. A case in point was the understanding of Iban omens and the value they attached to them:

> They have the Brahminy kite as the father of all omen birds and he has seven sons-in-law who are the principle omen birds. You go to seek omens in the proper order from the appropriate birds before undertaking such major operations as beginning a rice farm, going on the war-path, or at different stages of building a house. If you intended to build a house you would go out at dawn and seek to hear the white-rumped Shama, which is called the 'cool' bird. He sings away with a liquid song in dense trees or in the forest and he's often to be found near houses. The practice is to find an odd number of birds on the left for women and an even number on the right for men, and if you don't get these on the first day then you have to go out on another day until you do or abandon the site.

The problems of coming to terms with these taboos could be considerable: 'When certain birds crossed your path in a certain direction then there was nothing for it but to turn back. It was not merely that you yourself might meet with disaster but that you might bring disaster on the whole of the community that you were staying with – and you didn't want that. So it could be very inconvenient indeed.' But to know and to respect these and other omens was one way of maintaining the easy relations between *tuans* and natives that was characteristic of Brooke rule, for 'it was the custom that if you just wanted a chat with the DO and a gossip, you went along to his house in the evening. The door was always open and there he was, surrounded by people from up and down the river. So you went in and you chatted and talked late into the night. It was the same with the Resident. He wasn't a sacrosanct, remote figure as was the case in other places.' This mingling of the races was most striking to outsiders. Richards recalls an occasion after the Second World War when he was Resident in Pontianac and had a visitation from a representative of the Indonesian Embassy in Singapore:

When he arrived he was told by the guard on duty that we were all down at the bazaar having lunch, so he went off there and he found the Resident, the European District Officer, a couple of Malay and Iban officers, the policemen, the trader and his family and several others, including the boatman, all sitting round a table having a jolly good lunch. This man came in, sat down and goggled. I asked him what was the matter and he said that he'd never seen anything like it. His own people had never in a life-time of service sat down to eat with the Dutch and he had never imagined that people of different races would sit down together – particularly Europeans sitting down with the boatman – to eat.

Another characteristic feature of Brooke rule was the emphasis placed on travel as a means by which close contact with people was maintained. This was just as important in missionary circles as it was in government, and the style of travel was really no different. 'Every month you set off with your ecclesiastical supplies and a carrier and a boatman,' explains Peter Howes:

You paddled away, making use of the tides, until you got to your first Dayak longhouse, which would always be on the bank of the river. Then you would spend at least one night and possibly two nights in the longhouse, taking an evensong while you were there and a mass, and next morning hearing confessions and also instructing people who wanted to be Christian. Then you would go back to your boat again and travel further up-river, a matter of two or three hours, to the next longhouse – until eventually you got right up to the headwaters in the hills, where the water was perfectly clear and often very shallow. Finally, when you reached your last longhouse you'd cut back down-river. A journey of that nature could take you away for ten days or even three weeks.

Similarly, at the Sarawak Museum Edward Banks made a point of travelling around the country as often as he could, either on collecting expeditions or in answer to a specific request:

A District Officer would say, 'Something's wrong with the turtles on Turtle Island this year.' They used to have about five or six million turtle eggs every year and some years there weren't any. So you trotted off and you had a look at these islands and totted it all up and you came to the conclusion that due to rough weather the turtles hadn't come up. And then there were the huge caves full of birds' nests from which the Chinese make their birds' nest soup. They were very valuable; about a pound weight of nests would fetch you a quid – so it was quite a lucrative trade to the local people. But sometimes there was a hell of a lot of them and at other times hardly any. Everybody said that the locals pinched the nests and sold them. But again it was traced to a rotten winter or a rotten summer.

But what gave Banks the greatest pleasure was going up-river to collect specimens:

You took ship up-country till you came to, say, the mouth of the Baram river, where there was a District Officer and a little fort and from there you started off by boat up-river. These were very long boats, made out of one tree trunk, perhaps thirty or forty feet long and built up on the sides with planks and I suppose they put twelve or fifteen paddles on each side, two abreast, with a fellow behind to steer. Mostly, in those days, you used to row to the next village and then men from that village would take over. They didn't exert themselves terribly hard because they'd got a long row to go, but they paddled along quietly, and they chatted among themselves. Somebody pointed out a snake or a fish or a bird or a pig or something like that, and you sat in the middle and had a chat with all and sundry. The paddlers were Muruts or Kayans. They'd got long ears with rings in them and long hair and just a little g-string round their waists and I used to give them tobacco and odds and ends; you didn't actually pay them cash because they didn't know what to do with it but they were quite pleased to come along. And so it went on from one village to the next. When you arrived in a village they pulled in alongside the bank where there was a notched tree-trunk ladder going up the bank, with the houses built on poles on top of the bank. And generally, the headman came out to greet you and say, 'Hallo, come up.' Then you whizzed up this awful notched log, if you were lucky, and you were taken in and sat down and everybody wanted to know where you came from, and where were you going to and what were you doing and how many children had you got and all the rest of it. And there you stayed the night.

The style of travel was just as important as the method. 'The Brooke tradition was very firm,' declares Robert Nicholl, who after the war became one of Sarawak's first Education Officers. 'Every officer who travelled lived with the people. There was no question here of setting up half-a-dozen tents and dressing for dinner in the jungle as the great proconsuls did in Africa. That was out as far as the Brookes were concerned. You stayed in the longhouse and you lived with the people.' The difference between Sarawak and Malaya, as Bob Snelus saw it, was that 'we behaved like natives. We accepted Dayak conditions as they were. I always insisted on having my bath in the river first and then got into my *sarong* and *baju*.'

After this evening swim the guest was expected to eat with the
headman or one of the other families in the longhouse. 'They were
always exceedingly kind and hospitable,' recalls Peter Howes:

They would kill fowls for you which they had running about outside the longhouse by the score and these dreadful Dayak fowls
took an awful lot of getting through because one might just as
well have been chewing on sticks of rubber. But plates and dishes
would all be spread on great mats on the floor and if you were
well up-river you would be given a fresh banana leaf and a great
quantity of rice would be dished out into it for you. Then you
folded your legs so as not to prod your neighbour to left or right
and then you just reached with your fingers out into the various
bowls and selected such titbits as you fancied. Your neighbour, if
he felt particularly well disposed towards you or if he felt that
you were not doing justice to the fare, would pick up some titbit
and hand it to you or stick it on top of your rice. Once you got
more familiar with people, the great thing was to offer them the
sort of titbit that they couldn't chew – the foot of some fowl or
else its head. You'd pick this up and hand it to your neighbour,
then he'd feel duty bound to make an effort to eat this thing, so
he'd pull the comb off it and pull the eyes out and do his best.
But he might hand you in return the foot and then you'd be
caught as well.

Once dinner was over such official business as required to be seen
to was speedily transacted so that the evening get-together, known
as the *randau*, could begin. 'All the up-river people had one dis-
tinguishing characteristic common to them all and that was their
hospitality,' declares Snelus. 'Whenever the Dayaks were visited by
the District Officer celebrations invariably took place.' They began
with the singing of an ode of welcome:

The whole community would be sitting in a circle and you would
go and sit beside the head of the longhouse and then his wife or
perhaps his daughter would come along with a large glass of
borak, rice wine, and sing an ode. The theme was always one of
welcome but translations showed just how poetic they were. The
lady would end her ode and then offer you the *borak* which you
were expected to down in one. Then you would probably get
another lady who would come up and do the same thing – and so
it would go on.

As well as songs of welcome from the women, the men sang or
intoned what were known as *pantuns,* 'long verses recounting their
glorious past, the object being to liken their distinguished visitor to

their own heroes of the past, with some of the older men recalling
the number of heads they'd taken or the battles they used to have
against another village on the same river'. Then the District Officer
– or the chief guest – was expected to make an offering to the
spirits: 'Food of different varieties was presented to him and he
would have to pile them in a certain order onto a dish, which was
then put outside for the spirits to consume and to pacify them.'

Once these solemnities were over there was usually dancing and
more singing, either to the melodious accompaniment of the
engkerumong – 'an array of four or five brass gongs held in a
wooden tray and varying in size from six inches to twelve inches in
diameter' – or to the sound of the *sapeh,* the two-stringed mandolin
favoured by the Kayans and Kenyas. These two tribal groups produced outstanding singers – 'the only people in South-East Asia
who sang naturally in harmony' – and dancers. The men concentrated on war dances – 'there used to be competitions every two
years for the finest dancer on the Baram river' – while the women
did such dances as the bird dance, for which they 'put on the black
and white feathers of the crested hornbill with little clamps onto
their fingers and imitated bird moves – a bird ballet that was very
beautiful indeed to watch'. Finally there were wilder dances in
which everybody joined in a long column: 'The person in front performed various gyrations and everybody else followed and you processed round the longhouse.' These dances often lasted right
through the night – 'and all the time some lady would be coming up
to you and insisting on singing an ode and then you would have to
toss back yet another glass of powerful *borak*. It was very exhaust-
ing indeed and it only came to an end with dawn.'

For those who could sleep there were certain formalities to be
observed and precautions to be taken. 'As a man you would sleep on
the general *rouai*, alongside the bachelors,' recalls Howes:

Mats would be put down for you and you would be provided
with pillows and blankets if they were needed. You brought with
you your own mosquito net. In many of the up-river longhouses
there were next to no mosquitoes because the longhouse stands
high off the ground. But you really needed a mosquito net to
keep dogs out of the bed – because a Dayak longhouse contains as
many dogs as people and at night-time these wretched dogs
charge up and down the length of the *rouai* either in sport or in
battle and they are quite likely either to leap over you if you have
no mosquito net or come up and nestle close to you for warmth's
sake. Also, underneath the floor of the longhouse all the chickens
roost, very often in bamboo cages. They scratch vigorously from

time to time and you can get used to that – but in certain hours of the night and early in the morning the cocks crow furiously and in any one longhouse there may be anything from thirty to eighty or even a hundred doors – that is families – each with its own cocks and hens and pigs and things all rooting around under this house, so that the noise and the scratching and the cock-crowing and the pigs grunting and the yells and yelps of dogs and their pitter-pattering backwards and forwards across the floor do tend to make for a somewhat disturbed night. You find too in certain communities that while the first five minutes on the mat is restful you then become aware of an increasing irritation and if you switch on a torch and look at the mat you may see it covered with hundreds of bedbugs. The great aim of any traveller in a society like that is to get instantly to sleep, because if he is not asleep in the first five minutes the chances of getting to sleep afterwards are practically nil.

In 1941 the Rajah and Ranee celebrated their Silver Jubilee in Kuching:

It was a most memorable and extraordinary evening. All the *kampongs* were lit by hundreds and hundreds of little oil wick lamps made out of pieces of green bamboo and the Malays all turned out in their best clothes; the women in their gold embroidered *sarongs* and looking ravishing, like a lot of butterflies. The Rajah and Ranee drove around through cheering crowds, all pressing against the car to make quiet but heartfelt remarks of greeting. It was a lovely evening and a lovely occasion. There was no question about it at that time; the Rajah was enormously loved.

In their turn, the Rajah and a great many of the *tuans* who served him also loved Sarawak and its people: 'When I left the country in 1963 the best known of the Dayaks was a man called Temanggong Juga,' recalls Bob Snelus. 'I first knew him as a young *penghulu* and in some ways it could be said we grew up together. He always came on my trails of the Dayak villages in the district of Kapit and he always insisted on accompanying me, and eventually we went through the ceremony of becoming blood-brothers by cutting each other's fingers, making a little incision and drawing a little blood. It's a very simple little ceremony but it's rather touching – and not often done.'

7

PAX BRITANNICA

*It may be that some of those peoples, Malays, Day-
aks, Chinese, were restive under the British rule,
but there was no outward sign of it. The British
gave them justice, provided them with hospitals and
schools, and encouraged their industries. There was
no more crime than anywhere else. An unarmed
man could wander through the length of the Federated Malay States in perfect safety.*

Somerset Maugham, *Preface*
The Complete Short Stories, Vol III

THE exercise of power and responsibility came easily to most young
men reared in Edwardian and Georgian private schools, where 'the
whole idea was that you built up petty power and then you moved a
stage higher and it was knocked out of you and you started again; so
that we were all already as boys well accustomed to taking on power
when it was offered and to losing that power when you moved elsewhere.' What made this assumption of power even easier was that
'no difficulties were put in one's way. In those days because one was
an Englishman one didn't have any difficulty in exerting one's
authority. It was accepted straight away. Whether we liked it or
not, they looked upon us as power points, as persons slightly apart.'

This is as true of a manager of an estate, an administrator or a
captain of a Straits Steamships vessel. 'Our word was law and that
was all there was about it,' declares Captain Percy Bulbrook. 'You
weren't curtailed in any respect – not in those days.' It was this freedom of action that James Morice most enjoyed as an officer in the
FMS Customs and Excise: 'You were your own master. If you got
fed up in the office you could go away for the day to your outstations and nobody would say a word.' And it was the same sense

of liberty that Bob Snelus felt when he first became a District
Officer:

> Being a DO gave one an enormous boost. It is one's first real taste
> of power and power wielded on one's own without anybody con-
> tinually breathing down your neck and wanting to know what
> you're doing and what you're not doing. And, in those days, the
> work of a District Officer was remarkably varied. The District
> Officer was in charge of the prisons and had to turn out the pris-
> oners. He was also the magistrate, so that having remanded a
> chap in prison he then had him come up before him in court and
> had to decide whether he was guilty or not guilty. He was also
> responsible for public works, for maintaining such roads as there
> might be in the district and drains and so forth. And all this quite
> apart from his main job of generally administering the people in
> this area – touring around finding out their troubles, resolving
> their problems, settling their land disputes and collecting the
> head tax – which was the only tax in Sarawak in those days.

This bewildering range of responsibilities was by no means confined to Sarawak. When Richard Broome was appointed District
Officer on Christmas Island – 'a little island south of Java about
four days' steaming from Singapore, whose great claim to fame is
that it is a wonderful deposit of phosphate from bird-droppings
which have occurred over millions of years' – he was also gazetted as
'Harbour Master, District Health Officer, Magistrate, Coroner,
Chief of Police, Inspector of Machinery and a whole host of other
jobs which didn't occupy one's time much but for which one had to
have powers in case something cropped up'.

However, what Sjovald Cunyngham-Brown remembers as an
'idyllic noon-tide holiday on the part of the Malayan Civil Servant'
– where he was 'a little king unto himself in his own district' – was
slowly coming to an end. With improvements in communications
and increasing centralization of government the administrator's
powers were gradually being reduced. Many of his responsibilities
were taken over by a fast-growing number of independent departments and services:

> We would have been nothing had it not been for the police, the
> Education Services, the Health and Medical Services, the Survey
> Department from New Zealand, the Mines Department that dis-
> covered all the areas for private interests to exploit, the Agri-
> cultural Department – who were practically the originators of the
> wealth of Malaya – to say nothing of that most silent, unobtrusive
> and generally forgotten arm of government known as the Public
> Works Department.

It was the PWD, 'with all their roads, their bridges and their brothers-in-arms, the Electrical Supply Department and the Wireless and Telegraph Services, that quietly brought a civilized country into being. There was nothing that the PWD did not do. They created all the furniture for the government offices and bungalows – and built the bungalows themselves.' Indeed, all the British territories in the East shared the same joke about the kapok tree being known as the 'PWD tree' – 'because it looks as if a PWD engineer had built it'.

Inhabitant (pointing to Kapok) :—That's a P.W.D. Tree.

Stranger :—Why do you call it that ?

Inhabitant :—Because if the P.W.D. built a tree, they'd
        build it like that !

One of the classic jokes of the East. From *Straits Produce,* 1926

In territories like Sarawak and British North Borneo this build-ing-up of the infrastructure took longer to achieve, allowing some curious anomalies to persist rather longer than they did on the peninsula:

That meant that in a gambling case, for instance, the chances were that you had led the police raiding party and the people caught gambling illegally had then been brought before you as a magistrate. If you put them in jail, you were in charge of the jail, and you were also the prison visitor. This system – or lack of sys-tem – was open to all kinds of abuses, but people did the best they could, and you simply changed your attitude with the diffe-rent hat you were wearing. One minute you were a raiding police officer and next minute you were the magistrate, and you tried to set aside the fact that you knew the chap was guilty because you'd caught him the night before. In those days they seemed to accept all this.

In more typical circumstances an administrator's duties were in accordance with his experience and qualifications. In the MCS a cadet could expect within three-and-a-half years – having passed the required examination in law and language – to become a 'Passed Cadet'. He was then eligible to 'act' as a junior assistant in a number of jobs that were graded as Class Four posts, graduating in time to Class Three jobs. His magistrate's powers were similarly graded, with strictly-defined limits as to the sort of cases he could try and the severity of the fines and sentences that he could impose. By the time he became a District Officer he would have become eligible to exercise full magistrate's powers.

However, it was rare for an officer in the Malay States to spend all his time out in the districts: 'Establishment Officers watched each man's career and his list of jobs very carefully and they would say, 'That man's done enough in a district or out in the *ulu* and it's high time he came in and got some discipline and tidied up in the Secretariat.' Spells of duty out in the field usually alternated with periods in the Federal or a State Secretariat so that in time almost every officer acquired a wide range of experience.

Almost all administrators had to spend a certain amount of time in the magistrate's court and those who found the work to their taste were encouraged to read for the English bar so that they could con-centrate on court work or even transfer to the Legal Service. Dur-ing his first home leave in 1935 William Goode took time off to be called to the bar at Gray's Inn and when he returned as District Officer, Raub, had much of his time taken up with court work which he rarely found tedious, 'probably because we went to the heart of the matter and reached a decision. We must have made mistakes but at least justice was quick: somebody could commit an offence on Tuesday, be hauled up in court on Friday and the whole thing would be over by Saturday afternoon.' The courthouse in Raub was typical of many district courts:

> It was a large, airy, white-washed brick building, with plenty of windows all round because we had no air conditioning, just a *punkah* being pulled over our heads, and an elevated bench on which the magistrates sat. Then in front of you, you would have the local police officer, who did the prosecuting. Very rarely in places like Pahang would there be a lawyer for the defence; the accused or the defendant had to defend himself. This meant that the magistrate on the bench had to try and make sure that the defendant's case was put as well as possible.

Only in the larger towns and the Straits Settlements was the full majesty of the law displayed – as Cunyngham-Brown experienced when he became for a spell Fourth Magistrate in Singapore:

> The whole of the old Havelock Road Police Court had so great an aura of faded dignity surrounding it that it was almost ludicrous in its grotesque formality. There was an enormous Sikh at the door, who'd salute crashingly as you stamped up the steps to the pillared, green-painted police court – and into the chambers behind it. There one waited for the appropriate moment to go up the steps into the court and behind the great big table on its dais four feet above the court itself, and as you waited you heard the murmuring of people in the court, which would hold about five hundred people all sitting in rows and was very seldom less than crammed to the edges with people standing at the back and everyone waiting in expectation, chattering away and eating peanuts until the magistrate came in. Then a tremendous noise; the bashing of a stave on the ground by another enormous Sikh. '*Diawm*,' he would shout, meaning 'silence'. Everybody stood up and there would be dead silence as you came in, bowed to left and right and then sat down. In front of the magistrate's bench there was a Mr Surattee who was the Clerk of the Court, with his own clerks sitting on a green baize table underneath one, and he would jump up and give you the right legal references to any point in doubt. At one's right hand side there was the box in which the accused or the defendant was to sit or stand, with the lawyers at the next table to Mr Surattee's own table. There were *Hokkien* translators and Cantonese. All the Indian tongues, Tamil and even Telegu were also frequently spoken in the court,

Punjabi because of the Punjabis' money-lending proclivities, and Hindustani as a matter of course. Consequently, we were fairly well kitted up with linguistic ability in that court. And, as time went on, a certain relaxation would be permitted to creep into this fearful formality.

However, there was one occasion when the relaxation went too far:

I remember particularly one morning after a long weekend spent sailing my little boat across the Malacca Strait when I'd got abominably sunburnt, and so in the absolute safety and security of my seat, knowing that I had a big baize curtain hanging down over the table's other edge so that nobody could see what I did, I undid my belt; what a relief! I then listened to a long discourse on the part of the counsel for the defendant and opened a few buttons. And, when it came to a little further cross-examination with the plaintiff's lawyer, I took a bold step: I slipped off my trousers, lifted my shirt and gave myself a really good and satisfying scratch. I couldn't understand what was happening in the court. There had been a certain murmuring from earlier on but now a positive uproar suddenly broke out. I saw small boys standing on tables at the back pointing and screaming, as the three uniformed police were banging the floor, shouting 'Diawm! Diawm everybody!' And Mr Surattee, turning around to see why there was all this fuss, jumped up with a face of horror, opening his jacket like wings, and said, 'Sir, they've taken the baize away to be cleaned!'

For the policeman who had to take on the prosecutor's role in the smaller courts there were also lighter moments. Guy Madoc remembers how the courthouse at Kuala Selangor had 'a roof of jungle fibre, no walls and just an earth floor. Occasionally at important moments when I was addressing the magistrate on the bench in great fluency, I would look up and staring through the roof would be the faces of three or four monkeys. Whilst scratching on the ground just in front of the dock where the prisoner was lounging, would be five or six chickens which had come in from the farm across the road.'

The language of the court was always something of a problem. 'Most of the cases were heard in the vernacular and this was a very slow and sometimes very difficult process,' declares Madoc. 'I myself spoke only Malay, in which I became sufficiently fluent to be able to deal directly in questioning witnesses and the accused person. But if you were dealing with Indians or Chinese, then you had to work through an interpreter.' With such difficulties misunderstandings of one sort or another were inevitable – as Alan Morkill once discovered when called upon as District Magistrate to hear a deposition from a man who was said to be dying:

> Under the Indian Evidence Act, a dying deposition could be admitted as evidence and I was asked to go down and take one from a Chinese. I found him – an enormous Chinese – lying in a bed, apparently speechless. He'd complained that he'd been assaulted and I had to ask him whether he thought he was going to die. I don't know how the interpreter put my question to him but he obviously thought I was threatening him with death. He thereupon leapt from the bed and ran for it, pursued by the Inspector of Police.

The cases heard in the magistrate's court covered an enormous range – 'anything from riding a bicycle without a lamp or hawking without a licence to much more serious cases to do with theft or even murder, which, after the preliminary enquiry had been held, would go on to a higher court'. It was Madoc's job to investigate every sort of case before bringing it to court:

> We were expected to investigate such trivial criminal offences as the theft of five coconuts, worth about a dollar, and much more serious cases like gang robbery. In the first years of my life in Malaya gang robbery was far too prevalent an offence because we were going through a world recession and so many people, particularly Chinese, were out of work and desperate for money. Amongst the Chinese, there were also ritual murders which were quite terrifying things. I had to investigate one when I was still very raw. I was called out about three o'clock in the morning, marched for miles through semi-cultivated country and eventually came to a half-derelict hut on the bank of a stream and there was lying a poor old man who had suffered the death of a thousand cuts, which is a Chinese ritual form of murder. He had nothing like a thousand injuries on him actually, but he was very thoroughly hacked up indeed.

Working in conjunction with the law courts in the Malay States were native courts presided over by Malay *hakims* who dealt with all matters relating to *adat*, Malay social custom and religion. For the Chinese the closest equivalent was to be found in the offices of the Protector of Chinese. 'It was a system whereby any Chinese had direct access to a senior member of the government,' explains Richard Broome. 'The Assistant Protector sat at his desk in a very large open hall with seats and benches in front of him. Then nobody could stop a Chinese coming straight in and spouting out what his trouble was. You tried to get his grievances settled and it also taught you plenty because one got a most wonderful insight into Chinese life.' The disputes that Broome and his colleagues handled could be divided into either domestic or labour cases:

The labour cases were of people who had not been paid their wages, because labour on the rubber estates and on the tin-mines was recruited through Chinese contractors and they weren't all honest men. The labour sometimes would go on working for this chap for months and then discover that he had absconded with all the money owed to them. You used to come down in the morning to the office, and see about a hundred women outside your office, and your heart sank because you knew it was an absconding contractor case. They'd say 'What about our wages?' and they always supposed that the Protector had a magic wand. Sometimes you got some money out of the contractor but very often you had to go on negotiating until you got the management to pay out a percentage.

Many of the domestic cases also followed a set pattern:

It was usually started by a woman who came in and said, 'My husband beats me and I want you to divorce me.' So you sent the husband not an official summons but a little standard letter in Chinese saying, 'Be at the office of the Protector on such and such a day' – and invariably they came. There was no legal obligation on them whatsoever, but they came and you used to have to try and sort out these things. It was like being a marriage counsellor as much as anything else. And they ended up nearly always with our either arranging a divorce, or else persuading the woman to go back. All these proceedings were conducted openly before the whole audience but the Chinese never seemed to worry about privacy in that respect at all.

The statutory powers of the Protector of Chinese were few, except in relation to the protection of women and children and in such matters as looking after the welfare of *Moi Chai*:

Moi Chai means little sister and in those days girls in a Chinese family were not very highly thought of as compared with boys and if they had enough in the family they had somehow or other to dispose of the excess girls. What they did was to make arrangements with a richer family so that girls would be taken over, usually at about six or so, to be brought up as domestic servants and eventually married off. Now you could not at the stroke of a pen get rid of an ancient Chinese custom like that, so what was done was that all these *Moi Chai* were registered and every single one was visited at least once a year – and in many cases we were able to rescue girls from an extremely unpleasant existence. In the Protectorates we kept what were known as *Po Liang Kuk,* which literally translated means 'preserving virtue establishment' and these little girls were brought up in these homes and eventually married off quite successfully.

One other power available to the Protector of Chinese – 'seldom used but it was a good threat' – was the right to photograph people: 'If you got a really nasty customer or one who was truculent, you could order him to have his photograph taken. It sounds a fairly mild thing, but the Chinese hated that, because these photographs were often put up on boards with the name underneath and the reason why his photograph had been taken. It originated with the Chinese secret societies because we had to have photographs of all the chief members.'

In Sarawak the closest equivalent was the Court of Requests, where all the races could come to lay complaints or seek redress of one sort or another. Justice was also rather more informally arrayed than in Malaya; the law courts were simpler and often little distinction was made between the DO's office and the courtroom. When he travelled the court went with him: 'You *were* the court. You took a policeman with you as a matter of course and you simply went and heard disputes. You didn't keep notes on each case because the great majority of these were customary law cases where there was no point in keeping a record, although you were expected to record anything of general interest in your travelling report.'

Customary law in Sarawak – whether Chinese, Malay or Dayak – affected the DO's work to such an extent that he nearly always sat with assessors – 'prominent local people well versed in customary law' – beside him on the bench. 'The law was contained in what we knew as the Green Book, which contained orders made in almost minute detail by the Rajah,' explains Anthony Richards:

> It even included such things as orders that anybody originating in Sarawak was not to appear before any European officer in a building wearing a hat of Western style – because local people do not doff hats. And with the Green Book there was a Black Book which had all the minor regulations. We used an adapted Indian Penal Code and apart from that it was said that where the law of the land was silent then English common law should apply. But of course a great many of the cases were affected by local or racial custom. You couldn't apply English law to Chinese inheritance, for instance. A case I remember particularly was that of two widows who appeared in my office one morning, two middle-

aged Chinese ladies, who came the length of the office holding hands. They said, 'Sir, we have come to report the death of our husband.' One of them came from Singapore, the other from the station I was in. They had never met before, but the old man had died and they came to sort out the inheritance, in a perfectly friendly manner. I took advice from the local Chinese leader – the *kapitan China*, as he was called – and sorted it out as fairly as I could, but they were happy with it.

The main difference between the law of the land and customary law was that the latter's main function was to satisfy the parties concerned and not to administer the law for the law's sake: 'The fact that a man was killed did not affect the necessity to pay the ritual amount of brassware or money in order to perform the rites and make the peace, so it didn't really help to put a man in jail or to string him up.' There were, however, certain problems in dealing with customary cases:

The oaths or affirmations used in the court were not regarded as binding by the local people. Muslims would take oaths in the mosque and the Chinese used to take an oath by killing a black cockerel. With the Ibans you could require somebody to call down death and disease and poverty upon himself, but that wasn't really used at all; you simply had to weave your tortuous way between the tissues of lies on both sides. But the chief confusion for outsiders was that they telescoped time. They would relate something that happened five years ago as if it happened last week and so you could go very badly astray on this. But then these customary law cases were not court cases as we understand them; they were really debates and arbitration. A magistrate who knew how to do it would simply listen until everybody had talked themselves to a standstill, and then when they began to dry up he would give his decision in such a way, hopefully, that both sides would accept it. And only if they did accept it – whether it were a fine or an instruction to do something – only then would the decision stick, because if one side disagreed with it, they would simply go away in a huff and come up with the same case next week. And that was why one of our judges, who was formerly a District Officer, laid down (probably in the club house, I think) the rules of court for longhouses. They were very simple: 'Not more than three persons shall speak at any one time, and no drinks to be served until after a decision has been made.'

Sarawak was also said to be the last country where trial by ordeal continued:

It almost always arose over land disputes or over heirlooms, where you would get such a barrage of perjury on both sides that the District Officer and his assessors were utterly unable to reach any conclusion at all. Both parties were absolutely right. If it reached a stalemate, then the parties could appeal to the trial by ordeal. Each party picked its champion, and then the whole court adjourned down to the river. A spot was picked where the river was deep, the two champions dived in and he won who could stay under water longest. And no one would ever dream of questioning the verdict.

The rich mixture of races and cultures in the Malayan archipelago inevitably meant very different views on what did or did not constitute a criminal offence – neatly exemplified by the dubious proposal that Jim Morice received in his post one morning while working in the Customs and Excise Office in Kuala Lumpur:

On opening this, out came a typewritten letter with a photograph of a young Chinese girl. It was from a Chinese lady offering me her daughter in marriage on certain conditions which she outlined. The first was that I was to give her daughter a dowry of three thousand dollars, roughly three hundred and fifty pounds. The second condition was that I should find employment for her son in the department. And the third and last condition was the mother was to live with her daughter in my bungalow! I happened to have to attend a licensing board meeting at the Chinese Protectorate later that day and, being a friend of the Protector of Chinese for Selangor, I passed over this letter and said to him, 'See what I got this morning in my post!' He had a look at it and said, 'That's nothing new. Just a minute.' And out from his drawer he produced several other letters on similar lines. 'You leave this letter with me and I will deal with the matter,' he said. Later on I heard that he'd had the pair up before the Protectorate Court. He'd admonished the mother and he'd sent the daughter to a home for the protection of young girls.

The confusion of attitudes was most obviously apparent in such sensitive issues as bribery and corruption, where 'the Asians were corrupt according to our lights, no doubt, but not necessarily according to theirs'. Here the gap between British standards and others was at its widest and – as far as the government services were concerned – not easily crossed. 'The whole basis of our education was that we should always remain completely incorruptible,' declares John Davis. 'One of the great points about the British Empire was that although we were powerful, difficult, bossy people who may have been intensely disliked by the inhabitants of the countries which we ruled, they accepted it simply because they knew we were not involved. Very, very few British people would be involved in corruption because, even if we had an inclination towards being corrupt, there was nothing really that they could offer us that would have had any great significance.'

It was said, however, that 'certain departments of government were more open to bribery than others' and there were two major scandals associated with government officers in Malaya in the 1930s. The first involved corruption in the Department of Mines and resulted in several 'very senior and respected officials being imprisoned – which was a bit of a shock to the community in those days'. The second shock came in the form of a purge on homosexuals, who were 'ruthlessly banished from the country' – provoking a number of scabrous jokes in the process. Ipoh was said to be a centre of homosexual vice where 'the Volunteers were not prepared to fall in in the front rank' and, similarly, the Blue Funnel steamer taking the victims of the purge back to England was said to have 'entered Penang harbour stern first'.

There were strict rules forbidding the ownership of land or shares where private interest might conflict with public duties, but the regulations concerning gifts and presents to government officers were less specific, so that 'the question of where to draw the line was always being discussed amongst us'. Early on in his career Guy Madoc was shown how to deal with the problem without causing offence by one of his seniors:

> Around Christmas time I was in his bungalow when up came a rickshaw with a man from the local grocery shop. He had with him a whacking great case which he brought in and said, 'This is a gift to the *tuan*.' The *tuan* looked at it very suspiciously and he turned to me and said, 'This happens every year, you know.' It contained bottles of whisky, brandy, plum-pudding and so on. 'We can't accept these things,' he said. 'But I always accept a token amount. Now here are apples and bananas which are going to deteriorate anyhow, so I'll accept them and the rest is going back.' And he handed it to the man and said, 'Take this back to your master and wish him a prosperous Christmas.'

Much of the responsibility for the prevention or control of various activities that one section or another of the community considered harmful fell to the Customs and Excise. It was they who saw to it that no licences for the sale of liquor were issued to Muslims in the FMS, who were forbidden by their religion to consume or deal in liquor. Jim Morice was once called upon to deal with a complaint from the Sultan of Selangor that a Muslim grocer's shop in KL was selling liquor to Europeans. He investigated and found that 'when the shop's European clientele ordered their groceries they also put on their list of requirements, gin, whisky and so on – and to oblige them the grocers used to purchase the liquor from a Chinese licensed retail shop opposite and then send the liquor out with the other goods to their customers'.

From time to time Morice's duties also required him to take part in various raids – against opium dens, illicit stills or smugglers:

> One of the oddest raids that I was on was when I was stationed at Muar in the State of Johore. I had a long journey to a Chinese village up-country with an informer who took me to a Chinese temple. We entered the temple premises from the back and heard a Buddhist service going on – tomtoms and gongs with a priest intoning. We had to look behind the altar which was covered by a wall and we found an illicit still with jars of *samsu*, which is Chinese wine made from yeast and molasses and rice. Having collected all these exhibits, we waited for the priest to finish his service and when he came to the back to disrobe we collared him and removed him and his exhibits without his congregation being any the wiser.

Life was in many respects 'very easy' for the British in South-East Asia in the inter-war years 'because we exercised power reasonably' – and certainly there were few challenges to British authority. When an occasional inter-racial dispute flared up the authorities 'sat down on it like a ton of bricks' – but otherwise there were few signs of unrest until 1937 when a series of strikes and riots – which had their roots in continuing low wages in the rubber and tin industries but were organized by the largely-Chinese Malayan Communist Party – hit Kuala Lumpur and other towns. 'These riots were a shock to me and to a lot of people in the country,' declares Richard Broome, who was closely involved in events at the time. 'They were a shock because Malaya was normally a happy and peaceful place – one of the happiest countries you could think of – and there was precious little politics at all.'

Nor, to all appearances, was there much desire for self-government. Returning to Malaya after a four-year spell in South India as an emigration controller, Sjovald Cunyngham-Brown found the peninsula still remarkably untroubled by politics: 'There was not the remotest desire throughout Malaya for independence. There was certainly a sense of nationalism in the Malay States, yes, but the nationalism was to Kedah, to Perak, to Kelantan, and so on. These were the nations to which the Malays, who were in the majority in all these states, were giving their unyielding loyalty. But in the Straits Settlements nobody wanted in the least to be independent from anybody. They'd already had eight generations of belonging to Britain. More "dependence" was what they wanted.'

In 1935 King George V's Silver Jubilee was celebrated throughout the Empire. 'My colleague and I were given fifty dollars to decorate the office,' recalls Cecil Lee:

> The great Corinthian columns were swathed in the Union Jack and stag-moss from an estate. When we'd done it we pushed off to Port Dickson and on the way down all the little villages and the *kampongs* had little pictures up of the King and Queen and I suppose that was happening throughout the Empire. Then in 1936 George V died. I was down on a coastal estate when we got the news and a planter and I went along to the club and solemnly lowered the flag. And I suppose that, too, was happening throughout the land and other parts of the Empire. Of course, I realise now how privileged we were – but, I must confess, I didn't realize it at the time. It was the twilight of the colonial calm and it was all so peaceful, so placid. I remember an old hand saying it was our best colony: it was healthy, there were lots of sports, there was no great internal strife. It was a halcyon, idyllic period when I look back on it and afterwards it was never quite the same. I'm afraid for me, in the words of Browning, it was 'never glad, confident morning' again.

For many of those who survived the great catastrophe that was about to break over them these years immediately before the outbreak of war would seem, in retrospect, 'golden years' – and, in Cunyngham-Brown's experience, full of strange ironies then impossible to conceive:

> In the winter of 1943 I was with a collection of survivors from a vessel that had been torpedoed. We'd been dragged out of the sea after seventeen hours in a somewhat sorry condition; we hadn't any clothes on to speak of, some had none at all, and in the morning we were lined up by the Japanese to be marched to the Happy World Internment Camp in Happy Valley in Singapore, which was no more nor less than the accumulated gash heaps of the entire city. As we were marching towards this in a tropical deluge of rain, the streets running with water, our beards soaking wet and drenched, our long matted hair hanging over our faces and hardly a stitch on our bodies, we passed the Havelock Road Police Court. There, standing elegantly at ease as usual and conversing condescendingly with some minute but rather pompous

captains and colonels of the Japanese Army, stood no less a person than my handsome Sikh. And as he looked somewhat contemptuously at this miserable gang of semi-human creatures shambling past in the rain, his eye caught mine. He couldn't say, or acknowledge the fact, that he knew me, obviously, but he did the one thing that restored my confidence more than anything in the whole of the war. His feet banged together in a salute as though he was killing a mosquito between them, he looked me straight in the eye, and then relaxed back to go on with his smiling conversation with the Japanese captain and colonel. When the war was over I did attempt to seek him out in order to shake him by the hand and say, 'Thanks for what you did.' Alas, I never found him.

8

CAPTAINS AND KINGS

I was already the man in command. In that community I stood, like a king in his country, in a class all by myself.

Joseph Conrad, *Youth*

IF there was one group of Europeans in South-East Asia and the Far East who were a breed of men apart it was the sea captains and river steamer captains: the China Coasters who commanded the ships of the Jardine Mathesons and Butterfield and Swires' fleets along the China coast and up her great rivers and, in the South China Sea itself, the masters of the shallow-draught, coal-fired vessels of the Straits Steamship Company's 'little white fleet', based in Singapore:

> Butterfield and Swires and Jardine Mathesons had an agreement with the Straits: 'You don't run in our territory, we won't run in yours.' The other place that the Straits could never get in was the Dutch Indies, Java and Sumatra. That was strictly Dutch KPM. The Straits territory was as far north as Bangkok, right across to the Philippines, Zamboanga and Manila, down to Borneo, round to Sandakan and beyond the back up along Sarawak to Singapore. And then right up the Malacca Straits, right up to Rangoon and Moulmein and Bassein. That was all our territory.

> Percy Bulbrook joined Straits Steamships because of the slump in 1928 and Monty Wright some years later. Bulbrook was from an old Cornish seafaring family, with a grandfather who was a fisherman 'but also sidelined with a bit of smuggling' and a father who had left the navy to become a coastguard. After nearly a decade of sea-time in the merchant navy he found himself in a situation where 'even the sailors in the fo'c's'le all held Master-Mariner's Certi-

ficates'. The Straits offered 'security and steady employment – but, of course, you had to wait for promotions. It took me twelve years in the Straits with a Master-Mariner's Certificate before I ever went in command, and then, of course, there were quite a few old greybeards left when I joined and they resented us First and Second Officers because we were all carrying Master-Mariner's Certificates, the whole lot of us. All we were virtually doing was waiting for them to get out and we'd step in. There was quite a lot of animosity because the old greybeards had to put in a confidential report to the company every year and you didn't know what was ever said against you.'

Many of these senior Ship's Masters were 'real old salts who'd been in square-riggers round the Horn and even blackbirding' (illegally transporting Chinese to work as slave-labour in the South Pacific). One of the best-known characters was the twenty-two-stone Captain Caithness, who was said in his youth to have been either a Hudson Bay whaler or 'out of the Dundee trawlers, which was a hard affair in those days', and whose boast it was that he could pick up a coil of ship's rope and throw it across the deck. He was said to have a tremendous capacity for beer, being capable of drinking 'a couple of cases before tiffin with a few gin *pahits* to help it down', and was widely known as 'Captain Allsopp'. A 'dear old lady passenger' was said to have inadvertently given him this name: 'They asked her how she'd enjoyed the trip and she said, "Well, it was very nice, but this Captain – I think his name was Captain Allsopp – kept saying to his 'boy', 'Allsopp, boy, Allsopp'."'

At sea the Ship's Masters had almost unlimited powers: 'We were allowed complete freedom with regard to our decisions and they were never questioned by the management. For instance, sometimes you'd get an obstreperous – to use a nautical term – passenger, getting on the booze and probably interfering with the women. Well, you could send for him and say, "Right, I'm putting you ashore here." Finish!' But back in Singapore there were frequent disagreements with the management in the person of the Straits Marine Superintendent, particularly, as Bulbrook recalls, on such matters as uniforms:

We used to wear what the navy called Number Tens; long trousers of white twill, the *tutup* jacket that came up to the neck with brass buttons and the *topee* that the boy had starched up. You ordered the suits by the dozen and you could get through five or six in a day, all dirties, when you were supervising work on the cargo. Then some lad home on leave had to go to Harley Street on some trouble he had and mentioned this *topee* business and the doctor said that sunstroke came through the eyes. So then we all went into dark glasses and threw off our *topees* and reverted to our uniform cap, much to the disgust of the Marine Superintendent. But the greatest shock of all was when our navy decided that in the Eastern Station the day uniform could be white shorts and stockings and open necks. So I got half-a-dozen suits made and was very proud of them. The Marine Superintendent used to come aboard about six in the morning to do his rounds of the ships and, as Chief Officer, I went to the gangway to greet him. He looked me up and down: 'Go and get dressed,' he said. There was a hell of a row about it but we won the day.

Life was by no means made easy for the junior officers. There was no shore accommodation for bachelors and during their first term of service there was no official leave: 'We didn't get a single day's holiday in our first five years and the only way you could get any holiday was to be sick and then they put you in the hospital. We rather resented that because although we were doing all the ports we couldn't get around inside the country.'

Nor was there much mixing with the European business community in Singapore. The company provided its officers with their own club and 'if we got fed up ashore we said, "All right, the so-and-so mail's in – the German mail, the Dutch mail, our mail. Let's go down there, boys!" And we'd pile into rickshaws – because the

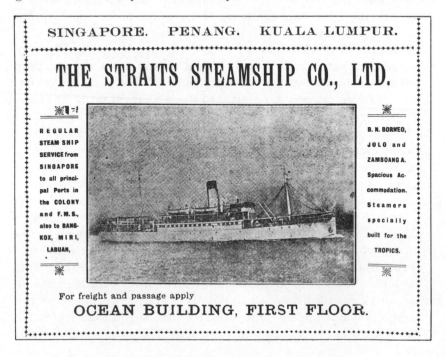

only means of getting around was by rickshaw – and go aboard. And if the bar bloke knew you were sailors, then you'd get everything cheaper. But the *Raffles,* the *Adelphi* and the old *Europe Hotel*, they combined and got that all stopped, because we were doing them out of business.' However, with the Straits time ashore was always limited since 'the voyages were short, with short stops in port', and in consequence, 'it was a life with one foot on the gangway and one on the shore all the time'.

Starting as Second Officers, both Bulbrook and Wright spent their early years with the company getting to know the various ships' runs:

> You were put there on one run, say, for two months and then it depended on how much knowledge you could get into your head. If it was a small run, after a couple of months you were shifted to learn another run and then shifted again, until you got to be Senior Chief Officer. Then you could say, well, I'm here for about a year. So you circulated – and we had a saying that if you didn't like the ship the only way you could get a transfer was to paint your cabin and as sure as hell you'd get a shift, because you wouldn't be there to enjoy the cleanliness of it.

On most runs the ships spent a day in Singapore and then one or two days at sea, working up the east or west coast of Malaya and down again, carrying general cargo and passengers on the outward run and returning with local produce: sheet rubber, tapioca, wood and copra. The major run was to Borneo and back:

> The ships would have a week in Singapore and then be three weeks away, calling at various ports along the Borneo coast – Miri, Labuan, Jesselton, Kudat, Sandakan and on to Tawau. The scenery from Jesselton round to Tawau was very beautiful because the Malawadi channel was strung with islands, some belonging to the Philippines, some to North Borneo; some were inhabited and some not. The channel was narrow and it was as though you were sailing on a multi-coloured sea, ranging from deep blue to green where the reefs showed through, with the islands set like jewels here and there. At the approaches to Sandakan there was an island called Pahala, which used to be the leper settlement for British North Borneo. The cliffs were red in colour and when approached just before sunrise they seemed to stand out in a vivid colour, gradually changing as the sun rose.

Some of the ports were just coves where all they had to export were a few bags of copra:

If they wanted the ship to stop they would hoist a signal – usually a bucket on a coconut tree – and the ship would anchor off-shore and they would bring their produce out to the ship. The ships carried their own tally-clerks under the charge of a *chin-chu,* the same as a *comprador*, who on behalf of the company would purchase the produce at the market price. And where there were no banks the ships used to act as the bank. If the District Officer required some money he would give the Master a chit for the required amount and the Master would give him cash from the safe. Each port had some form of club for the European inhabitants but there was no other real diversion except the Straits ship when she came into port, so the housewives would come down and buy the bread, meat and dairy produce from the ship's cold storage and make use of the dining facilities in the saloon. An invitation from a Master or a Senior Officer to join him for dinner was much sought after and people also used to book tables for dinner or lunch on board. And this friendliness between the ships and the local inhabitants was something that was enduring.

On these runs the stops were usually during the daylight hours with most of the sailing between ports done overnight, when 'large areas of the South China Sea, being phosphorescent, almost seemed to be alive. But there was always plenty of marine life, with the porpoise and dolphin gambolling and swimming close to the bows, almost seeking companionship. Various coastal areas, especially off the rivers, abounded with sea-snakes, all venomous and extremely lively, and very often when the ship was anchored and waiting the tide to cross a bar into a river and fishing lines were put over the side, these sea-snakes seemed to be the main catch.'

The sand-bars across the river estuaries always presented a serious hazard to shipping, particularly when the north-east monsoon whipped up the smooth water of the South China Sea into a fierce 'chop' that was 'most dangerous because it came from all ways and pounded the sand hard as iron'. This was still an era when navigational aids were limited to a few lighthouses so that the Straits' captains depended to a very large extent on their own skills and experience – 'all you had were your eyes, your ears and your blinking brains'. It was their proud boast that they always performed their own pilotage: 'We in the Straits never took pilots, even in Singapore, where the junks were the bane of our existence when the tide was strong and there was no wind.' They had also to know the rivers 'like the backs of our hands, which was no mean feat as the channels were always changing. In order to turn the ship around one usually drifted six to seven miles down the river in the course of turning, a process made more hazardous by odd outcrops of rocks here and there. But everyone fished up in the putty some time. Bouncing off the bank was an accepted fact and being stuck on a bar was an accepted fact. Nobody worried.'

Every captain had his own method of gauging his ship's approach to the shore. 'You had to pick out your own distinctive landmarks and it was a bit awkward if they chopped down a few trees here and there. Some of the rubber planters used to do that. Up the Perak river there's a little creek named Daley's Creek and this chap Daley he had a big rubber place up there. He'd fallen out with old "Talky" Roberts at the club and so whilst he was away Daley cut down about five of the trees that were most important. Of course, old Talky Roberts went ashore!'

Other local aids were also enlisted – particularly at night: 'There was one point in North Borneo in particular where we used to get close to within half a mile of the shore which we could not see in the dark but were guided past by a local dog that invariably barked, and depending upon the loudness of the bark we could gauge our nearness from the shore.' Even fireflies glowing in the dark could help to show where the river banks were when the ships were travelling up- or down-river: 'These passengers used to say, "How the hell can you get down the river?" They'd step out from their cabins or the bar or the saloon and peer over, but of course we weren't in the glare of the ship's lights.'

Even the smallest Straits' steamers carried a large crew drawn from several races but nearly always divided by occupation: 'The officers held British Certificates and were recruited in the UK. The crews were traditionally Chinese in the engine room and catering departments and Malay seamen on deck, as well as Chinese labour – eighty was the average on our small ships – to load your ship and unload, because we had our own crowd to discharge that ship. We used to pilot up to the wharf and if the cargo coolies on shore were too slow we'd say, "Get on with it, boys."' As well as the crew each ship had its complement of passengers: 'Up to forty First-Class passengers, a couple of dozen Second-Class and up to three hundred and fifty Deck-Class. We also carried on deck livestock in the form of pigs in baskets, hump-backed cattle, chickens, fighting-cocks and on occasion the odd circus.' Each ship also had to have three galleys: 'One for Mohamedans, one for Chinese, one for Europeans. The Chief Steward bought all the victuals and Europeans in the First Class used to have eight-course dinners – beautiful *makin*. The Master made sure he had a damn good cook on board because that attracted the passengers – and they made their bit out of it, too.'

Although the ships' runs always followed the same pattern and timetable there was very little monotony in the work: 'It was always different; the wind, the tide, the currents. There was always some factor which made the berthing of a ship different from the time before. And whether it was an old ship or a new one, one always had pride in whatever ship one was appointed to.' Occasionally there were moments of drama and even tragedy – as in the 'affair' of the *Klang* in 1930:

That was a very bad affair. Old MacDonell was Master – a gentle old bible-puncher he was, a bearded bloke and fairly elderly, who was going to retire when he got back. The *Klang* called into Port Swettenham and then on to Penang, had a night there, and then back to Singapore. She sailed at four o'clock and they got out to Keppel Heads, the entrance to Singapore Harbour, and in the meantime the deck crowd was settling down. She had about six hundred deck passengers and they each had a little cane mat which they put down on the deck and that was their bit of space. Well, by the time they got out to Raffles lighthouse, some Malays decided it was time to say prayers to Mecca. They weren't going to wait for the sun to go down, they were going to do it a little in advance. They had lain their mats down and, unfortunately too, they were *Hajis* – that's to say they'd just come back from Mecca – and in those days they used to stain their whiskers red with red lead. They went to the ship's rail at the stern to *Al-Allah* to Mecca. I don't know how long they were, must have been about a half-hour as usual, and back they came. But in the meantime, another fellow had picked up their mats, thrown them in the scuppers and put his down. Of course there was an argument and the next thing – out with the *kris*. And they started stabbing. The Mate was up with the old man on the bridge and they had another six miles to go before you get around Kapis to go up the Straits of Malacca. And the first intimation they got that there was something wrong down on the decks was when all these deck passengers, women, kids and all, began trying to get up on the prom deck. In the meantime, a *kemudi* – that's a Malay term for a helmsman – who was off duty having his *makin,* his food, saw all this and managed to climb up over the awning spars onto the bridge and told them that some fellows had run *amok*, and were foaming at the mouth like mad dogs. So the Mate said to the old man, 'I'll go down and see what I can do.' And the old man said, 'No, you'd better leave it to me.' So down went the old chap and he met these two coming along the deck, which was clear now because all the other passengers had crowded the other side to get

out of the way. In the meantime, they'd scuppered three or four
that were lying round the decks bleeding. The old man went up
to one of them, put his hand on his shoulder to ease him down
and this fellow just – sheesh – disembowelled him there and
then. Then he and the other fellow got busy with a few more. I
think there were seventeen altogether, seventeen Asians anyhow
and old MacDonell. The Mate on the bridge didn't know what
was happening, so he got hold of this *kemudi* and asked him to go
over the awning and look down and of course he did and came
back and told him, 'The old man's *sudah mati* – the old man's
dead.' So the Mate put the ship hard over and came back to Singapore. They got in off Johnson's Pier and had the police flag up
and it took the police nearly a good half-hour to get off. In the
meantime, the two *amok* fell out with each other and one got killed by the other one. But that left one who was still roaming
around and even ran down the engine room. That's where the
Chief Engineer got his – luckily he felt the knife coming in and
put his knee up, so he was all right; they stitched him up. The
European Inspector brought a couple with a rifle; they boarded,
the Mate bawled down from the bridge what was wrong and they
saw this bloke and they put four bullets into him. That didn't
stop him, but they got him in the launch and he didn't die till
they got him on the pier. Now, the bold European passengers
had locked themselves in their cabins. Among them were a lot of
army officers, too, and they had revolvers, guns. Oh, it was
hushed up; it had to be, but that was the *Klang*.

Piracy was no longer a serious threat to shipping in the South
China Sea but it was still a risk on the more distant runs to the Philippines and to China. Straits Steamships had a subsidiary company running three passenger-cargo vessels between Rangoon,
Singapore, Swatow and Amoy – which meant passing a notorious
haunt of pirates just north of Hong Kong known as Bias Bay. Since
the most successful ploy used by the pirates was to infiltrate on
board as passengers and then take over the ship at an opportune
moment, many of the merchant fleets operating along the China
coast employed White Russians as guards on the ships. The Straits
preferred to arm its senior crew members instead:

The officers all had arms issued from the armoury consisting of
Webley-Scott revolvers and Greener shotguns and were stationed behind grilles separating the officers' accommodation, the
bridge and the engine room from the rest of the ship. Once the
ship had cleared Hong Kong northward-bound, we were in contact with the Anti-Piracy Control to which all ships on the coast

reported, sending our position every two hours and our expected
time of arrival at the next port. If this transmission was not
received then the Anti-Piracy Control was expected to take
action. Despite these measures a number of ships were successfully seized and taken to Bias Bay, to be looted and their passengers held for ransom.

Few can have experienced quite as many hazards in the course of
their careers as Robert Williamson, who retired in 1947 after
twenty-six years with the Indo-China Steam Navigation Company.
Nearly half his service was spent on the longest of China's rivers,
the Yangtse:

> The Chinese always refer to the Yangtse as the *Ta Chiang* or the
> Great River, because it is the greatest river in China and it is the
> great highway of China as it traverses the country from east to
> west. It rises in Tibet, it flows south until it reaches the moun-
> tains of Yunnan and there it is deflected and turns and flows back
> north again for about a hundred miles. It then skirts the base of
> the great Cheng-tu Basin which in past ages was an inland sea.
> The Yangtse flows on the southern edge of it down to Chungking
> and then through the generally hilly country for about two hun-
> dred miles. For about a hundred miles it flows through
> tremendous gorges – the Yangtse Gorges, until it leaves the
> mountains at the port of Ichang and then flows down through the
> great central plains of China right down to the sea.
>
> The river begins to rise usually about May, but the first rise is
> a false rise and is due to the melting of snows in Tibet. But
> shortly after that the monsoon rains begin and then one gets the
> summer rise which begins to gradually build up. All the tributar-
> ies and the side streams are flooded, they all pour down into the
> main river and they build up enormous floods right up until the
> latter part of August. In the autumn the rains begin to ease off
> and the floods drain away until you get to December. Then
> December, February, March are the months when the river
> reaches its lowest level. Some years the monsoon rains are
> heavier than in others, but in one year – I think it was 1921,
> which was my first season of navigating a ship on that river – we
> had a very high river and at the entrance to the Wu Shang Gorge,
> which is the longest of the gorges and twenty-five miles in length,
> I recorded that the river had risen to just over two hundred feet
> above its winter level.

In 1921 Bob Williamson began a four-year tour as a Ship's Master on the five-hundred-and-fifty-mile stretch of rapids and gorges
known as the Upper River:

The Master has to be on the bridge the whole time. He goes on the bridge when the ship gets under way at the crack of daylight and he's on the bridge until he brings the vessel into the anchorage in the evening. We carried Chinese pilots, local junkmen who knew the river intimately but only from a junkman's point of view. They knew every danger, they knew every change of level one had and they actually acted as pilots, but it wasn't safe to allow them to handle the ship, because they knew all about handling a junk but nothing about handling a steamer, and many accidents on the Upper River were due to the fact that inexperienced Masters trusted those pilots too implicitly. Of course, these pilots had probably been born in a junk. They knew the river and absolutely everything about it and they were familiar with the stories and the legends – and every mile of the river has its legend. For instance, in the Windbox Gorge there is a sheer thousand-foot cliff and running up the face of this cliff is a zig-zag row of holes from the river's bank right up to the top of the cliff. This is known as Meng Liang's Ladder and goes back to some time in the era before Christ known as the Wars of the Kingdoms. Meng Liang's army was attacking up-river but the defending general above the Windbox Gorge had stretched chains across at low level so as to bar the river from an attack by water. So Meng Liang's men cut holes in the cliffs and inserted beams into these holes and by making them zig-zag, they made a ladder right up the face of the cliff, got up to the top and attacked the defending force from the rear and defeated them.

The whole of the gorges section, particularly, is full of links with the past history of China. Every rock and every shoal has its own name. The Windbox Gorge takes its name from the fact that on the high cliffs opposite Meng Liang's Ladder there are some boxes in crevices, the square ends of which look like Chinese bellows – but how these boxes got into these crevices nobody knows. It's a mystery. Then there is the Wu Shang Gorge, which means the Witch's Mountain Gorge. Wu was a legendary wizard who lived on a mountain before the river burst through the mountains and he is said to have blasted with his breath a passage through the rocks, to allow the river to flow through – hence it being called the Wu Shang Gorge. In a steamer capable of steaming fifteen knots it took six hours to make your way up-river through that gorge under very wild conditions, because you're bucking in this current which rushes off each point and shoots across to the next point and then the next.

Of the many kinds of hazards on the river the most serious were the rapids in the gorges:

When the river gradually falls in the autumn the gorges become very quiet and placid – a joy to navigate really. But then the rapids begin to show up at places where there are reefs stretching out from the shore. They become uncovered and between the reefs and the bank you get a very narrow channel indeed and a very swift rapid. At low level there were about thirty rapids and races, of which the greatest was the Sin Tan, caused by an enormous landslide in the seventeenth century, which almost dammed up the river. That leaves only a channel between the outer rock and the bank of less than two hundred feet where the sluice runs down so hard that no steamer can surmount it. So here we had to what we called 'heave it'; the steamer would steam into the tongue of the rapid and then a wire was thrown ashore on a heaving line and made fast to a rock above the rapid. This was then taken to the windlass and as the ship steamed and sheered to and fro so they hove-in the wire and the steamer gradually worked its way over to the top of the rapid and away.

Another hazard came in the form of other traffic on the river:

On the Lower River one could meet enormous great timber rafts coming down with a whole colony of people living on board who were handling the rafts. Then one would occasionally meet a convoy of ducks going down to Nanking where they were to be processed as Chinese ducks for export. The poor little blighters were made to swim down. They were herded together by the main junk following astern and by men in small single *sampans* who kept them going. In the evening they would herd them ashore and pen them up and in the morning they would set them afloat again and carry on. There were also convoys of salt junks coming down and above Chunking one could pass a small town where they made large pots and one would occasionally meet the potter on his way to Chunking to sell the pots. He bunged them up and made them watertight, he bound them into a raft with bamboos and then he took his place on board and travelled down to Chunking.

On the Lower River you'd get quite a lot of traffic, not much on the Middle River and even less on the Upper River, where you would only meet the odd steamer coming down and the junks, always close in at the bank going up but, when they came down-river, drifting down in the middle of the stream. Yet they very seldom interfered with the steamer and the experienced Master; he knew how the currents were running and when he saw a junk coming down he knew whether it would be set towards him or away from him and handled his ship accordingly.

The largest cargo junk, carrying about eighty or ninety tons of cargo, had a crew of twenty men who were called 'trackers' and these lads also handled the *ulos* – a side oar which is worked with a sculling motion, not a pulling motion. They couldn't work up any great speed but they could manoeuvre with the *ulos*, and Providence has so arranged things that in the winter at low level in the gorges you usually get an up-river wind. The current is slack, probably not more than one or two knots, so with a good up-river wind, the junk could sail up, using one great sail which they hoisted. At the same time they worked their *ulos* with a peculiar chant that they had which was the equivalent of what we used to call in sailing ships 'whistling for the wind'. This was a wild 'Hoo-hoo-hoo' while on the smaller junks that were rowed with great sweeps they would chant 'I-eee-yah!'

Now when the junk came to a rapid, then all the trackers went ashore and they had a tow-line from the mast-head of the junk – not from the bow because of the rocks. It was hoisted about half-way up the mast and made fast and the trackers then spread themselves along the bank and then they had to haul the junk over the rapid by main force. And in a very bad rapid, like the Sin Tan or the Sin Lung Tan, the New Dragon rapid, and the Ya Tan, which was the Wild Ass rapid – and was a very wild ass indeed at times – on these very, very strong rapids, they would be reinforced by local boys who would come down and form themselves into gangs under a leader and hire themselves out to the captain of the junk, who would hire as many extra men as was necessary to haul the junk over that particular rapid. It was a hard life being a tracker; where there wasn't enough wind then they had to go ashore and haul the junk up by main force. For miles and miles they would be plodding along, and they didn't haul with the hands; they had a canvas strap built round the shoulder with a short length of line which they toggled onto the main tow rope so that they hauled with their bodies and when it got to a tough spot they would go down on hands and knees and claw themselves along from rock to rock!

The third major hazard on the river was also a human one:

China was a very wild and lawless country in those days. There were several of the so-called war-lords who, every year, were campaigning against each other, trying to get control of a principal city like Chungking or Wanhsien where the people could be taxed. These people were quite a curse and as there was no law and order, the country was infested with troops or gangs of what were actual bandits. They just went off looting all on their own and so we had to be very careful of the places where we anchored. We had a night watch that we set and we had enough rifles on board for our own use and our pistols, too. The ship's bridges were also enclosed in bullet-proof steel all round the bridge with flaps which had loop-holes in them so that we could enclose the bridge in armour. They were arranged on quick-release hooks so that the flaps could be dropped at practically a second's notice. One could come round a corner where there was fighting on between the various war-lords and if one came across a gang of them on the march, sometimes they would just shoot at the ship out of sheer wantonness!

I can remember one occasion when I was going up-river some hundred miles below Chungking. I had to cross from one side of the river to the other to avoid central dangers and on the opposite bank was a small village and there seemed to be some commotion going on. I looked through my glasses and I saw that there was a bunch of bandits looting the village. There were a couple of long-gowned gentlemen with their hands tied behind their backs – the local merchants that they were robbing – and there was quite a hoo-ha. The head of the gang was sitting on a large rock practically at the river's edge, directing the whole proceedings. As we turned across the river, heading towards the village, he looked round. Then I saw him shouting to somebody obviously asking for his gun. The gun was handed to him and as soon as I saw that I knew that he was going to have a pot-shot at us as we began to go in fairly close. So I thought I'd spoil his aim and got my own pistol ready – and sure enough, he swung round and fired a round at the ship. As soon as he had fired one round, I fired at the rock on which he was sitting and hit it and he threw up his arms and went off backwards. Before they could recover themselves and send a few stray shots after us, we'd rounded our stern and were well on our way.

During his four years on the Upper River Williamson was based on Chungking, which was still largely untouched by the outside world:

On the first evening I arrived in Chungking with a brand new ship and I was up in the office. When I arrived back on board there were two little Chinese girls sitting in my accommodation, so I said to my boy, 'Who are these?' He indicated that the management had sent them and said, 'Well, you need a little home comfort.' So I gave the little girls *cumshaw* – which is a gift – and they went ashore again. Then we used to go in the evening through the streets in our sedan chairs – because there were no rickshaws in Chungking in those days – and with our bearers carrying a hand lantern, to the Chinese theatre. And this was real, real China, quite untouched by any outside influences, where life went on as it had done throughout Chinese history.

The Upper River was capable of offering moments of great beauty:

There was one place in the middle of the Wu Shang Gorge where there was a side stream and in the late autumn when the gorges were quiet and the violent period was over, it was possible to anchor there. Then just at the peep of day one would heave up the anchor and ease the ship out into the mid-stream and steam up-river and you'd be in deep shadows still. But at one particular place there is a gap in the cliffs and you could see a ten-thousand-foot peak in the distance, bathed in the rosy light of early dawn, and that is a picture one never forgot – just the snoring of the waters and that glimpse of that distant peak so green and beautiful against the pearly sky.

But, inevitably, there were also moments of great tragedy – as in the story of Freddie Brandt, a British subject with a German father and a Chinese mother, who was a fellow-captain on the Upper River:

Now on the Upper Yangtse there was a lot of smuggling of opium and Freddie was up to his ears in this business. I would never have anything to do with it. But Freddie, unfortunately, also became involved in an arms racket. There was a war every summer in Szechwan between the warring war-lords. The man who was in Chungking had control of all the taxes so the man who was up in Cheng Tu would bring his army down and they would have a war to see who could chase the other one out; so of course there was a great demand for arms and unfortunately Freddie became involved in the arms racket. I knew about the opium – everybody knew it – however, the arms I didn't know about. But I was in Chungking, it would be in the autumn of 1924. Freddie's little *Tzeit Swei* was anchored on the opposite shore from Chungking when I arrived in the late afternoon and I sent a *chit* across to Freddie to come and dine with us, myself and my crowd. So Freddie came over and we had dinner together and after dinner it was dark by that time and I said, 'Well, Fred, you don't want to go back to your ship, doss down on my settee and I'll send you over in my *sampan* in the morning' – because he was

due to sail next morning at daylight. So he did. I got into my
bunk – because it was only a small cabin in a small ship – and
Fred turned in on my settee and we lay and chatted. Now he was
a married man and he had two children down in Shanghai, and as
we yarned I said, 'You know, Fred, I don't know why you carry
on up here on this Upper River. You've got plenty of money.
Why don't you chuck it and go down to Shanghai?' 'Oh,' he said,
'I must finish the season, I must finish the season.' So I said,
'Well, you must have a lot of enemies up here you know, with all
these rackets.' One skipper had disappeared over the side and
there had been some nasty business, so I said, 'You get back to
Shanghai, man, chuck it.' 'Oh,' he said, 'I will, Bob, soon as the
season's over I'll be finished.'

Well, next morning I hauled my *sampan* away and I took Fred
across to his ship and I stood and I watched him while he went
on the bridge and hove up his anchor and as he turned around
into the river we waved to each other and that was that. Two
days later I was down-bound myself loaded for Ichang and I was
going through the last of the gorges, called the Yellow Cat Gorge
– it's about ten miles in length – and about half-way down, I saw
a little steamer coming into the lower end of the gorge and it was
the *Tzeit Swei*. This was Fred upward-bound again and as we
passed, of course we waved. Two or three days later I was up-
bound again and coming on through the second half of the
Ichang Gorge – I remember this sight well – in the Lampshine
Gorge, when a steamer came down and as she came down I saw
them with a blackboard. We hadn't time to signal to each other so
we always had a big blackboard on which you put any information about the river. One wrote on the blackboard and showed it
to the ship as you whizzed past each other. I saw the blackboard
coming out and read on it, 'Captain Brandt was shot at Kowchochin at such and such a time.' I thought, 'Oh, Lord'. Well, I
got up to Wan Sien and the British gunboat was there and the
captain came on board. He said, 'I'm very sorry to have to tell
you that Captain Brandt has been murdered. He was shot and
thrown over the side but his body has been recovered and is lying
in the Joss House in Kowchochin and I want you to stop there
and pick him up and carry him on to Chungking.' I said, 'Yes, of
course I will.'

I arranged my sailing from Wan Sien to arrive up there just
before nightfall. I anchored and I sent my *comprador* – what we
would call a purser, but they always used the old Portuguese
term out there of *comprador*, the buyer – to the headman of the
village, telling him that I was commissioned to carry Captain

Brandt and would they kindly send him on board first thing in the morning. I said, 'Take plenty of money, *comprador*, you pay the headman all the expenses of recovering his body and fixing him up and the coffin and the *cumshaw* on top.' At daylight a terrific hoo-ha started up ashore as Fred had a really good send-off from the Joss House with firecrackers all the way down to the beach. The coffin was then put on board a big *sampan*. They brought him over to the ship and up on deck and away we went. And that was the end of poor old Freddie Brandt.

After nearly five years on the Upper River Bob Williamson moved down to Shanghai, where he served for nine years as the Indo-China Steam Navigation Company's Marine Superintendent. But the Upper River was an experience that could never be forgotten:

It was my life and I loved every minute of it. I was an Upper River Master, which was recognized as a very difficult and at times hazardous occupation. And it's a source of great pride to me that my name in Chinese was Wei Ling Soong (Williamson) and that I was known as Wei Twon Ju. Twon is the ship, Ju is the overlord and that is the Chinese word for a captain of the ship, so I was Wei Twon Ju and I would go ashore in Chungking and I would hear the Chinese say, 'Who's that old foreigner?', and somebody would say, 'Wei Twon Ju.' It meant that I was Captain Wei and that was that.

9

THE MEMS

They played tennis if there were people to play with,
went to the club at sundown if there was a club in
the vicinity, drank in moderation, and played
bridge. They had their little tiffs, their little
jealousies, their little flirtations, their little celebra-
tions.

Somerset Maugham, *Preface,*
The Complete Short Stories, Vol III

As far as marriage was concerned most Europeans had little option
but to follow the standard convention:

At the end of your first contract you were called in by a director
in London and he said, 'I'm pleased to inform you that you are
now permanent staff. You've served four years; we think therefore as directors of the company that you should get married and
you've got four months' leave in which to find a wife.' This was
rather difficult in those days, but you were twenty-eight or
twenty-nine and you were getting a good salary by that time, so
the best thing you could do would be to go to a teaching hospital
in London, hang around outside and pick up a nurse. That was
the quickest way of finding on four months' leave a girl with
whom you might get some association going and then be able to
say, 'Would you like to get married?'

If only a minority of bachelors succeeded in finding prospective
brides on their first home leave, that was hardly surprising. Many
more marriages took place during the second long leave or during
the second term of service, often within twenty-four hours of the
bride-to-be setting foot on Straits or Malay States territory. The
'export' of fiancées for these 'beach weddings' was regarded as a
risky business – and not without reason: 'If you didn't take her

through the Red Sea on the P&O yourself she was almost bound to fall for somebody on the ship,' declares Gerald Scott. 'So very often these chaps from the rubber companies and the tin-mines who were exporting their fiancées from England – an awful lot of characters in my day in Singapore – they'd nip up to Penang and then the girl would come down the gangplank with some shipboard romance on her arm and they'd have to give the wedding reception they'd planned as a wedding present to the girl.'

But not all the single women who landed at Penang, Port Swettenham or Singapore came out as intended brides. Increasingly, from the late 1920s onwards, single women were being recruited by the Educational and Medical Services. In 1927 Mary Culleton, who had trained as a nurse at Guy's Hospital during the First World War, joined the Malayan Nursing Service. Her first three years in Malaya were spent in Batu Gajah hospital as a nursing sister, looking after the European women's ward and dealing for the most part either with maternity cases or malaria. It was malaria that presented the most serious threat to the health of the community. Quinine-based treatment had little effect: 'You had temperatures up to one hundred and five degrees easily and you sweated so terribly that you had constantly to be changed. It was very common to get it – and that's what got me finished earlier than that I would have.'

After a particularly bad bout of malaria Mary Culleton was invalided out of the service in 1930. However, in the meantime, she had met and become engaged to a rubber planter named Hugh Watts – 'we met at the Station Hotel, Ipoh, where the sisters were invited to a party. There was a group of young rubber planters also having a party and they said, "Let's all join together."' After a period of recuperation in England she returned and was married at Port Swettenham – 'a quiet wedding with the minimum of fuss and a wedding breakfast at the Rest House'.

Tamsin Luckham and Dorothy 'Tommy' Hawkings came to Malaya as teachers. Both had relatives in the Far East: Tamsin Luckham a brother in the MCS and a sister married to a Bousteads' executive; Tommy Hawkings a cousin in Malaya but with far stronger family connections with China, where her grandfather had gone out as a missionary in 1875 and where she herself had been born and educated. At the start of the Second World War she moved down to Malaya to open a nursery boarding school for European children in the Cameron Highlands, driving up through 'great tropical rain forests with orchids hanging from the trees'. She was struck by the 'peacefulness of life' in Malaya: 'After all the tragedies I had seen in Shanghai when the Japanese entered the Chinese settlement – old men and women with stones tied to their feet being thrown into rivers, young girls being taken off to be raped over and over again and then shot – Malaya seemed so calm and quiet. Everything was running so smoothly and it really was a dramatic change from the turmoil of life in China.'

In the Cameron Highlands she met Peter Lucy, a young planter and Manager of Amhurst Estate, who was on local leave. In November 1941 she moved down to Kuala Lumpur and saw a lot more of him:

We had a wonderful time together and I remember the evening when we walked through the Malay village in Kuala Lumpur after a dance and there were great stalls of what we call *makan kechils*, small eats, and kebabs on sticks that the Malays were making over the fires. This was about four o'clock in the morning

SARAWAK GOVERNMENT OFFICES,
MILLBANK HOUSE,
WESTMINSTER, S.W. 1

TEL. WHITEHALL 3226

G.635   5th June, 1946.

Dear Sir,

        With reference to your letter of the 30th May, I have received a telegram from Sarawak that your request to marry is approved.

            Yours faithfully,

            J O Smith

            Government Agent.

            *Rec & ack
            7.6.46.*

In this instance leave to marry was granted three months before the required eight years of service in Sarawak had been completed.

because dances in Malaya seldom finished before dawn, and it was there that Peter proposed to me and we became engaged.

Tamsin Luckham had started her teaching four years earlier in an Anglican mission school for girls in Kuala Lumpur. She too had been greatly impressed by a landscape that she first saw from the open cockpit of a Tiger Moth, piloted by a friend of her brother's who flew her down from Penang:

The jungle that covered so much of Malaya wasn't very colour-ful. It was rather grey-green – although the new leaves were always red, surprisingly. But looking down on the tops of trees you saw bright birds and flowers that usually you saw very little of unless you went to a hill-station. The mountains looked very, very blue – I suppose because of the atmosphere – although at mid-day the light tended to drain all the colour from things – that flat light with the sun overhead and no shadows.

Her school had an English headmistress with a staff made up of Eurasians, Indians and Chinese and about five hundred pupils:

This was a very well-thought-of school so we got the daughters of very well-off Chinese *towkays,* but also we had the daughters of anybody who could pay the very, very small fees that were needed, because it was a government-aided school where the government paid the staff. The majority of the girls were Chinese but there were also Sikhs, Tamils and Eurasians. There were no Malays because the school wasn't in an area where there were Malays and Malay girls tended to go to their own Islamic schools – although they thought convents were very ladylike.

After only a year at the school Tamsin Luckham found herself acting headmistress while the head went on leave. Her only moment of crisis came when a tiger was sighted near the school grounds:

I was a bit taken aback because these schools, being in a hot climate, were completely open, so there was no way of shutting doors or anything like that without a tremendous palaver. I thought, what happens if the tiger walks into a school of five hundred girls? But I said, 'Oh well, I don't expect it will come this way' – and it didn't come that way. The next day I saw a Baby Austin car with the girls absolutely crowding round and I said to them, 'What's all this about?' And they said, 'Oh, that tiger was shot and he's selling tiger meat. If we have that, it'll make us good and strong.' So here we were in a mission school and all the girls buying tiger meat to make themselves big and strong!

Being young and unattached in Kuala Lumpur had obvious advantages: 'I was very lucky because as an unmarried girl I was welcomed into all the clubs without paying anything. We were entirely supported by the men, who were so pleased to have some girls that I got all the facilities of the clubs for nothing, which was a big thing because I was terribly badly paid, of course, and I wouldn't have been able to afford going to the clubs otherwise.' As well as being entertained at the clubs she was also taken out to the Chinese dance-halls which were usually to be found in amusement parks. It was at one of these that she was introduced to Richard Broome, one of her brother's colleagues in the MCS, who later became her husband.

Another notable group of young single women in the Malay archipelago were the daughters of Britons already working there and who came out to join their parents as teenagers when their school-days were over. One such teenager was Una Ebden, who came out at her mother's insistence at the unusually early age of fifteen, soon after the war in Europe had started: 'I arrived in Malacca where my father was Resident Councillor and went straight from school into this glorious atmosphere of grandeur, with the sentry saluting you as you went in the front door and a car with a Union Jack and police saluting me. It seemed very grand and I was so impressed.'

Driving up from Singapore to Malacca through the Malayan countryside she had been greatly struck by the humidity and its 'encouragement to growth':

> It was like a large greenhouse, so that everything was green and of enormous growth. Then there were splashes of colour against the green; bougainvillaea which was purple; next to bougainvillaea, organe; next to that yellow canna lilies. Everything ought to have clashed but it didn't. It looked gorgeous, like a great bed of azaleas. The Malay women wore the same clashy clothes but they also looked gorgeous; where a white skin would look simply dreadful they looked really beautiful. Then the stars were so bright you could almost read by them and when the moon was full you could read. The strange thing was that the moon was sideways. Instead of a man in the moon it was a rabbit. I remember seeing that and thinking how funny it was. And of course swimming at night in Malacca swimming pool, which was just a fenced off bit of sea. As you waved your arm out of the water it dripped fire and you could see everybody splashing around in a great mass of fire and phosphorus.

Even at fifteen Una Ebden was able to enjoy the advantage of being one of a greatly sought-after minority: 'I was rather lucky in having a good friend who was exactly the same age, the daughter of the Dunlops' representative there. We had a very good time together, because there was no shortage of dates. We were taken out dancing, swimming, on picnics, anything we wanted – there were people queuing up. Oh, it was absolute heaven and very bad for the character, I know, but being good friends we were able to enjoy it all together and revert a little to childhood sometimes and have a good giggle.' When the climate became too oppressive she was able to escape with her family to the Cameron Highlands, which was fast becoming the premier hill-station of Malaya: 'It was five-and-a-half thousand feet high, which meant that it was still nice and warm during the days but that the air was fresh and you had wood fires in the evening and blankets on the bed, which was a treat. There was a golf course and lovely walks and horses to ride and a dance in the hotel every Saturday night.'

It was 'a lovely, carefree, irresponsible life' for a teenager. Yet Una Ebden was very conscious of the role played by her father and others like him: 'I saw my father as a man dedicated to Malaya and to the Malays, for whom he had a lot of time – good-natured gentle-men, was how he used to describe them – and I do think that he was typical of the MCS as a whole; the country was their only interest.'

For those who came out East as newly-weds – new *mems* know-ing very little about the country or what to expect – life was not quite so carefree. Nancy and Guy Madoc had grown up together on the Isle of Man: 'He then went out to Malaya and we wrote to each other. He used to write me long, glowing accounts of the country and how interesting it was and sent me wonderful photographs, and I began to get very interested, thinking it was a romantic place to live.' When Madoc returned on his first home leave the two met up again, became engaged and got married. During their honeymoon in Somerset Nancy Madoc had a foretaste of what married life in Malaya could be like when her husband had an attack of malaria: 'He had a very high temperature and would wake up shouting, and that worried me to death.'

The Madocs sailed for the East, to be met in Penang by a smell that Nancy found 'so frightful that I couldn't believe it. I said in a horrified voice to Guy, "What is that terrible smell?" And he said, "Oh, that's durian. That's this wonderful fruit that they all think so much of." Then Guy took me straight to the *Runnymede Hotel* – a lovely place with everything that could be luxurious, with fans and servants – and we had ice-cold mangosteen, which is another fruit and it really was lovely. There were no mosquitoes, and a breeze blew through the room and I thought, "Oh, this is lovely, I am going to love this country."'

They had already been told that Madoc's next posting was to Kuala Selangor:

The other officers on the boat said, 'What a dreadful place to send a young bride', so I began to wonder. However, Guy was reassuring and said, 'Oh, it's a lovely place and we'll be all right. We've got a bungalow and we've got a cook and we've got an *amah*,' and so I made up my mind that it would be all right and off we started. We drove and drove and drove, and at every little *atap* house that we passed on the way, standing way back in the jungle paddy, I would say, 'Is our bungalow like that?' and he'd say, 'Oh, yes, it's a bit better than that.' Eventually we got to Kuala Selangor and stopped at the bottom of a flight of eighty steps and that was the only way to get up to the bungalow, so we trudged up and Ah Chi, the Chinese servant, met us with his wife and small boy. It was a nice bungalow, perched on a hill, but our outlook was just the rather muddy Selangor river and the mangrove swamps really as far as you could go. The police station and *padang* were just below the hill, which was a consolation, because I could actually hear Guy sometimes in his office, but I was very homesick at first. I really was pretty miserable and it took me a long time to get used to it.

To her initial dismay this new life was not at all what Nancy Madoc had imagined it would be:

I used to wonder how I could have been so foolish as not to realize that of course it wasn't going to be a glamorous state of going to the club and being amongst a lot of other women, because Guy's letters had more or less told me that he wouldn't have liked that sort of life anyway. But we had a very old-fashioned bungalow; there were just kerosene lamps that had to be lit every night and a terrible old bathroom with slats on the floor that you could look through and see just the ground underneath – and, of course, every time I went into this place I saw snakes coming up through the slats in my imagination and it really took me a lot of courage to go into that bathroom. Then I was alone an awful lot of the time and I used to imagine things, I suppose – in other words, I got the jim-jams. Every terror that I could think of was there; a snake under every chair, a spider under every cushion. And it wasn't all imagination, because one day when we were down on the beach, I was standing under the casuarina trees watching other people who were still in the water surf-bathing when I became aware of a kind of tickling on my shoulder. I was in a sleeveless dress and I didn't think anything of it; I just reached up and shook my shoulder and then a clammy sensation began to grow upon my arm and I looked and there crawling from my shoulder down my arm was a beautiful vivid green snake. I have often heard people say they were stiff with fear and I was; my lips stuck to my teeth and I couldn't shout, I couldn't do anything. I just shook it off and I turned my head and there was our faithful Majid who always came with us. He saw that I was terrified and came running and cut the snake in half.

But as Nancy Madoc grew accustomed to her new role she began to realize that the country was not full of terror – and her confidence grew to the point where she could accompany her husband into the Malayan jungle without any qualms.

An important stage in the process of cultural acclimatization was learning the language. The tradition – particularly among government servants – was that *'mems* spoke Malay. In those days all servants, shopkeepers and market people, all – whatever their nationality – spoke Malay. It was a very simple type of Malay, but that was how we communicated and in fact servants didn't think it was correct in those days to speak English.' This was not something that most *mems* found easy at first – and Nancy Madoc was no exception:

Guy tried very hard to teach me the basic words to say to the servants and I used to repeat them religiously every evening. I got my accent more or less right but the time came when he had to be away overnight. I was rather nervous, but he said, 'You will be quite all right with Ah Chi. All you have to do is to tell him to lock everything that will lock,' and he told me what to say which I, faithfully, thought I knew well. So when Ah Chi came into the room and said goodnight, I said, 'You must *kenching sini, kenching sana, kenching sini, kenching sana*', and I went on saying this to Ah Chi, whose face never altered. He didn't let on by any indication at all that I was saying something quite wrong and off he went, back to his quarters, which are always at the back of a bungalow in Malaya and eventually I heard him laughing hysterically, and his family all laughing and laughing, and I thought, 'That's funny, why are they laughing?' So when Guy came home he said, 'How have you been?' And I said, 'Oh, I was all right, but when I told Ah Chi "*kenching sini, kenching sana*" they just roared with laughter.' And then, of course, Guy roared with laughter. What I should have been saying was *kunchi* which means lock, but what I was saying was *kenching sini, kenching sana*, which means, 'pee here, pee there', so no wonder they laughed.

There were many genuine and deep friendships between *mems* and their household staff but they took time to develop. One of the hoariest jokes in the Far East was about the Englishman who returned with his bride and introduced her to the servants: 'He said to his houseboy, "Boy, this lady here belong my wife," and the boy grinned and said, "Yes, master, yes, yes." But early next morning she felt her shoulders being shaken by the houseboy who said, 'Missie, belong five o'clock. More better you go home now.'

Rather more typical was the close relationship that existed between Tamsin Broome and her household servants – who were all Chinese:

The nice thing about the Chinese is that they're always so sure that they are very, very superior people and therefore there's none of this difficulty which I think one got in India over servants. Our cook was marvellous, for instance. He could cook English, or Chinese, or anything you asked. He also did the marketing and that kind of thing. The *amah* knew how to bring up a newborn baby and she taught the baby nursery rhymes in English and sang to it and so on. So though I was never able to have long conversations, because my Malay was not really up to that and nor was theirs, we were still very, very great friends and I think that we both felt that we were on a par. Now it wasn't quite the same with the other servants. We used to have a gardener – nearly always a Tamil – and gardeners in Malaya were the bane of my life because I love a garden and you could have a beautiful garden in Malaya, but whatever kind of gardener you had they always said they couldn't speak a word of either English or Malay and therefore they went their own way, whatever you wanted. On Christmas Island we had a Chinese gardener but I had to do everything through my husband because he wouldn't speak a word that I could understand. When Richard said plant vegetables he would nod and then you would say, 'Why weren't they planted?' He'd say, 'Oh well, the moon wasn't right,' or something – and Tamil gardeners were exactly the same: 'We don't understand English, or Malay' – and so they went their own way, endlessly cutting little tiny beds in the middle of your back lawn and filling them with marigolds and such like. So you never really got what you wanted. But of course you moved so frequently that however hard you worked you probably never saw the advantage of your garden.

Later the Broomes took on a houseboy, Ah Chuan, whom they had first met on Christmas Island when he was working for another employer – 'because on Christmas Island we had a very nice custom where if you were ever asked out to dinner it was taken for granted that your household staff would go too'. Here, as in Sarawak and other more out of the way stations, the houseboy would help to hand round various canapes – known as *makan kechils* or 'small eats' – serve at table if he was needed and then join the host's staff for their own dinner. After the Broomes moved to Penang Ah Chuan appeared at Richard Broome's office:

> He walked in and said, 'I've come to work for you.' I said, 'But we're not employing anybody else at the moment. We've got the cook and the *amah* and we reckon that's enough.' 'Ah yes,' he said. 'But Mrs Broome is going to have a baby and then the *amah* will be fully employed and then you will want me.' Of course, he was quite right but this was, we thought, a secret – and he had worked it all out. Like most of the domestic servants he was a Hainanese and my language was Cantonese, so I was a little doubtful but in fact he spoke quite enough Cantonese and Malay and so we could get on.

When the Japanese invaded Malaya, the cook and the *amah* went to join Tamsin Broome in Singapore. Richard Broome was then asked to join a special forces unit and told Ah Chuan to go: 'I said to Ah Chuan, "You'd better get off, because you'll be quite all right if you fade into the Chinese community here." But he said, "Oh no, I want to come with you." I said, "It's dangerous, you know," and he said, "Yes, I realize that but one has to die somewhere and I'd rather die in your company, please" – which was a very delightful thing to hear anybody say, so he finally came with me when we sailed for Ceylon.' When Broome later returned to Malaya by submarine and was landed secretly on the coast, Ah Chuan was forced to stay behind in India. However, he trained as a wireless operator and made three unsuccessful trips by submarine to try to join Broome. He then got himself trained as a parachutist:

> Eventually the time came when we were to receive our first drop of men and supplies from an aeroplane, and it was a most fantastically exciting moment. We were on this dropping zone, lighting enormous fires in case they shouldn't see us, and down these bodies came. And the third one to come down was Ah Chuan. I didn't know this, but he came marching over in full regalia, with his uniform and his parachute wings on, saluted smartly, brought out a cigarette case and said, 'Have a cigarette! I know you've been waiting for one of these for a year.'

On duty in the bungalow the servants were always immaculately turned out: 'Even if they lived in the tiniest little hovel, their clothes were starched and they always looked beautiful when they came out. The men wore these starched white *tutup* jackets, which were always tight up to the neck, and white Chinese trousers. Then the *amah* wore either a white or blue *baju*, a short-sleeved and rather long blouse, and loose Chinese trousers, sometimes patterned but usually black.' It was considered to be rather bad form for the *mem* to visit either the servants' quarters or the kitchen:

> The whole business of overseeing meals was done by word of mouth. The reason was that one trusted one's staff to be clean and reliable and to handle food properly. But also the kitchen would be one of about four or five rooms rather like cells but made quite comfortable by the boy, the cook and the water-carrier, who would be lounging about on their veranda in fairly casual clothes. When you called or summoned your boy he would be very quick to put on his trousers and jacket and come in, but he wouldn't be wearing them when he was in the kitchen quarters and so one didn't go there. Then if they had wives and children they would also be living there at the back so it was an invasion of their privacy to go and see them there.

Much of the cooking was done on the simplest wood-burning stoves, or even over open fires. Ovens were frequently shaped out of the ubiquitous and invaluable kerosene (paraffin) tin – 'a square, deep tin like a large biscuit tin which was very much a common-place item in the East'. Yet with this primitive equipment miracles in the way of cooking were performed by the better cooks – although it was also true to say that a lot of the food came from tins. There were additional drawbacks to a high standard of cuisine in the form of a climate that very qickly turned food bad and encouraged weevils and maggots: 'Flour and rice had to be spread out in the hot sunshine on a mat and these creatures would then crawl away. Then the flour would be sieved and it and your rice would be put back into their containers.' There was also a permanent battle to be waged against ants. 'The two things I found continually trying all the time I was in Malaya were ants and mosquitoes,' admits Nancy Madoc:

> The mosquitoes never stopped biting me; everywhere I went I had to have a smudge stick which is one of these coils that you light. It sends out a sort of spicy incense smell and it does keep the mosquitoes away. But it was the ants that really got me down because they were everywhere. You only had to drop a spot of sugar on the floor and in no time there was a trail of ants coming towards it and dragging it away. They got in amongst your handkerchiefs and they were in the food unless you watched like a

hawk. You put the legs of your food-safe into bowls of paraffin and unless you did that the place was just a teeming mass of ants. They also went for flowers and plants and I eventually decided that Malaya was built on an antheap, with ants everywhere.

Such little difficulties were never enough to discourage the high degree of entertaining by which members of an often widely-scattered European community kept in contact with each other. On more formal luncheon and dinner parties the *mem* had to ensure that the table was properly arranged so that government officers were seated in accordance with their rank, beginning with the most senior man present being placed on his hostess's right and his wife on the host's right. But with the official and non-official worlds so closely connected, such formality was rarely taken too seriously. And, increasingly in the Thirties, the old custom of dressing for dinner no longer prevailed except for the more formal dinner parties: 'Generally all we did was to change into decent clean clothes in the evening. There had been a time when this business of changing regularly for dinner really did maintain; it had something to do with the discipline of keeping up one's self-respect. Inevitably it got simplified but still people felt that a certain standard was needed if one was not to let oneself go completely. This even happened later on in prison camp, when some of the men always managed to shave somehow, whereas others grew their beards and whiskers right away from the beginning.'

Both in the towns and in the *ulu* the most popular means of entertaining at home took the form of the Sunday curry tiffin, the only significant difference between town and country being that in the towns, where there were more women present, drinking gave way to eating a little sooner – 'but never before two o'clock'. The food was the same throughout the archipelago:

When you went in you started off with mulligatawny soup, and then a really good hot curry with a lot of *sambals*, which were little side dishes like coconut, banana and fruit and all sorts of things like that to put on your curry, which was sometimes almost too hot but very good, a huge meal generally. After that you were expected to have your sweet, which was always a thing called *gula Malacca*, a cold sago with two sauces, one coconut cream and the other *gula*, which was palm-tree sugar of a very dark colour; an absolutely delicious sweet. After you'd had all that all you could do was long to get away and pass out on your bed for the rest of the day.

There was a very great difference between the everyday lives of the *mems* in the bigger towns and those who lived in more spartan surroundings up-country. In the former 'the community that one lived with and knew was entirely European and one lived for entertaining, for the club, and for seeing other people'. The bungalows were more comfortable and up-to-date and there were more creature comforts and amusements to hand. In the district, by contrast, most bungalows were built to the same basic pattern by the PWD and filled with PWD furniture, so that 'if you got a house that looked rather different you felt very pleased'. Beyond putting up her own curtains – 'which were never pulled but looked pretty' – installing her own plant pots on the stairs and veranda, adding one or two of her own pieces of furniture and her own pictures on the walls, and making sure the servants kept the house clean and the floors polished 'with a mixture of beeswax and paraffin applied with a coconut husk', there was little a *mem* could do to make a real home for herself and her husband. As a junior *mem* she was expected to toe the line and to defer to the senior *mem* of the district who sometimes would 'help the younger wives under her and give them advice as regards running their homes and in the way they ought to behave towards the local people' – but who also in some instances 'made it her business to pronounce on the behaviour of others'.

When Madeline Daubeny came to Sarawak as a newly-wed in 1933 she expected to find a small European community 'full of backbiting and scratching'. Yet although 'people came from every conceivable social background – which in those days meant so much more than it does today – this was completely swallowed up in the ordinary fellowship and friendship of living in a small place together. Most of the men had made it fairly clear to their wives before they brought them out what they were coming to, so they made friends with each other and were pretty happy. Very few marriages broke up and there were almost no romantic scandals.' It was equally apparent that there were really two kinds of *mems*:

Some of the wives came from very limited backgrounds and they were usually the ones who were disturbed and upset by conditions. They'd been given no idea what to expect and they did have problems – although I don't think we had the Somerset Maugham type of *mem* who was responsible for the stories and reputation that *mems* had all over the place. Of course, there were one or two who were difficult. There was one I know who used to keep her husband from going to the club when she didn't want him to by making him change into pyjamas early for dinner. But the wives who went up-country were a different kind of woman on the whole; they were usually the ones who had some idea of what they were going to cope with and so they did cope.

Madeline Daubeny was herself one of Sarawak's first generation of 'outstation wives' who accompanied their husbands to the more remote district headquarters up-river, and her husband, Dick Daubeny, was one of that heroic cadre of administrators who had gone out to Sarawak straight from school: 'Dick was nineteen when he first went out in 1921 or 1922 and after a very few months from then on for the next eleven years he was in places where he was practically the only European. The isolation was so great for these young men and they were such boys.' She had known his parents for some time before she actually met their son:

I'd always heard about this adored son who was due to come back on leave after nearly eleven years in the Far East, but when I did meet him and he told me how isolated and lonely and cut off his areas were I didn't like the sound of the life he lived. However, I fell in love with him and it was as easy as that. He had to go back in the autumn and I arranged to come out and marry him in Penang the following year, and during the time I was engaged Dick saw that I found out as much as he could arrange for me about Sarawak. He gave me books that were highly romantic and not at all reliable but they did give me the first idea that he was anxious that I should accept the existence of native 'companions'. This was something so eminently sensible that I saw no reason to create about it. Most English wives of that time were people like myself who were not easily shocked by this sort of thing. We were sensible enough and old enough not to be romantically influenced against the notions of such an arrangement but to accept it as something that was there and had happened and was past – and I must say very strongly that I entirely approved of this attitude.

However, the custom of keeping *nyai* did take 'a little bit of sorting out' when the first European wives began to live up-country:

Very soon a sort of convention was adopted which was that if you visited a household where there was a Dayak woman in the background she didn't appear. It was rather silly but it saved a lot of embarrassment because it is awfully important to remember the climate of opinion of the day. But it was a little disconcerting sometimes if you were having lunch with two or three men by themselves and a baby started to cry not so very far away. Of course, it was always accepted that this was the cook's child that was crying – although the children of these associations were always cared for by the fathers. They took their fathers' names and when they were older they were sent to the mission boarding schools so that they were properly brought up, even if the fathers did eventually separate themselves from their children and from that life.

After a couple of days in Kuching the Daubenys set out in a government launch, which took them out to sea and then sixty miles up the Batang Lupar river in Simanggang:

The whole European content of Simanggang had arrived to meet me and was standing on the wharf; there were three of them. I was of course not only the only woman but the first European woman ever to live there. So I was going to be a great nuisance to these men, who had never worried about their language, their behaviour, their alcohol intake or anything else and now they knew they were more or less going to have to – although they were very good about it, I must admit – because it was really awful for them to have a woman suddenly invading them. Anyway, we climbed up the steps onto the jetty and a prison gang of about eight men were then told to unload our luggage and I was appalled in my innocence and ignorance to see that two or three of the men had shackles and chains on their ankles. As I had just come from seeing a romantic film with Paul Muni in it, called 'I Was a Prisoner in a Chain Gang', this thing shook me cold. However, I soon discovered that the whole attitude towards prisoners was extremely light-hearted. There was a euphemism for being a prisoner which was *talong perintah* meaning 'helping the government', because all the prison gang normally did was to scythe the coarse grass round the area of the station, the official part of Simanggang, and the nine-hole golf course which was only a golf course by the skin of its teeth. In fact, I very soon discovered that one of them was going to be our *tukang ayer,* the scullery boy. He was not actually chained in the ordinary way, but he was a murderer, who had been given a life sentence for killing his wife's lover. His name was Jokmin, he was Chinese, he was absolutely splendid and we adored him.

However, some time later the Rajah came on a visit to Simanggang and to mark the occasion it was customary for the Rajah to grant certain favours: 'We were so fond of our Jokmin that we asked the Rajah if his life-sentence could be quashed. It was; and within twenty-four hours Jokmin had left us to go back to a life of freedom.'

Once settled into her bungalow Madeline Daubeny soon got used to the regular daily routine that begun at six with morning tea and fruit on the veranda:

Dick went off to the office at eight, before it was too hot, and I was then supposed to speak to the cook, Ah Kit, which was a frightful problem at the beginning. However, I very soon managed to learn the basic kitchen Malay, which was a very bad kind of Malay that all wives learned to speak, so that I was able to take down the cook's shopping list. Later on, of course, I spoke quite reasonable Malay so that eventually I was able to give him complicated and elaborate instructions on new recipes.

The Daubenys would have lunch together and then while her husband went back to his office – 'rather hot and disgruntled because the afternoons were very, very hot' – Madeline Daubeny would have a lie-off: 'On our beds we had a thing called a "Dutch wife", which was used throughout the whole East Indies. It was a firm bolster which you stretched a leg over and was very comfortable and cool.' Her husband reappeared at tea time, which was followed by a game of badminton or a round of golf with the other European men on the golf course or a walk through the edge of the jungle, 'because these settlements were just tiny clearings in an endless, interminable, tall, dense, wild jungle. Sometimes a hornbill would fly across the clearing and this was a most uncanny experience because it flew with a noise exactly like a very old-fashioned self-starter.' All round the outstation was the green wall of the rain forest:

The great feeling the jungle gave one was of enclosure because if you went into it you could only walk along known paths which were very uneven and very overgrown. It was a very 'Alice in Wonderland' feeling, because every plant would have a stem perhaps three or four inches in diameter and be fifteen or twenty feet tall, so what would have been a wild flower or a weed in an ordinary woodland as we know it, was grown to an immense size. At the same time it could be so sappy that one cut with a *parang* would slash it down very easily indeed. But jungle walking was limited only to paths that were little tunnels through the jungle, something like the tunnels that a pheasant makes through an English field, with the trees themselves making a close ceiling high overhead, a hundred and fifty to two hundred feet up. Any flowers there might be were quite invisible way overhead on the jungle ceiling and the only reason you got to know that they might be there was if there were one or two dead blossoms on the floor of the jungle. It was a very strange world; a secret place and very alarming. There were always birds calling, whistling, mocking, but seldom seen. The one thing you did see fairly often were monkeys, because they travelled about in such tribes that you heard them and then you looked for them and usually saw the movement of the trees and branches as they flung themselves around.

Twilight and dusk always came with predictable regularity – and with it the visitors of the evening:

That was the signal to go and sit on the veranda and have a drink, although, as often as not, we sat in the sitting room, because of the mosquitoes. I got almost bitten to death when I first arrived. Mosquitoes love somebody new and I don't know why I should have tasted better but I clearly did, although eventually I got hardened to it and it didn't worry me too much. But these evenings had one particular highlight which terrified me the first time it happened, and always made me jump a little bit. After darkness had fallen, one could be sitting quite quietly talking or reading and suddenly there in the large open door would be a party of some six or eight Dayaks always dressed in the proper Dayak rig; a beautifully draped scarlet loincloth, black and silver calf and wrist bangles and some superb tattooing on their coffee-coloured skins. Even the old men looked fine and the young men were very striking. But when you'd no idea they were there it was extremely alarming. So they would be welcomed in and given little tots of neat gin which went down with a smack. Then they would have a long talk to Dick about their own troubles and worries.

Not every *mem* appreciated these visitations: 'Many years later one of our District Officers got engaged to an English girl from Malaya and when she saw this ceremony of the Dayaks arriving for the evening drink and chat for the first time she was appalled. She'd come from a rubber garden where her planter family had always kept the "natives" at bay.'

Sometimes after the last visitors had gone the air would be filled with the sound of drumming late into the night:

I never got used to the drums, they were always romantic to me and they would be either for some wedding or perhaps there would be a party going down-or up-river to a celebration with the drums going as they travelled. The drums were really brass gongs and the most elaborate kind was called an *engkerumong* which was an array of about four or five held in a long straight wooden tray. They varied in size and note and they would play the most beautiful diatonic scale on them.

There were exotic sights to be seen at night, such as 'a tree in the grounds alive with fireflies, much more beautiful in their flickering way than the glow-worms of England' or the nocturnal antics of a pet honey bear that 'used to shuffle round the bungalow at night crying for honey and attention and which kept us awake and had to be given away'.

For Madeline Daubeny, as for many young *mems,* the 'great problem was how to occupy my time. I hadn't yet learned to become a gardener, which I did later on, but I did love drawing and so I drew a great deal. But I wasn't actually lonely. I was an only child, fairly self-contained and able to amuse myself – but it was difficult without plenty of books. I missed books very much indeed – far more than I missed people. In fact, it wasn't until long afterwards that I realized that in six months I'd never even seen another white woman. Then, fortunately I suppose, my first pregnancy intervened and that changed the whole situation.'

Shortly before the baby was due the Daubenys were moved to a new posting in Kuching but otherwise no concessions to her condition were made or expected: 'Nobody gave me any warning whatsoever about possible snags or miscarriages. The only thing I was told was that I ought to walk as much as possible. So I was blissfully unaware of some of the things that could just possibly have happened to me, which was just as well, since the journey back to civilization took anything from a full thirty-six hours to two days and a night and there was no medical help whatsoever in our place except a partly-trained dresser who could bandage or carry out first aid.'

Another Sarawak administrator's wife was Daphne Richards, who found that pregnancy and motherhood were a great help in breaking down social barriers when her husband was away on tour and she was left on her own:

> If I was lonely and wanted to talk to someone in English I used to walk to the Roman Catholic mission which was about a mile away and I often met people from the *kampong* or the bazaar on my way and they would say to me *'Makan angin ka?'* which means 'Are you taking the air?' or literally, 'eating the air', and I would say, 'Yes I was.' Then they would say, *'Selamat jalan'*, which is, 'Good luck on your path,' and I would say, *'Selamat tinggal'*, which means 'Good luck to you who is staying behind.' They were always very friendly, the people there, and when they saw that I was pregnant they'd always enquire about this and be very interested and want to know where and when the baby was going to be born.

Three of her children were born in Sarawak and their presence always aroused great interest:

> I remember on many occasions someone stopping me – probably a Chinese who didn't speak Malay – and asking me a question as

to whether it was a boy or a girl and either not understanding what I said or not believing it and finally undoing the baby's nappy to have a look to see whether it was a boy or a girl. They frequently commented on how big your baby was for its age or how well it looked and they would therefore ask questions as to how you fed it and they were most surprised to find that a European woman breast-fed her baby. I quite frequently visited either Malay or Chinese or Iban houses and I would feed the baby there to great interest. It was the natural thing to do and no one thought anything of it.

There were, of course, disadvantages in bringing up a European child in the tropics: 'You couldn't wrap a restless baby up; I tried this once or twice with the very thinnest of cotton sheets and found the baby absolutely covered in prickly heat next morning – but, on the other hand, it was certainly an advantage in that babies needed very few clothes.' Illnesses could be 'quite frightening because the children developed high temperatures very quickly and as for most of my time I was in an outstation where there was no doctor usually within fifty to a hundred miles. This was quite scaring because you just didn't know what might happen.' Then there were such diseases as hookworm, 'so you couldn't let your child go around bare-foot, which they very much wanted to do', and the rare but ever-present risk of being bitten by a scorpion or a snake:

When my daughter was about two years old, I remember, my husband and I were having our breakfast and she'd gone down the steps just outside the house where we could hear her laughing like anything. After a minute or two we wondered what on earth she was laughing about, so we went out to have a look and outside at the bottom of the steps there was a narrow drain and she was leaning over and there was a kitten with her and the kitten was pawing at something. We went closer and saw what the kitten was pawing at was a very large scorpion and my daughter was reaching down to pick this up. Fortunately, we caught them in time because the bite of a scorpion of that size could have killed a child of her age and it certainly would have killed the kitten.

Madeline Daubeny had a very similar experience with her son: 'Instead of putting him in his cot while she prepared the bath the *amah,* for some reason, put him on a bed. When she'd finished bathing him she threw the towel on the cot and a black cobra came out of the cot and slid through the bathroom and out.'

Despite the dangers and difficulties many European children thrived in the tropics: 'My children now look back on their early lives in Sarawak with great affection and almost as a sort of paradise,' declares Daphne Richards. 'Their first language was Malay and when we spoke to them in English they would always answer in Malay, because we were frequently the only Europeans where we were living and their companions of their own age were always children who spoke Malay or possibly Iban.' There were infrequent trips to the Malayan hill-stations and more frequent visits to the palm-fringed beaches that were never far away. At Christmas the branch of a casuarina tree served as a Christmas tree and a traditional Christmas dinner would be celebrated with locally-made plum pudding and cold-storage turkey from Australia.

But a time always came when the children had to be sent away: 'When the children reached the age of seven or eight they really needed to go home to school. Although there were local mission schools in many places the standard was not very high and children who were kept out later than that found they were very behind when they got home.' Their mothers had then to make a decision between staying with their children in England or with their husbands. The choice was never easy and many compromised, spending some time in England until their children had settled into their boarding schools and then returning to their husbands. 'It seemed to us at the time that there really was no other choice,' states Daphne Richards, 'but my children took it quite for granted because their friends were doing the same sort of thing.'

The European *mem* certainly had her critics. There were those who saw her as coming between her menfolk and the land in which they had chosen to spend their working lives. But if there was 'the occasional *mem* who lived a rather frivolous life and only occupied herself with her own home and surroundings and parties and socializing', then there were also others who in increasing numbers learned to take discomfort and physical hardship in their stride, and who made an effort to 'become involved in the local community, finding voluntary work to do and getting on very well with all members of the community'. They were themselves pioneers in their own way. 'We lived through things without noticing what was happening,' declares Madeline Daubeny, 'yet there was certainly a very great drama in the way we were living when I first went out there. Looking back, it's strange how we took it all for granted'.

10

THE FOUR SISTERS

*This account of childhood in Malaya between the
wars was first broadcast – in a more extended version – on Radio 4 on 25 December 1982 as the last
programme in the first series of* Tales from the
South China Seas. *The four sisters were the daughters of the rubber planter Mark John Kennaway
and his wife Dorothy.*

SUSAN: There were four of us daughters actually, my sister Ann,
followed by my sister Elizabeth who was born in England on
leave. And then Pippa and then myself, Susan, born in 1928.

ANN: We used to laugh at my father because – coming out from
England – Escot was a kingdom of its own and my father was the
ruler . . . Escot was surrounded by jungle. And he was always
fascinated by it. He would look at the blue hills in the distance
and say what wealth was underneath . . .

SUSAN: My father, Mark John Kennaway, when he was nineteen
was given the opportunity to go out to Ceylon under the manager
of a tea estate and learn what he could of planting methods. He
embarked for Ceylon in 1899 and the family he left behind was
typical of many young men who went out to the East in those
days. He was the second son of a country clergyman in North-
amptonshire. They lived in a nice old rectory with old oak furniture and their days were spent, the women certainly, doing good
works, attending church services and serving afternoon tea in the
drawing room, and I think many men like my father must have
escaped from that kind of life with relief.

ANN: Well, my father was not exactly the black sheep of the
family, but he was less docile, I think, than the others. They

used to pack them off to the colonies in those days. Then after about three years, he went over to Malaya, where Mr Wrigley had just discovered that rubber could be grown. And my father went over to see what the chances were.

SUSAN: His devoted family came to see him off. We have a photograph in our album of him on that day. His father was wearing a clerical black hat and a black suit and his step-mother and sister with their wasp-waists and large picture hats. A Salvation Army band had also come on board to see off one of their number and my grandfather insisted that they joined in the hymns, as it would do equally well for my father. And it's easy to guess their apprehension at that time because the estate he was going to, Batu caves, was an area notorious for malaria and diseases, and they could possibly have never seen him again. About a third of the work-force had been carried off by malaria and in fact most planters reckoned to spend one week a month laid up with malaria.

Looking at our photograph albums there are so many pictures of clearings of the jungle and small rubber trees being planted and a proud young man, my father, standing looking at them. It was a very exciting time. There was a feeling of expansion and something new in the air – one can sense it from looking at the photograph albums. In 1909 he took over a small rubber estate and called it Escot Estate, after his uncle's house in Devon, whose forebears had been in the East India Company at the end of the eighteenth century.

ANN: I remember that the steps from the front door led up to the hall at Escot in Devon, there were always big pots of ferns and flowers on either side. And my father had done the same thing, in a Malayan way, at Escot Estate.

SUSAN: There was always a porch to cover you from the tropical rain and you went upstairs – the house was built on stilts – up a long flight of steps with lots of flower pots everywhere – and upstairs you went into a huge veranda room.

ELIZABETH: When we got to the top of the steps there was an enormous veranda and in the middle of it there was this very, very ornately carved Celanese table with elephants' tusks for feet which had been a wedding present to my mother. The doors that led off were stable doors. They swung to and fro and I never learned to shut a door for ages afterwards when I got back to England.

ANN: Escot Estate as such was simply jungle. And gradually the jungle was cut down and rubber trees were planted. And he went back to England to try and raise money later on for this wonderful new development.

SUSAN: On his leave in England he was given the chance to place so many shares in the Sicily Rubber Company, which was floated in 1904, and he did a grand tour of his relatives who were rather stiff-backed and he begged and implored them to buy but they refused to take them up, and only Jones, the family butler in his uncle's house in Devon, bought some and I'm glad to say he became later a very wealthy man.

ANN: Well, by 1910 or 1912 there was a tremendous rubber boom. And when he went back home on leave the second time, he was richer than any of his family put together.

SUSAN: It was very much a life for a man. There were no European women in the district at all. And the first woman came out and reigned, as my father said, for one year. And the second one came out and when she arrived she unpacked her things and the first lady came round to ask her if she could help her and she said no. So when the second lady had unpacked she sat back and waited for the first one to call and a tremendous row broke out in the district with all the bachelors taking sides as to whether she'd called or she hadn't and my father very much enjoyed this.

ANN: My mother came from Yorkshire. Her father was a wine merchant who had gone bankrupt when she was about sixteen. And she went up to London and tried the stage, and she was very successful. She had a lot of push.

ELIZABETH: She was very much a person of her age, the 1920s.

ANN: And she did end up once playing the lead in the West End. It was one of our bedtime stories.

SUSAN: My parents met when my father was on leave in London and they became engaged, and my father went back to Malaya.

ANN: My mother came out two or three months later, and was married on the beach, as my father used to say, and then they went back to Escot Estate, which of course was very primitive. But my mother was very happy I'm sure, in those first years. They had a very good time.

ELIZABETH: Before I was born there was a river that used to run right across the entrance to the estate, and when it rained the river used to flood the bridge and nobody could get in. My parents used to take a bearer with their evening clothes and their bathing costumes, and when the river was in flood they would swim across the river with the bearer carrying their evening dress, and dress the other side of the river and walk, scramble, up a hill where the train crossed, and stop the train and go to Kuala Lumpur and have the evening out.

SUSAN: Rubber was booming and the smart young women of the Twenties came out as brides, and sisters came out on visits and

A WALL OF RUBBER

From the Kennaway family album: Mark John Kennaway (in straw boater) bids farewell to his parents as his baggage is stowed aboard the *SS Luitpold*, Southampton 1904.

A planter's bungalow goes up at the height of the rubber boom; Leonardo Estate, FMS 1911.

Beach wedding in Penang;
the newly-married Kennaways outside the 'E & O' Hotel, 1920.

Ladies' stand at the KL Races, c. 1928, always a
great attraction to planters and others stationed outside the Federal Capital.

On the veranda; the Kennaways and friends
at Escot, with the chicks lowered to keep out the sun's glare.

The four sisters; (from left to right) Pippa, Elizabeth, Ann and Susan,
together with their parents, the governess and the servants.

Servants of the Kennaway family in the early 1920s.

Bamboo rafts on the Bernam River, c. 1930; M. J. Kennaway's rafting parties were a popular feature of life among the planting community before the war.

pretty English governesses came out to look after the growing families, and romances blossomed and our photograph albums are filled with weddings and visits to the races and fancy dress parties.

And my father started the rafting parties of Tanjong Malim. He would have rafts made of bamboo and early in the morning they would meet at a point up the river and sail down, two on a raft, shooting down the rapids, with cold beer laid in various corners of the river to keep cool as they went down. And at the end they would all end up with a huge curry tiffin, I believe, at the Tanjong Malim Club.

My mother enjoyed that life very much, but she said sometimes that she felt she was enclosed by a wall of rubber on the estate, as the trees were surrounding the garden and stretched for miles and miles on end in every direction.

ANN: Being very much wanted, as our parents had married late in life, I think we were very spoiled. We had *amahs* to look after us and all the servants on the estate, as I remember, doted on us. We had Chinese *amahs* mostly, although Susan had a Malay *amah* who was called Denlora Perian, which I always thought was a lovely name. And I think we had a very happy, unspoilt, uncluttered early childhood.

SUSAN: Every time a new baby was born my parents would throw another bedroom and bathroom onto the bungalow and soon it became a very sprawling, very comfortable home. The stilts down below were filled in and a dining room was made and windows with shutters and there was a huge lawn outside of very coarse grass – it was quite a pride of my father's, this lawn – and a tennis court and canna beds. The cannas in Malaya were everywhere. They grew in people's gardens; bright orange and red flowers. And we had beds of them always round the house and there were some bougainvillaea and other plants I can't remember. And beyond the garden surrounding the lawns were the rubber trees – hundreds and hundreds of them in monotonous straight rows – these long alleyways of nothing.

ANN: The jungle was there. I just accepted it, as part of my background, where animals lived. My only fear, I remember, was tigers.

ELIZABETH: One day we woke up to find in the garden the marks of a tiger, footprints; he'd been walking through the garden.

ANN: And from then on afterwards, I always had this dreadful dream that there was a tiger over my cot! I remember we walked down to the end of the garden and I kept expecting the tiger to come – I never realized these marks in the ground were anything to do with him. It was a totally happy period.

SUSAN: I can remember my father calling for the 'boy' at four o'clock every morning for his cup of tea and his 'boy' who'd been with him for thirty years would bring it to him. There was a great understanding between them and he would have his tea and get up in his *sarong* and go to his desk and write for the next two hours.

ANN: Then we'd have tea on the lawn, which was one of the nicest times of the day 'cause it was cool. My father would go off and do his rounds. And then he would come back about nine, and we'd have breakfast, and then he'd go off again. And after breakfast I suppose we played about in the morning. Everybody slept in the afternoons till four. And by five o'clock or six o'clock we were down at the tennis club and it was getting cooler. We'd play around with the other children of the Europeans while the parents played tennis or drank at the bar, and then we must have been taken home about seven or eight and put to bed. Little beds and big beds, you know, with big mosquito nets.

SUSAN: And I can remember last thing at night lying inside these great white net cages and the lights faded down and all was dark and then the sounds of the jungle outside would begin to be heard – the jungle was never far below the surface in Malaya.

SUSAN: We have a photograph of the whole household, my parents and us, and the staff in the bungalow and there seem to be quite a number of them, standing at the back.

ANN: But Hi Ho was the constant one, he had five little sons and a fat wife.

ELIZABETH: Hi Ho the houseboy was really the key figure in the home. He was the man who employed the *amahs* for my mother.

ANN: And he was the one who appeared if you shouted and he would serve the drinks and serve the food. There was Cookie, he was a Chinese. Then there was the gardener who was called the *kebun*, I remember, he'd cut the lawn with a scythe. He was usually Javanese or Malay. And the chauffeur, or *syce*, he was a Malay. Father had a car, a large Ford, but then later on he bought my mother an Austin Seven as a present and there's a photograph of us all piled in this Austin Seven; father, mother, four children and the governess.

SUSAN: It was very comfortable, but there were disadvantages. All food had to be kept in meatsafes, standing in bowls of water, otherwise the ants would have got to the food in minutes. Home leave clothes were kept in tin trunks, otherwise they would go green with mould.

Unfortunately, in 1931–32 the price of rubber fell to five cents a pound and many planters were forced out of business.

SUSAN: We had to go back to England and my father stayed on and they were very bad days I believe.

PIPPA: My mother took a very small maisonette in London into which we all piled and we were extremely hard up. So much so that my father couldn't afford to join us.

ELIZABETH: My father, to keep the estate going, wrote out horoscopes which he bought from Woolworth's at sixpence each. These were a great success because the Chinese love anything to do with astrology and he made quite a lot of money which kept him going.

ANN: And my father came back to us every three years, or three-and-a-half years.

PIPPA: When he finally did come home I remember nanny saying to my mother, it's just as if he'd been down to the pillar box and come back; meaning that we had all accepted him so quickly and readily. He wasn't what I expected; a tall bronze man with a *topee* who could look well on a horse. He was a little man with a keen sense of humour and a huge trunk full of trinkets and toys and dolls and snuff boxes and all sorts of treasures that he'd brought home for us.

ANN: And those were lovely times. He'd arrive from off the ship with boxes of Turkish Delight he'd got at Simon Artz in Port Said, and Japanese dolls, I remember he brought back. And the time always went too quickly. He had to cram all the treats that normal fathers would give us in three-and-a-half years, into six months. And then, sadly enough, he'd go off again, on the P&O. We'd all be very sad after he'd gone. Although we grew up in London, my mother always talked as though our home was in Malaya at Escot. And all our plans were geared towards the life we would live out there, not an English life at all.

ELIZABETH: In the summer of 1939, when the war came, my mother decided to take Ann and I back to Malaya. The other two were left behind in England.

ANN: Probably it was one of the last P&O boats in the pre-war luxury style, and my sister and I had only just stopped being schoolgirls. We thoroughly revelled in all the luxury, the great long menus which we ate our way through.

At night after Port Said, there was no more blackout, and the boat deck was lit with coloured lights, and the band played and we danced with young naval officers. I think because I was seventeen, it was very romantic. It could never come again. But the beautiful sky, the stars in the sky and the sun on the sea, and you had this feeling that you were sailing away, away from the war in Europe.

My father drove us from Penang to Escot Estate. And it was strange coming back. Things that you'd forgotten about came back to you. And many faces were looking slightly older, like Hi Ho. My sister and I ran round looking in each room – I looked at my nursery which hadn't been used for ten years and was just – just there. The dining room was the same. The silver all set out on one side and kept clean. And the veranda of course had altered rather – sort of large divans, with brightly coloured cushions, and the pictures which were Renaissance beauties. The rhythm of life hadn't altered.

SUSAN: And my sister Pippa and I, who were at school in England, returned to Malaya in June-July of 1940.

PIPPA: I remember how delighted Sue and I were with the bungalow, we had no idea our family owned anything as grand. Over the next few days my sister and I were introduced to all the various servants round the house and were most impressed. We had no idea our father was so rich and important.

SUSAN: The boom days were over and life had changed quite considerably when we came back. Our wooden bungalow was definitely becoming old-fashioned, although it was still very much part of our lives. The bathroom attached to every bedroom was really a concrete floor with a galvanized tin tub and a *tong* of cold water which you could dip in and splash all over yourself, and when you wanted a bath you called out and someone brought a bucket of hot water up the backstairs and you could sit and wash yourself in this tin tub and end up with a wonderful douche of cold water.

There weren't nearly so many planters in the district of Tanjong Malim and the club had been built for so many more people and there were rows of chairs, long cane chairs with a hole in the arm for the glass, but they were never all filled and the magazines would be on the side tables and rarely read, I think.

PIPPA: I think my parents must have been quite hard put to occupy us, but my father was always very good to me in the way that he would always give me a game of tennis, both at home at the bungalow, and at the club. We also watched him at work on the estate and directing operations there. I remember saying to my father, why did he always have to shout at his staff and why did he never praise them for what they'd done? And he told me that if he did, they wouldn't do anything the following day.

I was thirteen and the novelty of being in the tropics and of being able to bathe in a jungle river and go to Kuala Lumpur and have shoes built for me by people who drew a line round my foot and produced them the following day – all this was terribly exciting. Our greatest treat was to go to Kuala Lumpur which we did I think most Saturdays.

SUSAN: We'd be shopping in the morning perhaps, having clothes made, taking patterns along and having them very skilfully made up into dresses and then in the afternoon perhaps we'd go to the cinema, and then drive home.

I remember one drive particularly. There was a lovely ring round the moon and these villages were bright and alive and there were children up at ten o'clock at night running about and stalls outside with people cooking and there was a smell of the East.

ELIZABETH: I can remember also the utter boredom and loneliness of it all, because I was only sixteen and like the heroine of *When The Rains Came* by Louis Bromfield, there was absolutely nothing and one had the feeling one was waiting for something to happen.

ANN: I loved the exotic flowers and the luscious fruits, and the feeling of the vast areas of jungle that man had never been in. And the rain; the storms were exciting, they came from Sumatra, with a sudden rush of hot wind.

Sometimes we would go and swim in the Slim River Pool which was a waterfall in the middle of the jungle. And we'd walk along the path with leaves, great big leaves barring our way. We'd push our way through and there, in the darkness of the jungle, was this lovely waterfall, where the water cascaded down; you could dive in and swim. That was Christmas 1940; that was the last Christmas that our family spent all together for a great number of years.

I suppose that life was never the same for me after that. It was the end of something – I never went back – and I never went back to that total family life, when I was a child in the family in my home.

So I took the night train, on 1 January 1941, down to Singapore – *very* excited because I thought my life was beginning.

ELIZABETH: When Ann went off to Singapore I was very envious and very determined to follow her.

ANN: I started off very patriotically, wanting to do war work and I did always have the war in mind so that I wasn't entirely frivolous, but you couldn't help being frivolous, there wasn't anything else but social life and very little cultural life. I'd met a young man in the Cameron Highlands and I realized that my office was going to be next to his, and of course I had fallen in love with him.

Raffles Hotel I went to quite a lot, there was always dancing on Wednesday nights and Saturday nights and although it seemed rather shabby in the day-time, at night-time it came to life with tables amongst potted palms with little individual lights, and we danced to tunes that had been hit tunes six months' ago in Britain like *In the Mood*, or swayed to *Begin the Begine*.

ELIZABETH: I used to feel terribly gauche and I remember one woman whom I saw, whom I admired very much, in a beautiful white dress one evening, and later she gave her life saving people from a ship which was full of women and children. She swam from the ship to the shore time after time after time with these women and eventually she sank, exhausted.

On 7 December 1941, Singapore was attacked and Malaya was at war.

ANN: Jerry and I had been at Tanglin Club all day sitting in the sun by the pool as we usually did on a Sunday, and in the evening we went to the cinema. I remember saying goodnight to Jerry on the mansion steps, a lovely full moon shining, and I went to bed, went to sleep. Four hours later I was in a deep sleep, and we heard the sirens; they woke us up.

My sister turned on the light and I remember spitting at her and saying 'Turn it off you silly, the war's begun' and she said, 'Oh no, look, the street light's on outside', and in fact everybody was saying that, saying 'Oh well it's only a practice, the street lights are on.'

ELIZABETH: At that moment there was a terrible bang and we all came running down the stairs to the hall. And we could – as the mansion house was on a hill – look down over the town and see the lights of the cinema going round and round, coloured: 'The Road to Rio', with Dorothy Lamour, Bob Hope and Bing Crosby.

PIPPA: I can remember seeing Japanese planes circling round our garden and waving to them thinking that they were our planes and being horrified to discover that they were Japanese.

SUSAN: I can remember too how we went down to the main road to wave to the lorryloads of troops who were going up north. And they gave us a tremendous cheer when they saw us. And it was shattering a few days later to see some lorries returning with very weary, tired-looking men and it was at that time I think I realized that something was really wrong.

ELIZABETH: Even though there was a lot going on in Singapore there was also a knowledge of what was happening. And there was the mounting terror which was creeping in.

SUSAN: We left our bungalow on Christmas Eve, my mother and

my sister Pippa and I, and made our way down to Singapore. I remember feeling any rate with relief that I wasn't going to go back to school for the next term.

ANN: On New Year's Eve, my mother eventually arrived in Singapore with my two younger sisters, and an aunt in what was then Rhodesia had cabled and said, 'Send them to me and I'll look after them, the two younger ones.' My other sister, Elizabeth and I said, 'Oh, we can't leave, we've got war jobs', and at the time it seemed quite right.

SUSAN: My father had stayed behind in Tanjong Malim with the local defence corps and he was told that he was too old to fight at sixty-two, so he left Tanjong Malim. I believe he was the last European to leave there, and he then made his way down to Singapore.

PIPPA: My sister was working at army headquarters and her commanding officer asked her to send my father to see him. They were very anxious to enroll men in the army who could speak the local languages and my father went along and was delighted to be told he could falsify his age and take on the rank of captain. This pleased him particularly as he had previously been a private in the Home Guard.

ANN: By January we had air raids in the day-time as well as night-time and I remember sitting in the Cricket Club one lunch-time when the sirens went. I looked across the street and I remember seeing a poor old rickshaw coolie looking rather bewildered as the sirens went, and the next thing was, there was a bang and I saw him lying on the pavement with blood coming out of his mouth. It was the first time I had witnessed death.

PIPPA: Despite the increasing frequency of the air raids my sister Susan and I managed to enjoy ourselves. We swam a great deal at the Tanglin Club and the Swimming Club. I honestly believe that my mother was the one person in Singapore who was quite certain it was going to fall.

ANN: My mother by then was getting desperate to get these children away and a woman said to my mother, 'Whatever boat comes, I'm getting on it with my baby, and if you like I'll take your two younger ones, because I eventually want to go to South Africa, and I will deliver them to their aunt.' So my mother agreed – that was how my two young sisters went off to Australia all by themselves.

PIPPA: We sailed off happily enough, unfortunately I can't remember saying goodbye to my parents or sisters, but we eventually arrived in Freemantle, and it was only during a visit to a post office, where I heard some English voices, that I suddenly realized that we were a long way from home – and for the first time I felt homesick and afraid.

ANN: I was totally in cloud cuckoo land. I imagined that there'd be a siege of Singapore and we'd endure it heroically, like the people of Malta and the British in the Blitz, but that day Churchill made a speech in the House of Commons, saying that there would be no help for Singapore, and I think that then reality took over because the following day most of the office had been evacuated; there was just a skeleton staff there. I saw my father on the steps of the Cathay Building, and he said to me 'You've got quarter-of-an-hour. You're to pack a suitcase, and I'm taking you to the docks.' And of course I argued, and said, 'I'm needed – I need to do war work,' and so on. And for once in his life he was absolutely firm with us and I went home; I didn't know what to pack, so I just packed the things I liked. My suitcase was stuffed with evening dresses, and my mother and sister were waiting and he drove us to the docks.

ANN: Elizabeth and I were to be put on a ship going back to England, but my mother was going to try and find a ship that was going to Australia. So I remember, we said goodbye to her and my sister and I went up the gangway of the *Duchess of Bedford* which had just been hit, and there we said goodbye to my father, which was really very sad because he looked so strange. By then, of course, he was in the army and in a very ill-fitting uniform with a holster – but no gun in it because they'd run out – and we weren't to see him until November 1945.

ELIZABETH: Ann and I walked up the gangplank into the ship and as we walked we could see my father standing in his ill-fitting army uniform waving goodbye, and my mother trudging along the edge of the dock towards the ships.

ANN: He was a prisoner of war, and spent most of the time in Changi camp. We never really found out very much about the worst things that went on there, because he always used to laugh about it and say he'd had very good food there and a very nice peaceful time and no school fees to pay.

SUSAN: He always said he must have been the worst bargain the army had ever had – three weeks' work and four years' pay!

ANN: The day we left was the day the Johore Causeway was blown up, and I remember seeing the smoke, columns of smoke going all over the island, and I remember looking to see if I could see the mansion where I'd stayed so excitedly the first day a year ago, and eventually the island disappeared altogether, and that was the last time I saw Singapore. I've never gone back.

The four sisters and their mother were eventually reunited in

*Southern Rhodesia. Mark John Kennaway survived his imprison-
ment in Changi prisoner-of-war camp and in 1946 Elizabeth, Pippa
and Susan went back with their parents to Escot Estate. However,
Ann never went back. Her fiancé, Gerald Scott, had managed to
escape from Singapore in a small boat and had sailed to Ceylon.
When the war was over they got married.*

THE FALL

*I have seen the mysterious shores, the still water,
the lands of brown nations, where a stealthy Nemesis lies in wait, pursues, overtakes so many of the
conquering race, who are proud of their wisdom, of
their knowledge, of their strength.*

Joseph Conrad, *Youth*

WHEN war broke out in 1939 there was no immediate threat to the
British in South-East Asia. The main feeling was one of impotence:
'A lot of us young men felt uneasy; we wanted to be in on the act if
we could and we felt increasingly uncomfortable that we were still
continuing our routine civil occupations and not making any real
contribution to the war effort.' Officials and unofficials alike found
themselves prohibited from leaving their jobs and joining the armed
forces, and when a number of younger Europeans took matters into
their own hands and made their way back to England to join up
,they were ordered to return to Malaya. It was made clear to them
that they would be more valuably employed in helping to produce
the vital war supplies of rubber, tin and oil.

But gradually the position changed: 'Everybody was watching
Japan in the East and when Tojo the war-lord came in we knew
pretty well what was going to happen. Nobody with any sense had
any doubt that the Japanese were going to attack Malaya. The only
question was when.' From the winter of 1940–41 onwards 'all ranks
in Malaya in all walks of life' began to prepare for war – 'within the
limits of our resources and our manpower and always giving first
priority to maintaining the economy and the output of rubber and
tin'. For Bill Goode this meant working in the Civil Defence Office:

> Raising air-raid wardens and organizing air-raid precautions, rais-
> ing a Home Guard with schemes for coast-watching, working out

with local authorities denial schemes to prevent valuable things like boats falling into the hands of an invader, getting out schemes for rice-rationing and making stores of food, deciding whether we should store rice or whether we should store un-milled rice and how we were going to mill it. This was going on at absolutely full blast, but always in parallel with the ordinary running of the country, which went on as normal. In my spare time I was a local territorial in the Singapore Volunteer forces, with most of my evenings and weekends taken up by parades with them. Then for two months, in June and July 1941, we were mobilized full-time and office work fell behind.

But if there was little complacency there was widespread ignor-ance, both about the state of Malaya's defences and the nature of the enemy. 'We didn't know the extent of the danger or how near it was,' declares Cecil Lee:

Nor did we know the capacity of the forces we had to resist it. Troops were coming in and it looked big but we didn't know that they were mostly raw Indian troops. So we really thought that the country was being adequately prepared – although some didn't. For instance, we had an estate up at Jitra, in Kedah, on the front line where the 11th Division had their defence works. We made arrangements with them for compensation but I remember the company board asking Jenkins, our visiting adviser – who was an old soldier himself – to let us know what effect these defences were having on the working of the estate. And I remember that he came back and said to me, 'They're just paltry. If those are the main defences of Malaya, thank God we've got a navy.'

In fact, Malaya's strongest line of defence was then being built up on Singapore Island, where 'we were all told that there would be in some mysterious manner a wonderful defence system worked out by the military'. These defences were concentrated on the southern part of the island in anticipation of an assault from the sea.

The impression of military invulnerability was heightened by the arrival of the battleships *Prince of Wales* and *Repulse* – but without any supporting aircraft: 'One was an ancient vessel and the other was fairly new but what good would they be without air-cover? They would be sitting ducks. We hoped and prayed we might get some air-cover – but no air-cover ever came.'

Public statements, put out for the best of motives – 'to keep morale high and to prevent people from getting into a panic' – made light of the increasing 'inevitability' of Japanese attack. Gerald Scott recalls how in Singapore 'notices of exhortation' appeared in all the banks signed by the Commander-in-Chief of the British Forces to the effect that the defences of Singapore and Malaya were not wanting and that the country could not be invaded. 'We believed this,' adds Scott. 'We didn't believe that the Japs could come in through the back door in gym shoes through the jungle and knock the place sideways.'

The fighting qualities of the Japanese themselves were also ridiculed. 'All sorts of things they told us,' Guy Madoc maintains. 'That the Japanese pilots were myopic and that their planes were not airworthy; and as December 1941 approached they told us that we'd be perfectly safe for the next four or five months, because the monsoon was blowing on the East Coast and there was no possibility of a landing from the sea during a monsoon. But I had lived in the monsoon on the East Coast and I knew jolly well that sometimes there were periods of complete calm for five or six days at a time.' When ships of the Japanese fleet began gathering in the Gulf of Siam early in December the government radio still remained 'fatuously cheerful and said they were on naval exercises – although everybody at naval headquarters was perfectly well aware that this was the beginning of the attack'.

Up in Kelantan Bill Bangs had been asked to form some local Malays into a frontier force to check local smugglers' paths through the jungle, in case the Japanese were planning to attack across the border: 'This was all put onto a map and worked very well – but, unfortunately, it was the only way the Japanese *didn't* come!' With only a few days to go before the invasion of Malaya was launched Bangs was sent across into Siam to find out what the Japanese were up to. Using the cover of a Seventh Day Adventist missionary – 'because I didn't think there was any such thing as that in the Far East' – he checked into a Siamese hotel, only to be greeted shortly afterwards by a Seventh Day Adventist from Sumatra who 'was very pleased to see me and asked me if I would take the service that evening!' After this false start Bangs went on to locate several airstrips in the jungle that had been cleared of undergrowth and were awaiting the arrival of planes from Japanese aircraft carriers. Convinced that the Japanese were poised to launch their invasion near Kota Bharu, Bangs slipped back across the border with all speed:

In those days the only way to get to Kota Bharu from there was to hire a Model T Ford and drive along the beach. This was the night of 6 December 1941. The waves were very big indeed and we had to keep stopping for the waves to go out, so when I got back I went to see Brig.-General Key of 8 Brigade and told him all that I'd seen and that the Japanese were supposed to be com-

ing that same night. But then I told him that it was quite
impossible, as I'd come along the beach and the sea was much too
rough and nobody could possibly make a landing. However, I
was quite wrong and they landed that night at one-fifteen.

Like many others on that same night of 6–7 December, John
Davis was woken by explosions as the first bombs fell on Singapore.
Even then the realization that war had begun in earnest was accom-
panied by disbelief: 'We thought that this was one isolated raid and
that we wouldn't hear any more about the war. With the wonderful
fleet we had, the Japanese wouldn't be so foolish as to attack
Malaya. The next thing we heard was that they had landed in
Kelantan – but then Kelantan was five hundred miles away from
Singapore and there were heavy forces and many airfields in
between, so that was alright.'

The Volunteers had been mobilized some days earlier. Peter
Lucy had 'just walked out of the bungalow for an ordinary parade as
I was accustomed to do once a week, leaving the house open and
everything in it – and never returned'. He and other members of his
armoured car unit were sent over to the East Coast to defend the
local aerodrome at Kuantan. Bill Goode was manning the defences
of Singapore – no longer as Assistant Commissioner of Civil
Defence but as a lance-corporal in the Singapore Volunteers, 'lost
in the big army machine and with only a worm's eye view – so that
my view of affairs became very limited indeed'. For the next two
months he found himself 'mostly engaged in digging holes in the
ground then being told by an officer to fill 'em in again or putting
up miles and miles of barbed wire and sandbag emplacements near
and just behind the Singapore waterfront, because my battalion was
responsible for the defence of the waterfront along by the swimming club.' John Forrester was similarly employed defending
Singapore's Tanga airfield: 'It's an awful thing to say but I don't
think anyone took it too seriously. We were sitting there on this
airfield for day after day after day. Nothing was happening and we
thought it was probably going to be rather like Europe, where
nothing happened for a long time. So we felt very comfortable sitting in this fortress and waiting for them to come and I think we felt
more sorry for the Japanese trying to come to us rather than anything else.'

But within a few days of the Japanese landing at Kota Bharu the
situation took a dramatic turn for the worse. 'I was then staying
with a chap called Claude Fenner,' recalls Davis. 'He came in in the
morning with the newspaper and said, "Look at this, John." And
there was the report of the sinking of the *Prince of Wales* and the

Repulse. It was unbelievable. I've never been hit so hard in my life. The whole thing suddenly for the first time became terrifying, because if the Japanese could sink our fleet like that, they could do anything. I think this broke my morale and I think it broke the morale of a tremendous number of people during the campaign, from which we never properly recovered.' There were others who were affected by the news in much the same way. Perky Perkins remembers 'the utter depression which fell on us at that time when these two great ships were sunk'. In Malacca sixteen-year-old Una Ebden was sitting for her School Certificate and at first the bad news came as something of a relief, because it now seemed unlikely that she would ever get the result of the examination:

> I remember walking back from the convent from that exam, feeling rather low and rather frightened, and overhearing an Indian boy, a youth of about sixteen, saying to a Chinese boy of about the same age, 'Cheer up, man, there'll always be an England.' And that's a thing I remember, because how badly let down those two boys must have felt later on, when the Japanese just overran the whole country.

Over the next few weeks there was some valiant fighting but to little positive effect. The Japanese consolidated their positions in the north and began to advance southwards, 'never using the deep jungle but using the roadside rubber estates which had all been beautifully mapped out by all the Japanese taxidermists, botanists, brothel keepers, amateur photographers – to say nothing of the Japanese estate owners and managers – who had come to this country in hordes before the war.' The news bulletins that Gerald Scott and others read out in the Malayan Broadcasting Corporation Studios continued to sound 'always very hopeful'. There was talk of 'firm stands' followed by 'strategic retreats' until it became increasingly obvious even in Singapore that 'we were in a hell of a shambles and that the Japs were coming down Malaya at a terrific speed'.

Up in Kelantan Bill Bangs took part in a number of rearguard actions as 8 Brigade retreated south: 'We were ordered to defend the crossroads at Mulong and were told "Last man, last bullet." This was the first time that I heard these orders, although I was to hear them many times afterwards. It usually meant that within an hour we would receive an order to retire once more.' When the fighting reached Kuantan, Peter Lucy found himself caught up in this same demoralizing process:

> We never did any defending at Kuantan aerodrome. We just sat there till the Japs arrived. Somehow or other they crept up

through the rubber trees and fired on us. Without firing back we merely got the order to retreat, so we jumped into our armoured cars and drove away. And this went on all through the country – retreating, retreating, although we never had any real reason for retreating. We were never defeated; we merely retreated on orders and the feeling was one of bewilderment.

Driving inland away from the coast Lucy's unit was ambushed: 'The Japs had expected us to be using that road and they were lying in wait as we passed. Their armour-piercing bullets just came into the car and whizzed around inside and everybody was hit. I was cut right across the back and another man had his leg broken. The armour-plating was just useless against the Japanese bullets.'

Meanwhile on the West Coast battle had been joined on the Jitra line in North Kedah – where after a few days Guy Madoc was ordered to gather his local police force and pull out:

When we got to the main road the whole of the army was streaming back, not in disorder but completely and utterly worn out. Every time there was a halt for any reason – a lorry broken down or run out of petrol – the whole convoy stopped and every driver went to sleep, or so it seemed. I spent my time hammering on the bonnets of cars with my swagger cane saying 'Get on! Get on! Get on!' Until finally at about four in the morning we reached the next big town, where I found my Chief Police Officer, and I had just about told him my tale when some goon came dashing in and said, 'The Japs have reached Gurun!' That was about fourteen miles up the road and it meant that they had done a big sweep round and had broken through the retreating column, so we all leapt into our cars and fled back another thirty miles – only to find that this ass had evidently had a nightmare. The whole thing was a fiasco, because next morning we had to go back. But at intervals over the next two months these retreats continued and I never seemed to settle down in any one place for more than about a week at a time.

One calendar month after the Japanese landing at Kota Bharu the Battle of Slim River was fought and lost. Kuala Lumpur was evacuated and the European women and children joined the growing number of refugees heading for Singapore. On KL aerodrome Cecil Lee and other members of his company of the Selangor Battalion of the FMS Volunteers were joined by British anti-aircraft gunners from Penang – who left them in no doubt as to what they felt about the Malayan campaign: 'I remember one of the gunners saying to me, "As far as I'm concerned, the Japs can have bloody

Malaya" – which gives some idea of the attitude and the lack of morale. By that time there was also looting and it was a pretty sorry sight to see people in the streets with stuff on their backs and bicycles – one fellow had a piano on a cart that he was taking along.'

Lee and some of his fellow-Volunteers were then moved to Port Swettenham to make up a new armoured car company:

> We were just put in them and told to get on with it and we proceeded down the coast road. I well remember passing a *padang* with a club and thinking that this was a society in dissolution. Then the Malays started to desert. Quite naturally, they were anxious about their families. We met one chap on the road and our rather intense commander got out his pistol and menaced this poor little wretch who was merely going home to his family. I remember seeing one dear old planter, Stephen Taylor, explaining to one of these Malays by the roadside, 'We'll be back, you know. It won't be long before we're back.' Of course, it was numbing to them to see the *orang puteh* – the white men – fleeing, and I'm told that after the war when they spoke of this they used the expression *tarekh orang puteh lari* – 'the time when the *tuans* ran'.

As they retreated down the coast they often found themselves billeted in abandoned bungalows, many still fully furnished: 'I remember seeing two chaps in their army boots and full kit lying on the double bed of a planter's main bedroom.'

When they reached Johore the various volunteer units were disbanded, the Europeans being attached to one or other of the regular army units. Lee found himself fighting alongside the Argyll and Sutherland Highlanders: 'There for the first time I met the real army, because although they were much depleted and battered they were still an effective fighting force. I remember when we had an air-raid one of the young Jocks saying, "Dinna run, man, dinna run!"'

The remaining Malays and other non-Europeans in the Volunteers were discharged and allowed to return to civilian life – where attitudes towards the war differed very much according to nationality. 'The Malays were not taking any great interest and can you blame them?' asks Sjovald Cunyngham-Brown:

> It was their country that was being rolled over by two vast overseas giants, who were fighting their disgusting battles in Malaya's own garden, smashing and destroying everything. The Malays had benefited by joining Western civilization and now they realized with horror that they were about to pay for it; this was what

happened if you joined the West – so they stood by. The Indians were mostly rubber estate workers who had no contact with what was going on. They lay doggo, hearing nothing, saying nothing and seeing nothing – and I don't blame them either. They were a little minority caught in a trap. The Chinese, on the other hand, were already at war with Japan. Their mother country was fighting Japan, therefore so were they, and the more virile of them were busy getting arms to go into the jungle to die fighting against the Japanese – as indeed they did.

At Johore Bahru, where Cunyngham-Brown was based while dividing his time between his work as Controller of Labour in Johore and his duties in Singapore with the Royal Navy Volunteer Reserve, 'a steady stream of old 1933 Morrises and other motor-cars, with children inside and baggage and perambulators on top' was making its way across the narrow causeway that linked Singapore to the mainland. As more refugees came south an enormous queue of cars and people developed at the bridgehead:

> During that time my friends and I in Johore Bahru met so many of our old friends and acquaintances from up-country that we had a sort of perpetual cocktail party that went on interminably in the garden and in the house as they poured in. We were bombed every now and then, usually in the evenings and not very close to us, but enough to put us under the staircase and under the tables, while we went on talking and saying things like: 'It'll be all right when we get to fortress Singapore.' 'Thank God we've got down here. Poor old Jimmy got killed at Perak, did you know?' 'She got away all right, but poor Jack got killed, you know.' They were all a little shaken and telling those short stories and so it became a rather macabre and everlastingly prolonged cocktail party.

Singapore itself was rapidly filling up. 'It was like a scourge of population – all European, I'm afraid,' asserts Una Ebden, who had come down from Malacca with her mother: 'We went to a boarding house called the *Manor House Hotel* which started to fill up and fill up with more and more people until they were sleeping in the corridors and on the verandas. What made it even worse was that the army kept on commandeering houses to billet the troops who were also coming down into Singapore, so the civilians were hard put to know where to go. We ended up at the Swiss Club, because there was nowhere else to go.'

The numbers were further swelled by troops arriving from overseas – whose officers were allowed to use the European clubs without paying subscriptions. Gerald Scott recalls an occasion when having got an evening off from his duties as a Volunteer he went to the Tanglin Club in his uniform – only to receive 'a note from some general saying that this was an officer's club and that Other Ranks were not allowed. I sent him a note back saying that as it had been my privilege as a member of the club to vote for serving officers becoming members without paying subscriptions, I was delighted to think that he was enjoying himself there!'

Soon the last of the British fighter aircraft had been destroyed – 'these poor little Brewster Buffalos going up with the Japanese Navy Zeros coming over in great clouds and shooting them down' – and, unopposed, the bombers were coming over – 'twenty-seven at a time, slowly and easily coming across the sky, fairly low down, and dropping their bombs wherever they wished'. Many were aimed at the shipping in Singapore roads – and to good effect. Trevor Walker watched the *Empress of Asia* sinking off Singapore Island, and with it all the transport and artillery for the newly-arrived 18th Indian Division, which had been trained for desert warfare but had been diverted to Singapore instead: 'They didn't know what a rubber tree looked like or what the jungle looked like. They were keen to do a job but it was all too quick and too sudden and they had barely got into position in Johore when we were told to withdraw.'

In Singapore town itself the bombing was not particularly heavy, but what was especially depressing to Tamsin Broome, who had arrived in an advanced stage of pregnancy, was the certainty that 'whenever you heard a plane you knew it was a Jap one'. On 5 January 1942 her son was born in Singapore Hospital, with a Chinese and a Malay nurse in attendance: 'It wasn't a very comfortable time to be having a baby. The Chinese nurses got terribly worked up whenever they heard bombs and rushed in saying "Take cover." But how can you take cover when you've just delivered a baby? But luckily he was very large and very healthy and nothing disturbed him.'

Richard Broome, meanwhile, had been ordered to report for special duty in Singapore a fortnight earlier:

I was told to go to a certain office which turned out to be the Secret Service. They said they wanted somebody to look after their agents in Singapore, and while they were talking there was the noise of packing going on and so I looked round and said, 'Well, what's happening here?' They said, 'Oh, we're getting out. We just want you to stay and look after the agents.' This rather took me back and I said, 'How many agents will it be?' And they said, 'Well, we've only got one at the moment.' So I went out with my heart in my boots – and there outside the door was another gentleman who said, 'Oh, you don't want anything to do with that lot. You come with us.' Now this was the organization which was eventually to become Force 136, and what they wanted was some Chinese speaker to escort groups of Chinese Communists trained in sabotage work up to the front line and hide them in the jungle. The Communist Party of Malaya, which had done its best to sabotage the war effort for most of the war, had changed sides and offered its services to the British Government and parties of these young chaps were now being trained in sabotage and fifth-column work. So for the next few weeks my job consisted of picking up these fellows, taking them up in lorries to as near the front line as we could get, finding them a hiding place in the jungle, giving them all their stores and trying to give them a bit of spirit by making speeches in Cantonese and waving my fist.

Soon he was joined by John Davis and between them they succeeded in putting out seven 'stay-behind' parties, with each journey to and from the front line growing shorter as the Japanese advanced on Singapore. Finally, on 31 January Johore was abandoned and the causeway was blown. 'The morning came when we thought there was going to be a battle for the bridgehead,' Lee recalls. 'But there wasn't. Contact with the Japanese was broken. First the Australians and then ourselves and the Argylls were ushered across the causeway. I remember feeling particularly happy – because we hadn't had any fighting, I suppose.'

By now the evacuation of the European women from Singapore by sea, which at first had been opposed by the authorities on the grounds that it would unnecessarily demoralize the native population, was almost completed: 'They were evacuated – but right at the end – and therefore there were tremendous losses.' Tamsin Broome and her two small children left on one of the last two large passenger liners to leave Singapore, the *Empress of Japan*, which sailed in January with 'two thousand women and children and one old man who had got left behind'.

But there were still quite a number of European women left in the city – including 'Tommy' Hawkings who was working as a VAD nurse at Alexandra Military Hospital. Within a few days of her arrival in Singapore she had received word that her fiancée, Peter Lucy, had been wounded – although not seriously enough to prevent him returning to his unit when it was pulled back into Singapore. The two met up whenever they could – and decided to get married: 'We both agreed that Singapore would stand forever.

Evening after evening Sir Shenton Thomas, the Governor, broad-cast that we were perfectly safe where we were, that we were to stay at our posts and were not to leave, so Peter and I agreed that we would be much happier if we were married and fought out the siege as a married couple.' Because of food shortages it was difficult to find all the necessary ingredients for a wedding cake, but the prob-lem was solved by the Bishop of Singapore:

> He and I sat in his air-raid shelter while he transferred a bag of currants into my lap for the wedding cake, which we then made in a friend's baby bath. There was no time to issue invitations so we put notices in the paper – which was still being printed just as if everything was going on as normal – asking all our friends and relations to come to Singapore Cathedral at two-thirty the after-noon of 7 February 1942, where Peter Lucy and Tommy Hawk-ings would welcome everybody they knew. That was exactly one week before Singapore fell.

Despite the bombing it was a 'perfectly beautiful wedding', which was followed by a reception attended by 'a whole contingent absolutely straight from the front line, some with arms bound up and some with mud on their trousers and boots. Many of the men we never saw again; either they were killed in the last few days of fighting or they died in prison camps. Many of our women friends, too, were lost at sea when their ships were bombed and sunk by the Japanese.' The Lucys' honeymoon consisted of two nights together, the first in an air-raid shelter and the second broken by 'the most tremendous barrage that anybody who had been in the First World War had ever heard. This was the Japanese crossing over onto the island.' In the morning Peter Lucy went back to the front line and his wife to Alexandra Hospital: 'Neither of us had any idea that it would be four years before we saw each other again.'

For the men who were still fighting it had now become a matter of simple survival: 'One lived literally from hour to hour, mainly concerned with eating and sleeping and getting a rest when you could.' From patrolling the Singapore waterfront Goode and his company were sent across to reinforce the Australians, who were falling back after failing to hold their defences on the north side of the island. 'We carried out a typical Singapore Volunteers opera-tion,' he recalls:

> We left our camp in trucks and we drove to the address we had been given. But when we got there we were met by our platoon officer, who'd gone on ahead and who flew into a fearful rage and told us that our approach was under enemy fire, so we should have got out of our trucks way back down the road and come up

in sensible open order to avoid casualties. Having made such a mess of it, we would have to darn well go back and do it again. So we solemnly got into the truck, drove back to where we should have got out and started walking in open order along the side of the road. Of course, we hadn't gone very far before a Japanese aeroplane came over and started machine-gunning the road. All hell was let loose; we were all terrified out of our wits, jumped into the monsoon drain, got covered in water and arrived with our morale rather at rock bottom.

Soon they were being mortared and taking their first casualties: 'We dug various holes, always with the mortaring going on, always moving about as you do in the army and going out on patrols after snipers in coconut trees and never finding them.'

On the high ground of Buona Vista Ridge overlooking the western perimeter of the city, where the Malay Regiment was dug in, George Wort first of all had a spectator's view of events. Then stragglers from various Australian and British detachments began heading back through his lines in disarray. A period of confused fighting and sniping followed until on Friday 13 February the command post in which Wort and other officers were conferring received a direct hit. Seriously wounded, he was carried up to the Gap rest house – 'a place where in the days of peace you used to take your girl friends' – to be patched up and then taken down to Alexandra Hospital, which itself was now almost in the front line. Here Tommy Lucy and the other nurses were packing up to leave: 'Everybody knew what Japanese soldiers did to nurses and so we were all ordered out by the matron.' They were driven straight down to the docks where that same day they sailed on an 'old tramper', the *Empire Star:* 'There was no food or water on board but in the *godowns* along the wharf they found cases of Guinness and cases of asparagus, so we sailed out on a brown haze of Guinness and eating asparagus. We were down in a hold with only one ladder to get out and with thousands up above and we were bombed the whole way from Singapore to Sumatra. It was a tragic journey and yet a glorious one in the spirit of the people who were on board.'

Just three hours after his wife had left Alexandra Hospital Peter Lucy was brought in, having again been wounded in an armoured car. Because the hospital wards were already full he and a number of other casualties were put into a spare room:

That night the Japanese attacked the hospital and we just sat there and listened to the screaming that was going on, not knowing exactly what was happening until a private soldier in the room got up and said, 'In private life I am a pastor in Norfolk but now I am a private soldier. As you all know what is going to happen very shortly I expect you would like me to say a few prayers.' So he said a few prayers along the lines that we were about to be killed and we then waited for the Japanese. The screaming went on and then it continued above us and eventually died down. We found out afterwards that our room was not a proper ward and the Japanese had thought it was a store cupboard and didn't come in – otherwise we too should have been victims of this tremendous slaughter.

George Wort also survived the Alexandra Hospital massacre: 'I woke in the morning to find that my arm had been amputated. All the doctors and orderlies had been taken away and we were on our own. I remember lying on my bed and the Japanese coming round the ward and taking whatever we'd got. They took my watch and it was all slightly tense and then they moved on.'

On the evening of the following day, 15 February, Bill Goode and his companions were given the news that they would be making a bayonet counter-attack close by in Alexandra Road: 'This filled us all with great apprehension; however, just as it was getting dark and we were getting used to this uncomfortable fact, we were summoned again and told to our amazement that we had capitulated. I was overwhelmed with emotion. I couldn't think how it could have happened. It couldn't be true. I found myself desolated by the fact, which was quite stupid because if we hadn't I should probably have been killed the next morning.'

All over the island other Britons were experiencing very similar emotions. John Forrester, whose unit of bren gun carriers had scarcely seen any action at all, greeted the news with disbelief:

We were sitting in a compound owned by a Chinese millionaire with our bren carriers all round us and thinking what a peaceful time it was when suddenly somebody said, 'Oh, we've surrendered.' We just couldn't believe it, because there was plenty of ammunition, there was plenty of water, and our bren carriers were full of petrol. We thought the man who'd brought the news about the surrender was some fifth columnist and somebody even suggested shooting him. We were particularly amazed and dumbfounded because, although we had been to various corners of Singapore Island, we had never actually seen a Japanese or fired a shot in anger. We had done nothing worthwhile to stop the capture of Singapore. We had done nothing.

After checking to see whether the news really was true Forrester and three of his friends decided to make a break for it. They made their way down to the Singapore Yacht Club, found a fourteen-foot sailing boat, rigged it with sails and worked their way through the defences and the minefields out to sea. There were others who had the same idea: Guy Madoc had been given permission to escape if he wished so he and another police officer went down to Keppel Harbour – only to find that the boat they were looking for had been scuttled; Edward Tokeley and two colleagues got a car and drove through what was now 'a ghastly scene of destruction and desolation' towards Thorneycroft United Engineers boatyard: 'There were fires all over the place. A lot of the street lighting was gas and I can remember seeing one of these gas cones broken in two, with the lighted gas spurting out.' When they reached the boatyard they came under mortar fire. There were no boats to be seen and so they were forced to turn round and drive back into the town.

Gerald Scott and some of his colleagues in APC were luckier, having already got away in their own launch a day or two earlier. John Harrison also got away – as part of a crew of a sailing boat that eventually got all the way down to Australia. Sjovald Cunyngham-Brown, Percy Bulbrook and Robert Williamson were out at sea when Singapore fell – all of them helping to ferry women and children and the wounded across to Sumatra. Bulbrook sailed on to Ceylon in the Straits steamship *Perah*, Williamson to Madras in the SS *Pahang*.

It was Cunyngham-Brown, second-in-command of a little vessel called the *Hung Jao*, who provided one of the best-known and happier rescue stories to come out of the fall of Singapore:

We were trudging along in the pitch-black night heading for Sumatra. I was leaning over the cab of the bridge when what should I hear but a voice saying, 'Going my way?' I saw something in the wash astern and yelled, 'There's a man in the water! Stop! Go astern!' My commander, Robin Henman, came up bleary-eyed from below and said, 'What's happening?' 'Man in the water,' I said, 'We're going to pick him up.' 'How do you mean? Did he say anything?' I said, 'As a matter of fact he said, "Going my way".' 'Full speed ahead,' said Robin. 'Sjovald, you're asleep, poor chap. Try to keep awake.' I said I wasn't asleep and I begged him to let me go astern for ten minutes. So we proceeded astern and finally the aldis lamps picked up something in the water. We came up alongside and what was it but a Fraser and Neave aerated water crate!

'Full speed ahead,' said Robin Henman, 'I've had enough of this bloody nonsense.' I said, 'Robin, *sir*! For God's sake let me go astern for another five minutes. There *is* someone in the water.' And sure enough, as we proceeded astern something did turn up in the water – a man sitting on a raft. We got alongside him and threw a rope over but he couldn't pick it up. So as it was my find I eased myself into the water and swam across to tie him on. As we got him alongside I looked at him and said, 'My God, Puck!' It was H. V. Puckeridge, a remarkable and well-liked character who was manager of a large rubber plantation in Selangor. He said, 'Oh, hello, Sjovald. Do be careful of my shoes, old boy, because they're practically new.' He'd got them neatly placed side by side on top of the raft as though it was outside his bedroom door.

After the sinking of their own vessel Cunyngham-Brown and Henman attempted to escape northwards in a catamaran but were eventually captured. After many months of solitary confinement Cunyngham-Brown was brought back to Singapore as a prisoner of war.

Richard Broome and John Davis also got away to Sumatra and from there went on to India – to begin training and planning for their return to Malaya as the spearhead of Force 136.

There were some who were offered the chance to escape but refused to take it. On 13 February Bill Bangs had escorted a senior Malay official – whose life would have been at risk under the Japanese – down to the docks where a naval launch was waiting to take him away:

An officer said, 'Get on, get on. There's no sense in staying.' But, having had a very fine time in Kelantan and loving Malaya and the Malays, I felt that if I rushed away now I would never be able to come back and face my Malay friends. So I did not get on the launch and stayed behind. It was a very silly decision because if I'd gone out I could have then been dropped back with Force 136 in the *ulu* of Kelantan and got all the Malays who knew me together and we could have done a lot of damage to the Japanese.

Elsewhere on the archipelago other groups of Britons were also surrendering to the invaders. There too, there were many – like Bill Bangs in Sarawak – who had refused the chance to get away when it was offered to them: 'You can't live among the people for years and then when the danger comes drop everything and leave them. I know it sounds daft but we felt that way. So we stayed, not knowing what was going to happen.'

The day after the surrender of Singapore all the British forces were marshalled together and made to march out to Changi, on the eastern tip of the island, where there was a civilian jail and the military barracks. 'We marched in endless line,' recalls Bill Goode:

We came snaking in to Newton Circus with the 2/29th Australians to whom we'd been attached, and immediately behind us was a regular battalion of the Gordon Highlanders who'd been a bit further up the line from us. All through the night we marched but I found it very heartening and encouraging on that long march to hear the regular tramp, tramp of the Gordons behind us and, of course, the pipes playing, which certainly helped me to keep going through that night. It was unpleasant to start with because we were moving through parts of Singapore that had been heavily bombed, where everything was in chaos, with bits of telephone line and overhead tram cables lying about in the street, vehicles damaged and overturned and the most ghastly stench of decaying corpses. It wasn't until we got out into the coconut estates and the country districts that life began to seem a bit more normal.

As they marched there was 'plenty of time to reflect upon what had happened and what could possibly happen in the future' – and there was particular sadness among those who, like Edward Tokeley, had spent nearly all their adult years in Malaya and had grown to love the country: 'The incoming soldiers had lost the battle but they didn't have the same personal involvement that we had, walking through Singapore as the vanquished, with the Asians – who didn't know what was going to happen to them – seeing you going.'

'There wasn't any jeering or anything of that sort,' Bangs recalls. 'A lot of Chinese, Malays and Eurasians along the way had tins of water and were giving the soldiers drinks as we went along – in spite of the Japanese trying to stop them. But we hadn't had any sleep for days and on this horrible march we didn't really know what we were doing.'

Some days later some two-and-a-half thousand male civilians, led by the Governor, made their own march out to Changi. 'It was a very long march and we were all ages,' remembers Madoc:

There were a certain number of schoolboys even and people up to the age of seventy. Some foolishly overburdened themselves, others somehow managed to scrounge room on a lorry for their mattress or whatever they had with them. But what moved us was that during that march the few Asians that we saw all turned their backs as we walked past them – not in disgust but because they didn't want to have any part in this.

The women were made to march, too, a couple of days later. We heard them arrive and clearly they'd put up a better show than us, because as they marched along the walls of this very grim prison we heard singing: *There'll Always Be An England*.

DE PROFUNDIS

ADJUSTING to captivity was not easy. Feelings of relief at still being alive quickly gave way to depression and forebodings about the future: 'To begin with our main anxiety was about our relations. Many of us did not know where our wives and our families were. The second thing – and one that took up a lot of our time – was walking around and meeting friends and trying to find out what had happened to friends, whether they were still alive, whether they too were trapped or not. And in the background was this overwhelming feeling that we probably kept to ourselves; what's going to happen to us – because there's nothing we can do which will make the slightest difference to our future. That was the sort of thing that came on you as you were trying to get to sleep at night, rather than something you talked about to other people.'

Although not particularly religious – 'scarcely any of us had gone to church except for weddings' – many of the internees in Changi Jail felt the need for spiritual support, and when it was announced on the first Sunday that a service was to be held in the exercise yard Guy Madoc and his colleagues dressed in what was left of their best clothes to attend: 'We expected to get spiritual support, we expected to sing good old hymns like *Fight the Good Fight* and *Onward Christian Soldiers* and we expected a sermon which said "Well done, you good and faithful servants". Instead we were shamefully betrayed by a senior clergyman of Singapore who preached a sermon that shocked and angered us, saying that we thoroughly deserved what had come to us and that we must treat it as a penance for our sins of omission and commission in the years that we had been in Malaya. So we left that exercise yard and I personally never went to church again.'

However, both the civilian internees and the prisoners of war soon had other more pressing problems to worry about. In Changi Jail Madoc found himself crammed with two other policemen into a small cell built for one: 'In the middle was a raised block which we called a sarcophagus on which the most senior officer slept, while we two more junior men squeezed in between the walls and the sides of the sarcophagus. This was all very well until the bed bugs started to infest us, because there seemed to be far more bed bugs on the wall attacking the junior officers than there were on the sarcophagus.' Similarly, in Changi Barracks nearby thirty-seven thousand British troops and fourteen thousand Australians had been squeezed into quarters built for only a fifth of that number. 'There was at first a feeling of every man for himself,' recalls George Wort. 'People grew their hair long and grew beards and that sort of thing. But within a very short space of time people realized that without some sort of discipline and organization none of us would survive. From then on people took more pride in how they appeared and we settled down to what you might call a military organization within the camp.'

Other camps were set up in Sarawak and British North Borneo, although in time the great majority of internees ended up in Kuching: 'Into this camp went everybody; people from Sarawak and Dutch Borneo, sailors from the *Repulse* and *Prince of Wales,* White Russians who had been taken off some ship, missionaries, bigwigs, planters, all kinds of people herded together — and it was very interesting to meet such a cross-section of people like that with different ideas.' Here and in the other camps gangs of working parties were formed and put to work as coolies. For a period Edward Banks helped to pull a bullock cart through the streets of Kuching, shirtless and barefooted: 'The local people's reaction to this was one of horror. They went indoors and hid their faces; they didn't want to see it. But I'll always remember a little Chinese girl — only a sawn-off little thing — who rushed out and gave me a bunch of bananas. The guards gave a yell and chased her but she was gone like an eel!'

In Singapore, too, many acts of kindness were shown by the Asian population towards the Europeans in the work gangs. Bill Goode remembers how 'as we marched through the streets on our way to work in the docks, a Chinese would run through the ranks of a marching column and shove a two-dollar note or a piece of bread into the hands of the nearest man — at considerable risk to himself because he could be very badly beaten up by the Japanese. They needn't have done it but they did and this sort of thing formed a bond between people like myself and the people of Singapore and Malaya, which was of inestimable value when later on we returned to Malaya.'

Peter Lucy also worked in the docks, as one of a gang of two hundred and fifty men based on Blakang Mati Island:

Our job was to unload bombs from the ships as they came into Singapore harbour, then take them across the water and stack them into the armouries on the island. They were all one-hundred-pound bombs and the order was one man one bomb; we had to stack it in the armoury and then go back for more – and this went on until the ship was unloaded, irrespective of how long it took. It was sometimes forty-eight hours non-stop except for an occasional five minute rest. It was very hard work and at first a lot of planters gave up the ghost. They were elderly and not used to hard work and it was too much for some of them. We were all treated as private soldiers and we had to do the work of private soldiers. There was no alcohol and no cigarettes and food was very scarce. We had eight ounces of dried rice a day plus whatever we could pick up from the Malays or anybody who could send over a banana or something that we could mix with the rice. We were able to catch snails and snakes and mix them up with the rice to produce some protein and sometimes we were able to collect some beans or sugar which had fallen out of the sacks as the cranes were unloading them. So those who were able to look after themselves and were optimistic, as I was, managed to survive. Discipline among the working-parties was maintained by the officers; some of the other nationalities weren't so well disciplined but we had a doctor who was an officer and one or two other officers and their orders were strictly obeyed, so discipline on the whole was good. Our attitude towards the Japanese, however, was simply to ignore them as far as possible. We just looked upon them as something completely out of this world. But they were always on top of you. You were constantly being told that you should have committed suicide before being taken prisoner, that you were the lowest of the low. If you tried to retaliate you simply got beaten up, so it was difficult to retain one's dignity. The men were rather inclined to be peasant types and if they could do anything to help the prisoners they very often did but the officers were always brutal.

The civilian internees in Changi Jail were rather more fortunate. For Guy Madoc the two greatest hardships were 'the lack of news from the outside world and from loved ones – and the lack of food'. At first the inadequate rations could be made up from supplies of tinned food brought in by scrounging parties from Singapore but eventually these extra rations ran out: 'The time came when the Japanese said, "If you want to eat you've got to grow it yourself." Fortunately at about that time they transferred us from Changi Jail, where it had been impossible to grow much food, to Sime Road, which was an open camp and where we cleared the scrub off the sloping hills and planted acres of sweet potatoes. Even so, by the end of imprisonment we were in a very bad state.'

In both the camps on Singapore Island great efforts were made to preserve a semblance of normality. Camp newspapers were produced, concerts and plays were put on and a wide variety of subjects were taught:

> We had an immense number of intelligent people in Changi, including practically the whole of the Education Department and so all sorts of classes were set up. You could even learn Swahili, if you wanted to. Everybody began enthusiastically by joining too many classes but there was a shortage of paper and pencils and gradually attendance at the classes dwindled. I myself had a mad idea that I might be able to escape and get up-country through Malaya and then through Siam, so I decided to start learning Siamese and I continued to do so right through the whole of our imprisonment of three-and-a-half years. I also started to write a bird book and I got great help from one of my cell mates who was put on the job of cleaning out the Japanese commandant's office. Every time he went in there he stole some of the best foolscap paper and brought it back to me. Another internee had a typewriter which he would lend me every Sunday morning and so gradually I built up quite an extensive bird book of more than a hundred pages. Another ornithologist who was a good artist added some illustrations and then we found a couple of French prisoners who were good bookbinders and they made a beautiful job of it. And this single volume of *An Introduction to Malayan Birds* had a very considerable circulation in Changi.

There was little direct contact between the two camps at Changi, although for several months Mervyn Sheppard and Bill Bangs managed to run an effective postal service between the jail and the barracks using a hollow bamboo. Then Sheppard was caught and tortured by the Kempeitai. As time went on, others in the jail were also tortured: 'Some were tortured to death, others returned to us in such a state that our doctors could only ease their last hours of life. I remember so well working in the vegetable patch one afternoon when the body of the former Chief Secretary of Singapore was brought back by the Japanese. Although we had Japanese sentries amongst us whose duty it was to see that we didn't slack, we all put down our tools and stood to attention whilst his body went by.'

At Changi Barracks the first major crisis came at the end of August 1942 when all prisoners of war were ordered to sign a document stating that they would make no attempt to escape and that if they heard of any other prisoner planning to do so they would inform the Japanese: 'Of course, everyone refused to sign this and as a punishment all the prisoners were put into Selarang Barracks, which had been built to accommodate eight hundred Gordons in peacetime.' The punishment backfired because, as George Wort recalls, 'everyone was in terrific form. We were cheek by jowl, we'd had to bring all our belongings with us so people were pushing beds and prams and everything, water was very short, food was very difficult to get and the lavatories didn't flush so open pits were dug, but the general effect of morale was terrific. However, after three or four days there was a great risk of dysentery and so our commanding officer ordered us to sign under duress, which we did, but it was a great morale booster in spite of the appalling circumstances.'

Then in October the Japanese started sending the first parties of prisoners of war away from Singapore by train. 'The rumours were that we were going up to the Cameron Highlands to grow vegetables,' remembers Cecil Lee. 'But we discovered eventually that we were going up to Siam to build the new railway. It was a long journey, travelling twenty-six to a box-car in great discomfort, and on the first night when we arrived at Seremban station the whole of the British Army seemed to be out relieving itself.' After four days and nights the passengers reached the railhead in Siam and then began marching up to the first of the makeshift railway camps.

Among the planters who worked on the railway were Bill Bangs, Perky Perkins and Hugh Watts. All of them had been Volunteers – as had been Edward Tokeley, Cecil Lee and Bill Goode:

> We built the first camp from nothing, clearing the jungle and putting up bamboo huts. It was a good camp site, high on the river bank with a marvellous view of the hills in the distance and the river in the foreground, in which we were allowed to wash. But we soon began to come up against the hardships of building a railway on inadequate rations. The Japanese communications were almost negligible so we lived for weeks on end on very bad rice – we thought they were sweepings from the floors of warehouses – and pumpkin stew. This and the long hours of work, coupled with the exhaustion of the march up, started to take their toll.

The first death 'created quite a stir', remembers Lee, who was working in the same labour battalion as Goode: 'He was such a nice young lad, a bank clerk fresh out from home and a Gordon Highlander – one of the poor lads shipped out to Malaya at the last minute and wondering what the hell they were going to do. He got dysentery on the way up and there was nothing for him. Of course, it became a commonplace thing but that was the first time and it struck home.' Their camp commandant was 'a very fine old colonel of the Sherwood Foresters' who 'by dint of a good deal of suffering and great courage established a domination over the Japanese lieutenant in charge, so our losses were much lighter than was the case with other camps higher up.'

But then came the period known as 'speedo' – because 'it was "Speedo! Speedo! Speedo!" the whole time' – which started just before the summer monsoon in April 1943:

> We started moving from camp to camp, to reinforce camps higher up which had been decimated by disease and illness, and this was when we really came up against trial and tribulation, because by then it was the monsoon and it was pouring with rain. We lived in mud and we slept under the remnants of tents which leaked like sieves. We got up in the dark, we went to work in the dark, we worked all day long and we came back in the dark, hoping to get some rice for an evening meal. Disease, of course, was rampant: dysentery, beri beri and malaria and then – most frightening of all – cholera. This really was very hard on morale because you could leave a sick friend in the morning when you went to work and when you got back in the evening you were told he had died. With people dying of cholera and the Japanese driving us harder and harder, it was a time when we couldn't help being seized with a most awful feeling of helplessness – because of our utter inability to do anything to influence our own fate. We were completely in the hands of these crazy savages, as they seemed to us, who had no understanding of our suffering. Our being deprived of the elementary trappings of civilization, living in filth and squalor, always having dirty hands, allays having wet clothes, literally walking about in excreta – these things didn't seem to bother them. That did depress us terribly and there were times when all of us began to feel that sooner or later we must succumb.

It was at this time that Edward Tokeley, who had remained in Changi suffering from loss of eyesight, was brought to work on the Siam–Burma railway as part of 'F' Force, made up of 'seven thousand half-beats – because, by and large, it was only the sick who were left in Changi'. 'F' Force had to march two hundred and fifty miles from south of Bangkok to Three Pagodas Pass:

> It was a ghastly march with thousands of midges that tortured one night after night, biting everywhere – you just couldn't keep them away from you. I got malaria after about the fifth day so I

had to be left at one of the staging posts and went up with
another party. So I was cut off from the bulk of my Volunteer
friends and found myself mainly with some Manchesters and
Argylls. I've always disliked since then the noise of the gibbon –
we call him the *wa-wa* in Malaya – with that soulful, whooping
noise that he makes, which did nothing to cheer one up when one
was walking drenched and hungry and miserable like hell out to
where you had to work in the half light of morning. Of course,
disease took control very quickly. A lot of people died through
cerebral malaria, screaming with agony. We got to the cholera
belt, where dozens died every day. I had a very bad go but managed to get over it and as a result I was asked to stay on and help
out in the cholera ward. I didn't particularly want to go out on
the railroad if I could avoid it so I stayed in the cholera ward and
my job for a very long time was throwing chaps on the fire and
burning them, because you had to get rid of the disease somehow. There were five Boustead chaps who went up with me on
'F' Force and I was the only one came out. I watched one of them
die; he turned his face to the wall and said, 'Go away, don't try
and annoy me. This is a mathematical affair and I am not prepared to wait.' And he just turned his face to the wall and died. It
really was a ghastly period and to me it proved that the veneer of
civilization is skin deep and that once you scratch away that thin
veneer you're left with the basic human being, who is unpleasant
in the extreme and where it's everybody for themselves. There
were very few people who really acted as Christians, very few.
The vast majority very much looked to themselves and for themselves.

For Bill Goode survival was living 'literally from day to day':

If you could get through the day's work without being bashed
up, if you could get something to eat and if you could get to sleep
then that was one more day done. And the fact that we were
living so close to the earth and such a brutish life meant that your
whole being was concentrated on pure existence, and so at the
very bad time you simply had neither the time nor the energy to
spend on mournful speculation about your fate; you only woke
up now and again to think 'Good Lord, we've been here another
year and we don't seem to be any nearer getting out.' Inevitably,
we became increasingly filled with what was really hatred for the
Japanese and for the Koreans who were our more immediate
guards. The Koreans got beaten up by the Japanese and then
passed it on to us with interest. But it wasn't all gloom. The
ordinary British troops, drawn from all walks of life and all sorts

and sizes of people, had something quite extraordinary about them when they were gathered together in a more or less disciplined body, whereby their natural spirit seemed to triumph over these appalling surroundings. So we had lots of fun at the same time, like the names that we used for identifying our guards: Arthur Askey; Joe E. Brown; the Rocking Horse; Dr Death, who needless to say was a medical orderly; the Kenyu Kid, who was a particularly vicious little officer, beautifully dressed and an absolute bastard when it came to knocking people about. These names were given partly in a spirit of morbid humour, which carried us a long way and over many months.

When the monsoon ended conditions improved and morale rose once more, but the cost in human lives was very great. Only half of 'F' Force's original work-force returned to Singapore: 'The troops there were horrified at our appearance,' recalls Edward Tokeley. 'We were absolutely emaciated and full of disease. I can't imagine that many were better clothed than I was and all I possessed was one wooden clog and a *japhappi*, which was a form of loincloth. I didn't have anything else.'

By now not all the British in Malaya were there as prisoners. In May 1943 John Davis had been set down off the coast of Perak by Dutch submarine: 'It was wonderful to come out on deck to the muddy, soft, warm smell of the Malay coast that I recognized and loved. We got into our folboat canoes, the submarine just gently faded away and we were on our own.' Davis and four Chinese companions rowed five miles to the shore. 'It was a curiously uneventful way of landing on enemy territory,' he recalls. 'We ran ashore on a sandy beach with a jungle canopy ahead of us and it was so quiet and so desolate that the first thing we did was to have a bathe! Then we hid the boats and lay down on the beach and slept soundly till dawn.' In the morning they set off into the nearby jungle and made camp. Then the Chinese went out to gather intelligence – 'to find out what was happening in Malaya and to see what had happened to the Chinese Communist guerrillas that we had planted in the country.'

While this first contact was being made Davis had nothing to do but wait in the jungle: 'It soon became apparent that I was really an obstruction to my people so I decided that the best thing was for me to go back to India to report the situation and come back as soon as I could.' Richard Broome went out on the next submarine and the two men met at a prearranged rendezvous: 'We put up a periscope at the right place and immediately I saw a junk and there was John Davis, with his backside over the stern!' A month later Davis returned to Malaya and was followed shortly afterwards by Broome. Contact with the Communists was now established:

> One evening a stranger was brought into our bivouac camp, a young man, probably not more than twenty-two or three, quiet and tallish. He was the Political Commissar for Perak and his name was Chin Peng. He just said a few things and then suddenly and abruptly he brought out a watch and said, 'Do you know what this is?' I said, 'Yes, that's my watch and I gave it to your leader when I put him down in South Negri Sembilan at the beginning of the campaign.' He knew then that I was the right person and I had confidence in him because he had been able to bring the watch back and from then on we got on famously together.

The object of their return to Malaya was to organize a fifth column behind the enemy lines in preparation for an Allied invasion, so mutual trust between the Communists and the British was essential: 'It was no good being suspicious of them or antagonizing them because we were in their hands in an enemy country and they were looking after us. Our only chance was to show full confidence in them in the hope that they would respond and give us their confidence – and this, I'm happy to say, is what happened.'

The Communists took Davis and Broome on a five-day march deep into the interior of the country where the guerrillas had a number of camps hidden in the jungle. Here they settled down to plan and prepare for the eventual return of the British. An agreement was reached by which both sides would co-operate for the duration of the war, with the British supplying arms as soon as it was practical to do so. In the meantime there was little to do but wait. 'We were sleepers really,' explains Broome:

> It was no use trying to do any sabotage while the Japanese were in occupation. The only result of that would have been a lot of innocent people murdered. So ours was really a political operation. The main trouble was boredom, unquestionably, because for a whole year we were cut off. There was only a very small chance of being killed by the Japanese because we would have had ample warning of their approach, so we were perfectly safe. But there was a definite danger, in my mind, of dying from disease, because we all had malaria terribly badly. Every now and then we had visits from one or other of the heads of the Communist organization but we were at a disadvantage at that time because we were being of no help whatsoever.

The one Chinese leader with whom both Broome and Davis got on well was Chin Peng:

He was the one man whom we were always delighted to see arriving in the camp, because he was a splendid person to be dealing with. He spoke a bit of English but we usually spoke to him in Cantonese, and he was the one Communist whom we felt to be totally reliable. You felt you could rely on his word and he was also an extremely pleasant character. He said to us once, 'Our objectives, of course, are not the same. We want to run the country, you realize that? But for the duration of the war our objective is the same, which is to get rid of the Japanese.'

During this first long period of isolation in the jungle Broome made a number of unsuccessful attempts to get past the Japanese in the plains in order to rendezvous with submarines:

On one of these occasions I was suffering quite badly from malaria and Chin Peng put me on his bicycle and wheeled me for about ten miles, so I always had a pretty soft spot for him. After the war we had several lunches together. His father had a bicycle shop in Telok Anson and as everything was very scarce in those days I did my best to get a special dispensation to import bicycle parts into Malaya simply for Chin Peng's shop, because if he'd really got established in that it's quite possible that he might have chosen a different course from the one he did, which was to become the number one leader of the Communist insurrection.

After a year and a half of total silence from Broome and Davis they were given up as lost by the leaders of Force 136 in India. Finally, they were able to get a radio going using a pedal-powered transmitter and contact was re-established:

We'd been written off and furthermore we were using out-of-date codes, so our chances of getting through were slim, but it so happened that one of the FANYS (First Aid Nursing Yeomanry) who manned the radio sets in Colombo was twiddling the knobs and she heard a signal. She reported this and there was a lot of laughter but after a bit of an argument they accepted the fact and realized that we were using out-of-date codes. The assumption was that we were in the hands of the Japanese, so they started sending over security checks on their messages to us. We didn't realize this so we didn't send the right replies, which merely increased their suspicion and they decided to class this as an enemy station. But fortunately we had a great friend from the Malayan Police in headquarters and he said, 'Oh, give them another chance.' So they sent over a message which referred to 'Tightarse', which was Davis' nickname, and to Tamsin, which was my wife's name. We then realized what had happened and so we concocted a fairly ribald message about 'Tightarse', told them to 'leave my wife out of this' and finally said, 'Are you satisfied now, you bastards? If you don't believe us, come and pedal the bloody machine yourselves.' No Jap could have made up a thing like that so they had a tremendous night out in Colombo on it – and after that things went absolutely splendidly.

Early in 1944 the first supply drop took place:

We got an army of thirty or forty Sakai aboriginals and with our own men helping we built up enormous piles of timber. Then we listened and listened and suddenly we heard the drone of planes in the distance. We immediately set light to these flares and the flames leapt up twenty feet into the air – we were told that they could be seen over the Straits of Malacca and that the whole of Perah must have been roused by them. Then the planes came round and dropped the men first of all and then lovely little weapons, small carbines which we'd never seen. So from that time on the whole scene changed and something like four hundred people were dropped in over the few remaining months of the war.

Davis also became aware that during his two years in the jungle the British Government's attitude towards the Communists had changed: 'They had become the natural enemy in the eyes of the British. But these Communists in Malaya were not baddies, they were our allies and this created tension – which became apparent immediately after the ending of the war.'

Some months earlier Davis had been walking in the jungle with a third member of their group, Freddie Spencer-Chapman, when they both heard a 'tremendous booming roar in the sky. There was a clearing nearby so we dashed out to look and there, unmistakably, were about twenty or thirty American Flying Fortresses, flying over on the way to bomb Singapore.' The same aeroplanes appeared 'like silver bullets shining in the sky' to Peter Lucy and his comrades still working in Singapore docks, and even though the bombers then proceeded to unload incendiary bombs over the city it was nevertheless 'one of the greatest moments of all', because it so clearly heralded the end of the war.

Yet liberation would come too late to save many thousands of prisoners. In the POW camp in Kuching more than half the occupants had died. John Baxter remembers how 'they were burying ten a day at the end and playing the Last Post over coffins that held two bodies at a time. Those who were still alive were walking skeletons, with no backside at all; where their spines ended their legs began.'

Baxter himself dropped from thirteen-and-a-half stone to eight –
but he survived: 'Age didn't seem to have much to do with it as far
as I could see. It was entirely mental. If you thought it was going to
end all right and you didn't worry, then you survived.'

The story was repeated in Sumatra, where Cunyngham-Brown
was one of the few who survived the building of a railway across the
island: 'We went across to Sumatra three thousand strong and we
built that railway for the Japanese. It ran for a fortnight before the
end of the war in autumn 1945 by which time we were just over
eight hundred strong.' Long before then the struggle for survival
had become one in which both prisoners and guards were equally
involved: 'The Japanese were no better to their own men than they
were to us and they equally were dying at great speed from malaria
and the absence of quinine and from under-nourishment.' Having
lived in Malaya and spent time in the jungle Cunyngham-Brown
was able to profit from his experience:

> I was accustomed to the sort of food people ate and I knew what
> sort of things one could collect from the secondary jungle
> growths around the camp that could be cooked and eaten. I used
> to bring in occasional dogs, cats, frogs or snails and loads of
> ferns, which have very good little edible tips on them, and
> attempt to persuade the British Other Ranks to eat this – but no,
> they'd rather not. And I'm sorry to say that whereas the Cockney
> would give a toothless grin and shove into his guts anything that
> was going, my own great Scotsmen, looking so noble and splen-
> did, would sit dreaming of the girl with the light brown hair and
> thinking of their beautiful Scotland and dying as quickly as they
> could. I was also the sanitary officer of the camp and they built
> for me very good closed refuse dumps with naval-fashion hatches
> on top so that everything was hermetically sealed and you didn't
> get flies in the camp and therefore we had no cholera. There was
> a quantity of bones from the kitchen in these refuse dumps and it
> was my practice to go down into these dumps at night to fossick
> about and collect them, so that I could grind them down and boil
> them to make soup for the hospital patients. This was a godsend
> as far as health was concerned and yet so many people said, 'No,
> I'm sorry' – and died as a result. Coming across me one night as I
> wallowed in the filth of one of these refuse dumps in my per-
> petual search for bones, a brother officer of mine turned away
> from me in disquiet with the remark, 'I'm sorry to see you like
> this. I only hope I don't go the same way.'

Here, as in many other camps, there was a secret wireless
receiver that remained undiscovered by the Japanese, so that it was

possible to follow the progress of the war in its closing stages. Then, just when it seemed as if the liberation of South-East Asia was at hand, a sinister development occurred:

> Our guards had become extremely unobtrusive over the last week and then suddenly they were withdrawn and a very savage bundle of Koreans came in who dragooned us with day-long digging of large trenches that were six-feet deep, six-feet wide and thirty-feet long. It wasn't until they started putting emplacements up at the ends of these holes for their machine guns that we realized that these were our graves that we were digging.

A last-minute reprieve came in the form of the atomic bombs dropped on Hiroshima and Nagasaki, which 'not only saved our own lives but those of millions in South-East Asia'.

In Changi POW camp Perky Perkins remembers how the hut commanders were sent for by the Japanese:

> We all waited anxiously to hear what the result was and then the hut commanders started coming back and we could hear cheers from Number One Hut and Number Two Hut and Number Three – and then our own hut, Number Four. Oh, how we cheered! The Dutch started to sing their national anthem which they'd often sung during the imprisonment, but we'd never sung ours. But then we started to sing *God Save the King* and at first the thing rather collapsed. Then we started again and sang it with great fervency.

For Peter Lucy in the Singapore docks the end came rather less dramatically: 'We got the news and so we waited for something to happen and after waiting for at least a week we took matters into our own hands. We went up and told the Japanese that the war was over, to which they immediately agreed. We then handed our tools to the Japanese soldiers and watched the Japanese doing our work.' But of the original working party that had come to Blakang Mati two hundred and fifty strong, only eighteen remained.

Over in Sumatra the surviving prisoners began to repair a nearby airfield. 'I was given the job of putting their airstrip in order with the very greatest speed with a hundred men,' recalls Cunyngham-Brown:

> The work went on from early dawn to late dusk and we made remarkable progress but on the third day some large aircraft came floating over and circled around the camp and the airstrip. The next day they came back and we realized they were the same ones because the front one of these three aircraft was a shiny, polished one which glittered in the morning sunshine. They

came lower this time but again they disappeared. On the third day we were still working as hard as we possibly could, filling in these trenches across it, but the runway still wasn't hard enough. But then to our horror and surprise the front one of these three planes came in just over the palm trees and made a landing, bumping and jumping in a cloud of dust across the airstrip and on into the secondary growth at the other end, where it made a successful turn and then worked its way out of the undergrowth again. I was furious at this and rushed over – losing every stitch of clothing in the process, because I was only wearing a small loincloth – so as to shout to the pilot, 'For God's sake don't let the rest in. Wait until we're ready for you.' But no, the door opened and an extremely attractive woman, elegant in the extreme in what I thought was a WREN uniform but was actually St John's Ambulance, was standing at the top of the gangway. I stood within twelve feet of her, stark naked, and as she came down the steps I said, 'I do apologize.' 'Not at all,' she said. 'What you need is a cigarette.' She held out a gold cigarette-case and I had my first English cigarette for three-and-a-half years. 'Do tell me,' I asked, 'what is your name?' She replied, 'I'm Lady Mount-batten.'

Later that same day Cunyngham-Brown was back in Singapore, astonished by the look of the average European: 'They were pink-coloured, fat little tubs of lard, all of them shining with sweat and good health.' Other prisoners also managed to make their way into Singapore. John Theophilus and a friend got a lift from Changi down to the docks: 'We'd all kept a pair of shorts and a shirt for just such an occasion so we looked quite respectable. We then went aboard HMS *Sussex* and had our first beer for three-and-a-half years.' George Wort also went into the city and called in at the Chartered Bank: 'I asked for my account and it was handed to me straight away, just like that!'

In Kuching Edward Banks made a point of searching out the Chinese girl who had given his morale such a boost in the early days of his captivity: 'I found that kid and gave her some emergency rations and later got her a job, because she was a bright little girl. She was the slyest little crook you've ever met, but the last I saw of her was in the arms of a British soldier, gazing up into his eyes – and the best of luck to her!'

The prisoners of war and internees were all to be repatriated as soon as transport could be arranged, but after being told that he was to go home and that he could be of no possible use in the meantime, Cunyngham-Brown decided to go back to his old post in Johore

Bahru. He made his way over the causeway and went to see M. C. Hay, an old friend in the MCS, who was now the Chief Civil Affairs Officer for Johore. Here he was made welcome and given a bath and a change of clothing – 'putting on the uniform of a full colonel in the British Army, which was all that M. C. Hay could let me have'. After dinner that night in the Residency, Hay gave Cunyngham-Brown a revolver and told him that transport was waiting for him outside:

> With a cigar in my mouth and seated very comfortably in the back of the car I proceeded up the road for fifteen or twenty miles until the headlights disclosed a chunky, tired Japanese general with his forces trudging along behind in the best order they could maintain. The car stopped and they came to a halt. I got out of the car and the general walked towards me. He gave me his sword and his ADC gave me his flag. He saluted, I responded, and I took his surrender.

EPILOGUE – STAYING ON

'I wish that the critics of colonialism could have been present when the British returned to Malaya after the Japanese surrender,' declares Richard Broome. 'Their reception was totally rapturous from all sections of the population. Three weeks after the surrender it was still going on; as I drove up-country people were coming out of their houses by the roadside and waving and cheering. The obvious relief on their faces was something terrific to see.'

The defeat and subsequent humiliation of the British in 1942 had indeed had an impact on the local population but, in Bill Goode's estimation, its effect was less than was later assumed to be the case: 'The first reaction of the population was one of overwhelming joy that the Japanese occupation was over and that the people they knew and had previously trusted had come back to help them recover from the damage done by the war, because that was the first priority – to repair power stations and water supplies, to get food in so that they could eat and cloth so that people could have clothes, and to get the economy going again.'

Under the aegis of a British military administration the former British territories in South-East Asia now entered a period that was known officially as rehabilitation. Returning to Malaya as a civilian official with the Ministry of Supply, John Forrester was flown up to Kuala Lumpur – to be met by a large contingent of Japanese troops drawn up on the airfield: 'Some very important general marched up to us and said he wanted to surrender. We said we knew nothing about it and all we were interested in was finding transport to Kuala Lumpur, so we couldn't help him.' In KL, Forrester and other officials began to take the first measures to restart the economy by getting large sums of money back into circulation and tracking down any supplies of rubber that could be exported: 'Then gradually the banks and the insurance companies came back and people returned after their internment and a period of leave and started up the plantations properly, and everything gradually came back to normal.'

All internees and prisoners of war had been repatriated to Britain after their release. Trevor Walker was one of many who returned to a family of whom he had had no word for three-and-a-half years:

I found my family living quite close to Dorking in Surrey, where the Guthries' office had been rusticated after being moved out of their city office. I made my number with the people in the office and told them that I'd done nothing for too long and should like to do some work. My chairman said, 'When you're fit, come and work with us two or three days a week and re-engage all the planters and the office staff. But nobody is to go back until he is fit and nobody must go back until he has been at home for six months.' So we did it gently and as best we could and one of the most remarkable things was the keenness displayed by almost everybody to go back.

John Theophilus' reactions were very typical of the great majority of planters: 'I'd been a rubber planter virtually all my adult life and I knew nothing else. I wanted to come back; I liked the country and the people and I wanted to get things moving again. It took a bit of time because the estates were mostly secondary jungle.' Returning to Sapong Estate in North Borneo John Baxter found gruesome scenes of devastation:

It was completely overgrown with weeds up to the branches of the rubber trees and covered in Japanese graves, which the pigs had dug up so that there were bones all over the place. There were only two buildings left standing and the labour remaining on the estate were skeletons, covered in scabies and ulcers and suffering from malaria. About ninety per cent of them had died. It was dreadful. But I found that my family, Susan and the small children, had managed to survive, which was really a miracle. They had managed to exist by fishing and planting *padi*. But it had been a real hard life for them and my youngest daughter had died just at the end of the war from malaria.

Many marriages also proved to be casualties of the war. 'Thousands of marriages broke up and it was nobody's fault,' declares Tommy Lucy. During the long separation from her husband she herself had often wondered how, if he survived, she would react to him after his release. The only news she had received during his period as a prisoner of war had been a single postcard containing a few phrases selected from a list drawn up by the Japanese authorities:

It was difficult to get together again because we had lived in such completely different circumstances for four years. The women had been in authority and in positions of responsibility all over the world, while our husbands had been beaten and treated despicably by a race that had no moral code in war whatsoever. So we had changed as people and it was impossible in many cases to readjust. Very many of our friends' marriages broke up and there were times when we ourselves thought we would have to divorce because we were not thinking in the same way as we had four years before. But we persisted; we were determined that we could make a go of it once we got back to Malaya, the beautiful country that we both loved and where we had met and married. As soon as we got back and the circumstances were the same, we found our old love for each other.

Peter Lucy's bungalow was still standing but all its contents had long since disappeared: 'We had to start from scratch with two deck chairs, two camp beds and a camp table, and we had to drink our first bottle of whisky in order to get a water bottle.' The bulk of the estate's original force had died on the Siam-Burma railway, but there were enough survivors to get the estate back in working order and within a matter of months rubber was once more being tapped: 'We then had about a year of the normal rubber planter's life – not quite so good as it had been before the war but still enjoyable.'

Throughout South-East Asia the war had taken a heavy toll among the civil population. In Sarawak, where food shortages and malnutrition had led to an epidemic of the skin disease known as yaws, Robert Nicholl was horrified to see 'these awful dripping sores all over people' when he first went up-river. Hitherto western medicine had been regarded as something to be avoided:

It was very difficult to get anybody to suffer the dangers of inoculation because that was generally associated with death, as was everything in the way of European medicine. But our hospital assistants stepped in with their hypodermic syringes and penicillin and when they had injected a few people with this ghastly disease and the sores healed up, then word very quickly spread up-river. Immediately people heard there was a cure down they came, all demanding injections. And that completely transformed the attitude of the people of the interior to Western medicine. People came down-river for days to the government dispensary, demanding cures for all sorts of things – even for bad dreams.

There was also an acute shortage of clothing material, which was ameliorated to some extent by relief supplies from America. Robert Nicholl was given some of these to distribute:

As I happened to be going up the Baram river, the District Officer said to me, 'Look, a group of Punans are coming to Long Akka; would you take up this bale of stuff and distribute it to them?' So I went up and, sure enough, in came the Punans, twenty-seven of them as far as I remember. One of the Kayans who was with me interpreted and explained that we brought this present from the people of America. Then we opened the bale and it was really quite a surprise because it consisted entirely of fur coats. However, the Punans had never seen fur coats before and were immensely thrilled by these extraordinary things, so we divided the fur coats into twenty-seven little bundles and the Punans drew lots and each was given his little bundle. And having decked themselves out in these beautiful fur coats, off they went into the jungle and that was the last we saw of them.

Another great advance was made in the eradication of malaria, using new forms of insecticide – with unexpected consequences:

Whereas formerly when you went up-river you sat amidst clouds of smoke conversing rather as fiends do in hell, now there was not a mosquito left and you could sit and talk in comfort. When you went to bed, however, you would be bitten not by mosquitoes but by rats, because the longhouses were overrun with rats. In killing the mosquitoes the anti-malarial teams had also killed the cockroaches, which were eaten by the cats, who seemed to find the deeldarin seasoning attractive. So, of course, the cats died, too. People were now being bitten by these wretched rats and up went the cry, 'For the love of God, send us cats.' And that was the point at which the RAF stepped in. Cats were assembled and sorted out, generally one tom and two female cats, and put into containers to be loaded on to planes with little parachutes attached. The planes then flew up into the interior, circled the longhouses and out went the container. The parachute opened and the cat container floated to the ground. And the cats, of course, found themselves in what could only be described as a cat's terrestrial paradise.

It was now quite obvious that the days of colonial rule were numbered. In Sarawak and North Borneo the first steps towards eventual self-government were taken in 1946, when both territories ceased to be independent fiefdoms of the Brookes and the British North Borneo Company respectively and were brought into the orthodox colonial fold. The only political issues that remained to be settled were the actual timetable of events leading up to full independence and the question of who should do the governing thereafter. In the meantime, it was generally agreed that the process of rehabilitation had first to be completed – as speedily and as thoroughly as possible.

The immediate post-war years were, for Trevor Walker as for many of his colleagues, the hardest-working years that they had ever experienced:

> Both in the office and on the estates we were bringing things back to the standards that we had known before the war. We were approaching normality again and it looked as though not only peace was returning but prosperity with it. The politicial scene was changing, certainly; there was an approach towards Independence and people were being politically more vociferous than they had been before – although in a very pleasant fashion – when out of the blue came the Communist uprising that became known as the 'Emergency'.

The Communist guerrilla forces which had co-operated with Force 136 and the British throughout the war had been disbanded in 1946 with 'all the face and ceremony that the army could give them'. Its leaders had assured John Davis that, even if their ultimate aim was the political control of Malaya, 'the day had ceased when they were going to fight anybody', so that the sudden outbreak of terrorism directed by these same leaders came as much as a surprise to him as to anybody else: 'We had always known that they would remain our political enemies. That seemed all right, but it was ironic that only two years later these people whom we had treated as friends should find it necessary to start the Malayan Emergency in a terrible manner with the murder of two planters up in Perak.' The rest of Davis' career in Malaya was to be spent fighting the predominantly Chinese terrorists, who had once more retreated into the jungle, and their leader, Chin Peng – 'this man who had been my greatest ally and who has always, I believe, remained a good friend'.

In many ways the Emergency proved to be an even greater test of fortitude than the Japanese invasion and occupation of Malaya. It was a long drawn-out affair, lasting for more than a decade, and if the end result was 'the only war ever won against Communists' it was certainly not won easily. But whereas in 1941 'we were all virtually pawns, admittedly giving some help to the armed forces but entirely dependent on the fortunes of the fighters for our lives, our homes, our businesses and our possessions', now the Europeans found themselves 'masters of their own fate', all actively involved in a war that 'reached into the most remote *kampongs* and affected vitally almost everyone. We were not relatively safe miles behind the front line. There was no front line; it was all round us.'

It was the rubber planters and the tin-miners who provided the easiest and the most valuable targets. 'On 6 July 1948 we woke up to the news of the killing of two of our friends in Perak,' recalls Tommy Lucy. 'We realized almost immediately that we were going to be the main targets for the Communist bandits – they were always called bandits – because if they got rid of the British influence on the plantations and in the tin-mines then the labour forces would be disrupted and the whole of the country would come to a halt.' But what the Communists had failed to take into account was that 'we were absolutely determined that we were going to stay'. After what they and nearly everybody else in the same position had gone through, the Lucys felt that there was no question of pulling out: 'I said in no circumstances would I leave,' Tommy Lucy declares. 'The Indian women have to stay and the Malay women and so the British women must stay too and take whatever is coming to us. We did not know what was coming to us, of course, but I wish people would not call it an Emergency – because it was a full-scale war.'

As far as the planters and tin-miners were concerned, the re-actions of the government to the first acts of terrorism were not encouraging: 'It was simply not realized by the authorities how vulnerable we were and how simple it would have been for the Communists to get rid of us all at a blow. It was only by a miracle of misjudgement on their part that we were not all killed in the first year.' Norman Cleaveland had returned to Malaya to resume tin-mining operations just outside Kuala Lumpur, after an absence of more than a decade. For the first three years of the Emergency he remained convinced that the Communists were going to win:

The confusion between the services and the civilians and between the state and federal governments was almost unbeliev-able. We were frequently admonished by the authorities not to panic and not to publicize the situation. We were very strongly told that we must not use the word Communist. They were not Communists; they were bandits. And all the while incredible things happened that made for a lack of confidence. For instance, immediately violence broke out we were told that we were on our own. I asked what would be available to us in the way of weapons and they said, 'Nothing.' The Chamber of Mines sent a signal of distress to London to get the Colonial Office to take action and the Colonial Office came right back and said that they had made an investigation and their records showed that there were plenty of guns and ammunition in Malaya. We returned a message saying they were dead right; there were plenty of guns and ammunition in Malaya but they happened to be in the wrong hands.

When the tin-miners took steps to defend themselves they met with government opposition:

Our Superintendent in Perak went out with a truck and an acetylene torch and gathered up all the armoured plate from the derelicts of the Japanese invasion and armoured some jeeps and other vehicles, including a jeep for the Kampar police which was promptly confiscated by higher authority. When we got these armoured cars to Kuala Lumpur we were told that they too were going to be confiscated and that the government were not going to permit any private armies in the country. I got facetious and said, 'Well, how about the Communist army? Was that private or public?' However, facetiousness got me nowhere so then Anglo-Oriental, which was the largest company in Malaya, said, 'Look either we get those armoured cars or we shut down the show' – which would have meant blocking off twenty-five per cent of Malaya's tin production. They then let us have the armoured cars.

After failing to get any help from the government over arms, Cleaveland turned to America for help: 'The first two Pan-American planes to arrive in Singapore after the war were loaded with guns and ammunition, not only for ourselves but also for the entire mining industry. Later we expanded our order and got further guns and ammunition for the rubber industry. It was an incredible situation because these two industries at that time were supplying more hard currency for the sterling bloc than any other.'

Vulnerable as the tin-mines were, they were not so isolated as many of the rubber estates and it was here that the highest casualties among the Europeans were suffered. One in five of the rubber plantation managers in the state of Pahang was murdered and over one hundred and twenty planters killed in all.

Peter Lucy's Amhurst Estate six miles outside Kuala Lumpur was attacked on innumerable occasions: 'This was a daily event and not an occasional sporadic attack, because walking past us to their store of guns in Batu caves they would take pot shots at us, either by day or by night, and this went on for weeks and months and even years.' Right from the start the Lucys had decided that maximum protection was essential: 'A splendid Canadian couple who were missionaries, ran a school for Chinese children two miles away from us and I begged them to protect themselves in some way but they said, "Oh, no, the Lord will protect us." It wasn't long before they and their children were burnt alive in their home by the Communists.' As well as building up an armoury that they reckoned to be second to none in Malaya, the Lucys also fortified their bungalow with a barbed-wire perimeter guarded by two Alsatian dogs and floodlit at night. Finally, as the government began to respond to the pleas of the planters and tin-miners for help, they received reinforcements in the form of twenty-six armed special constables:

> When the bandits attacked us the floodlights went on, we had all the guns and ammunition at the ready and we could fire and kill them before they killed us. At the first sound of a bullet my job was to rush to the telephone and see if the line was cut, then get out my bren gun and start firing. Another of my jobs was to fire a Verey light in order to get help from the Gurkhas who were stationed on a property near Kuala Lumpur. A sight I shall never forget is when you're lying there expecting to be shot dead and suddenly an armoured car full of Gurkhas with guns blazing and tracer bullets going into the rubber trees, comes up your drive and you know that you are safe.

As the months went by the attacks on the estate became more frequent and then, to make matters more difficult, Tommy Lucy became pregnant:

> I knew I was going to have twins and as the time drew near for their arrival my greatest fear was that a bullet would go into my tummy, so towards the end I would use the bren gun only on real emergencies. Otherwise, I used to go and lie in an old steel bath at the back of the bungalow, because pregnant or not I was absolutely determined that these devils would not get us. That attitude persisted until one night when there was a really bad attack and I was forced to use the bren gun and I must have twisted the wrong way because I suddenly felt a dreadful pain and as it was near my time I knew that I was going to give birth. My husband got out the armoured car and I was carried in, but with a gun as always by my side. As we went down the drive we saw the bandits in the drive ahead of us. There was obviously no turning back so Peter put his foot down on the accelerator and we roared and bumped over this road. Why the twins didn't arrive in the armoured car I don't know, but as a final gesture of defiance I put my pistol through the louvres of the armoured car and fired a shot and yelled, 'That's for you. You devils!' But we did get through and got to the hospital where I was safely delivered of two fine boys.

Amhurst Estate was made up of four divisions that were widely separated so that Peter Lucy was often away from the bungalow. Like other wives in the same position Tommy Lucy always had to live with 'the awful fear when your husband went out in the morning to do his rounds that you would never see him again'. Her fears were well founded, for visiting one of the outlying divisions one day with a visiting agent, Peter Lucy walked straight into an ambush:

> They opened fire with their sten guns as we approached. They short Clarkson in the stomach; the whole of the magazine must have gone into him because he dropped dead right at my feet. But for some reason I didn't get hurt and as I had a revolver I fired back and I presume I got a bandit because I've got his hat. Then I disappeared into a ravine and it took me three hours to get home – by which time the *Malay Mail* had appeared stating that Mr Clarkson had been shot dead and that I was missing presumed dead. My wife was in the house, having read the paper and surrounded by other planters.

After surviving a second ambush in which he shot dead a prominent guerrilla leader – 'I happened to have a twelve-bore shotgun over my shoulder and I just brought it down as if I was shooting a rabbit and got him in the head' – Lucy was warned by the police that he was a marked man. On the advice of the new High Commissioner, Sir Gerald Templar, and for the sake of their children, the Lucys very reluctantly took up the offer of a job in East Africa.

There seems little doubt that the arrival of Templar dramatically changed the tempo of the struggle against the Communists. His predecessor as High Commissioner had been ambushed and murdered in his car as he drove up to Fraser's Hill; an event that had shaken all nationalities in Malaya very badly but had also had the effect of forcing the British Government to take more positive action. 'Out came somebody who was almost unheard of – but with more powers than any soldier since Cromwell,' declares Guy Madoc:

> In no time at all Templar turned us upside down. He was a man who used four-letter words and he said, 'I'm going to put some ginger up —' Perhaps I'd better not say where he was going to put the ginger but he was absolutely the key figure in those years. He persuaded the Malay leaders that we were going to win and he persuaded us that we were going to win. He was a complete human dynamo; he drove himself tirelessly and he drove everybody else. Sometimes you'd feel you weren't really getting home to him; he was looking a bit tired – and then suddenly you'd say something and he'd come upright like a spring. He'd open the

bottom drawer of his desk and put his feet into it and start addressing you as 'Old cock'. Well, then you knew you were really home and that you were getting somewhere with him. I found, too, that he was a very superstitious man. One thing he absolutely refused to do was to drive up the road where his predecessor had been killed. He was always ready to go places and meet members of the Special Branch, high or low, but he refused to go up that road. He said, 'Nope. If I go up that road I'll be killed. I'll come in by chopper, old cock.' However, as far as I was concerned, one of the great moves he made was to say, 'Right, Special Branch has got to be separated completely from CID and that should be done in forty-eight hours' – and I found myself head of Special Branch.

The war against the Communists was being fought on both military and political fronts – and Templar assumed personal command of both:

In the first years of the Emergency the army really wasted a tremendous amount of energy by sending random patrols into the jungle which very rarely made any contact with the terrorists. The terrorist in the jungle had become as sensitive as a wild animal. He could smell cigarette smoke half a mile away and if you used brilliantine on your hair or used too much toothpaste he could detect that too. We had great difficulty in overcoming the British soldier's desire for cleanliness. But with the build-up in the strength of the Special Branch and its efficiency we got to the stage where every unit of the army could be gainfully used, either by denying a particular area to the terrorists or by ambushes.

It had been recognized for some time before Templar's arrival that the key to defeating the Communists lay in separating them from their food supplies and their sources of intelligence, which came primarily from the Chinese squatters living on the fringes of the jungle. This was the basis of the Briggs' Plan, which involved the resettlement of squatters in New Villages together with such measures as the formation of Home Guard units, food rationing and the carrying of identity cards. Although accepted by the government the plan was being implemented with considerable reluctance. Templar seized upon the Briggs Plan and gave it top priority:

So gradually we began to starve the terrorists from the jungle, while the Special Branch took good care to arrange defects in the food denial arrangements in some operational areas, so that our secret agents amongst the New Villagers could attract their terrorist contacts. Such places we called our 'honey pots', where the military and our para-military police could pre-arrange effective ambushes.

It was Templar, too, who recognized the pyschological value of what came to be known as the 'White Areas':

Almost fortuitously, we cleared the whole of Malacca territory and Templar said, 'Aha, now if we free the people of Malacca from practically every emergency restriction, including food control and food rationing, this will encourage the civilian population in other parts of the country to work for us against the Communists. It's a carrot that we can hold out' – and how right he was. Six months later we'd cleared the whole of the State of Pahang, which is almost continuous with Malacca, and within a year we'd got a complete White Area right across Malaya so that the lines of communication between the terrorists in the north and south were cut. Starting from the original White Area we then decided to take on Communist districts and wipe them out one at a time, concentrating all our intelligence resources and the best units of the army and knocking them out at a rate that varied between four months and nine months each. This was never done at random; always we went for a district neighbouring a new White Area, because you'd got to roll up your enemy, so that it was obvious not only to the civilians but to the terrorists, too, that there was a sort of inevitability about it.

At the same time the High Commissioner ensured that advances were maintained on the political front. The 'Malaysianization' of all the government services was stepped up and Whitehall was persuaded that Malaya should be granted independence sooner rather than later. In consequence, self-government in the Malay states and the other former British colonies came about 'easily and politely and gradually' and with remarkable goodwill on all sides. In Sarawak, for instance, 'an elite of educated people from amongst the people of the interior had been raised up who could take over from us. They were brought into government service and put to work under some experienced officer. Gradually, they took over and the experienced chap remained as an adviser and in the end they were on their own. The actual hand-over took place as soon as we had got them qualified.'

Malaya was the first to gain its independence in August 1957, but as the Union Jack was hauled down here and in other former British territories in South-East Asia there was little sadness among the British witnesses. Guy Madoc was one of the many Europeans who attended the *Merdeka* ceremonies in Kuala Lumpur:

We all dressed ourselves up in our full dress uniforms and went off to the stadium and saw this really magnificent ceremony, with the Malay police and Malay regiment marching with all the dignity and precision at which they are so adept. It was a moving ceremony; one that we witnessed without sadness but really with pride in what the British had achieved in the country and with a great warmth, too, because the Malays gave us expatriates due credit for what we did for them.

After all the pomp there were other more informal parties. In Penang John Forrester recalls how first 'there were speeches, a band played, the flag was lowered and everything was very, very formal. Then everyone, including the band, came into the bar and we had the most wonderful evening, with the Resident Commissioner dancing on the table and taking his shirt off.'

As the younger men that they had trained began to take over so the British officials went into early retirement; a few moved to other colonies but the great majority returned to the United Kingdom. They went with the satisfaction that they left behind countries that were 'prosperous and peaceful and well-governed'. They had stood for 'decent, not very efficient but well-meaning government that gave the very poorest man a chance to live and enough food to eat'. And if as rulers they had been 'sometimes pompous and stupid' they had also been, by and large, 'dedicated, intrinsically good and incorruptible'.

For those in commerce, of course, life went on very much as it had done before *Merdeka*. In 1960 the State of Emergency that had existed in Malaya since 1948 was officially lifted and all sections of the community were free to enjoy an inheritance that was in many respects the envy of a great many other newly-emergent nations. In business as in government, Malaysianization programmes ensured that more native Malaysians were brought into all the big companies. And in the clubs, too, the last racial barriers were lowered. When John Theophilus became President of the Sungei Ujong Club in 1959 one of his first acts was to write a letter to all its members: 'I said that there was nothing in our rules to stop Asians from becoming members of the club and that if any member had any objections to the club being open to anyone please would they let me know before the end of the month. I never got a single reply and therefore from 1 May 1959 the club became open to anyone from any community to be put up as members. Now we have over a thousand members of the club among whom there are damn few Europeans.'

Theophilus was one of a considerable number of Europeans who chose to stay on when the time came for them to retire. He did so quite simply because 'it was a bloody marvellous country'. Bill Bangs (now better known perhaps as Dato Haji Mohamed Yusuf Bangs) was another who had no doubts as to where his future loyalties lay: 'There was no question of my going back to England because I looked upon Malaya as my country and I had no further wish to go back to England.' He had been a Malayan citizen since 1948. Another planter who followed the same course was Perky Perkins, who built a house for himself on a promontory overlooking the Malacca Straits: 'I saw this lovely site and I thought what a wonderful place. There was a little holy place on this cape with a grave which people claim is the grave of Admiral Ricardo, a Portuguese admiral. So I had a *bomoh* come up who looked it over and said it was a lucky site and I built my house there and called it Bukit Tersenium – Smiling Hill.'

John Baxter, Hugh Watts and Mervyn Sheppard (now Tan Sri Dato Mubin Sheppard) also became Malaysian citizens. Datuk John Baxter now lives in retirement with his family in Tenom, not far from the estate where he first began working as an assistant fifty-eight years ago, taking little interest in the affairs of Britain other than following the sporting results: 'We have fifty head of cattle, a small area of cocoa and rubber and twenty acres of wet *padi* – which has been completely washed out in the last flood. I know everybody here and they know me and if I went anywhere else I couldn't possibly be as happy. All my children have turned out well and if you have a family that turns out well then you're a happy man.'

Captains Percy Bulbrook and Monty Wright became citizens of Singapore. Today Bulbrook lives with his wife in a modern apartment block overlooking a busy dual-carriageway that was no more than a bullock-cart track when he first came to Singapore. 'I just can't fit in the transformation that's taken place,' he admits. 'I had to give up driving last year: you just keep losing your way.' But he still keeps in close touch with the Straits steamers' captains who succeeded him:

> I always wig the younger generation that come up here to see me. I tell them, 'Cor, you don't know what bloody weather is yet. Wait till you go foreign.' I always joke with them and tell them what my father told me, that all the real sailors were killed at the battle of Trafalgar: 'You've got radar, echo sounders, push buttons everywhere. All we had was our eyes, our ears and our heads' – but, by God, I'd go back with them tomorrow if I could.

Sjovald Cunyngham-Brown is another expatriate, still based in Penang where he was the last British President of George Town and where today he has a small part-time export business in spices and other Malayan produce.

> It is one of those old perfumed trades where one has to have a bath to get the smell of cloves off one in the evening. And it often makes me laugh when I'm doing this job to think that this is where we came in, that this is exactly the way they were doing their job in 1686 on the territory of Ben Coolen in Sumatra, which was our very first possession in South-East Asia – young men in the East India Company collecting the cloves as I am, supervising the export of this precious commodity. That is an additional enchantment to a life that I find perfectly satisfying.

Robert Nicholl is now employed by His Highness the Sultan of Brunei and still gets visited by old boys that he once taught in Sarawak:

> It's surprising how gratifying it is to come across boys whom one first saw as urchins puffing hard at their cheroots and knocking back glasses of *borak*, and then taught in one's sixth form. Now they are very important people either in government or in commerce and so one feels that all those years in Sarawak were not only happy but fruitful. They were not wasted years.

When Guy Madoc retired from the police he returned to the United Kingdom, like the great majority of his colleagues. However, the country in which he had spent all of his working life continues to exercise a hold over him: 'At intervals a sudden urge comes to go back just to visit some particular place, such as my beloved district of Jelebu.' In 1976 he and Nancy Madoc returned to make just such a visit:

> I'd promised myself a trip in the jungle and I was in all day entirely on my own watching birds, cutting my way with a jungle knife. I came to a stream where some Malay youths were bathing and I sat and watched them. When they came out of the water they carefully examined my jungle knife. Then they said, 'You speak our language,' and I said, 'Yes, of course I do, because I was the officer in charge of the police district right here about forty years ago.' 'Oh,' said they, 'How old are you?' I said I was sixty-seven, 'Umph, when our grandfathers reach that sort of age they stay peacefully at home in their *kampongs*.'

NOTES ON CONTRIBUTORS

(Up to year of retirement in S-E. Asia)

Dato Haji Mohamed Yusuf 'Bill' BANGS; born 1903; Asst. Han Yang
Plantations, Johore 1926; joined Socfin 1927; Manager Kuala Pergau
Estate, Kelantan 1933; POW Changi, Siam–Burma 1942–5; Development
Officer, Kelantan 1948–54; retired 1967.

Edward BANKS; born 1903; joined Sarawak Service 1925; Curator Sarawak Museum; interned Kuching 1941–5; retired 1950; pubs. incl.
Naturalist in Sarawak, The Green Desert.

Datuk John BAXTER, CBE; born 1899; RFC and RAF; Asst. Sapong Estate,
British North Borneo 1925; married Kadazan wife, Susan; Manager
1938; interned Kuching 1942–5; retired 1954.

Richard BROOME, OBE, MC; born 1909; joined MCS 1932 Chinese Protectorate; Canton 1932–4; Asst.-Protector Penang 1935–6; DO Christmas
Island 1938–9; Force 136 India and Malaya 1942–5; Labour Dept.
1945–2; Ferret Force 1948; Sec. Chinese Affairs Singapore 1952; Sec.
Defence and Internal Security 1955; retired 1957.

Tamsin BROOME (*née* Luckham); born 1909; teacher Pudu English
School KL 1936; married Richard Broome 1938; three children born
Penang, Singapore, KL; after war taught in Johore Bahru, Ipoh, Singapore.

Capt. Percy BULBROOK; born 1903; apprentice Hain ss Co. 1919; joined
Straits Steamship Co. Singapore 1929; Ship's Master 1941; was service 1941–8; Master Red Funnel Heap Eng Moh ss Co. 1948–59;
Cargo Surveyor, Sec. Straits Merchant Service Guild 1959–71; retired
1971.

Norman CLEAVELAND; US citizen; mining engineer; mine manager
Anglo-Oriental and engineer Malaya, Siam, Burma 1930–2; Manager,
later President, Pacific Tin, Malaysia 1947–66; retired 1966; pub. *Bang
Bang in Ampang* (autobiog.).

Sjovald CUNYNGHAM-BROWN, OBE, Legion d'Honneur, OM France; born
1905; joined MCS, 1929, Penang 1930; Asst. Emigration Commiss.,
India 1932–4; Magistrate, Singapore 1937–8; Controller of Labour,
Johore 1938–41; POW Sumatra 1942–5; Depy. Res., Johore 1946–8;
Commiss. Lands, Resettlement Off., Johore 1950–1; DO Kinta, President Municipal Councillors, Penang, 1952–7; retired MCS 1957; pubs.
incl. *The Traders; Crowded Hour* (autobiog.).

Madeline DAUBENY; born 1905; married Richard Daubeny (Sarawak Civil
Service 1921–45) 1933; up-country 1933–4, then Kuching, Limbang,
Miri; two sons born Sarawak; husband's health damaged as POW, left
Malaya 1945.

Helen DAVIS (*née* Duin); born 1914; war service 1941–5; married John
Davis 1946; four children born Malaya.

John DAVIS, CBE, DSO; born 1911; joined FMS Police 1931; 1931–3 OCPD

Pahang; Canton 1933–5; CID Perak 1936–40; Force 136 India and Malaya 1942–6; transf. MCS 1947; Ferret Force 1948; Chinese Affairs, 'Emergency' 1949–53; DO Prov. Wellesley, Johore, Kedah 1954–9; retired 1960.

John FORRESTER; born 1914 Shanghai; joined Harrison and Crosfield 1937; based in Ceylon, Singapore, Penang; escaped Singapore 1942; Ministry of Supply 1942–6; rejoined H and C; retired 1969.

Una FORRESTER (*née* Ebden); born 1925; father MCS; lived Malacca, KL 1940–2; married John Forrester, India 1943; three children, one born Singapore, one Penang.

Sir William GOODE, GCMG; born 1907; joined MCS 1931; Kuantan, Selangor, Besut 1931–5; DO Raub 1936–9; Asst. Fin. Sec. Singapore 1939–40; Asst. Commiss. Civil Defence 1941; POW 1942–5; Secretariat, KL 1946–9; Chief Sec. Aden 1949–53; Chief Sec. Singapore 1953–7, Governor 1957–9; Governor North Borneo 1960–3.

H. L. H. 'Bill' HARRISON; born 1897; joined Osborn and Chappel, Ipoh 1919, mining engineer; Manager tin-mines, Siam 1921; Anglo-Oriental, KL 1936–55; escaped Singapore 1942; London Tin Corp. rehabilitating mines in Malaya 1945; Director, Exploration & Development Division; retired 1955; pubs. incl. *The Sarong and the Kris* (autobiog.).

Derek 'Bill' HEADLY, CMG; born 1908; joined MCS 1930; Selangor, KL, Kuala Trengganu, Muar 1931–6; DO Pekan 1937–8; seconded Palestine 1938–44; Force 136 Malaya 1944–5; Senior Civil Affairs Officer Trengganu 1945–6; Resident Labuan 1947; Commiss. Resident, E. and W. Coast, N. Borneo 1948–53; British Adviser Kelantan 1953–7; retired 1957.

Peter HOWES, OBE, PBS; missionary priest posted to St Augustine's, Betong, Sarawak 1937; Priest-in-charge Land Dayak District 1940–52; interned Kuching 1942–5; Warden Theo. College Kuching 1952–6; seconded Officer-in-Charge Padawan Dev. Scheme 1957–61; Archdeacon Kuching, Brunei and N. Sarawak 1962–70; Sen. Archdeacon, Asst. Bishop 1971–81; retired 1981.

Mark John and Dorothy KENNAWAY; four daughters born in Malaya; ANN born 1922, married Gerald Scott, APC 1946; ELIZABETH born 1924, married Bernard Davis, MCS Controller of Emigration 1948; PIPPA born 1927, sec. Defence Dept. KL and MOD Singapore 1948–56; USPG missionary Penang 1958–9; married Alexander Boyle 1962; SUSAN born 1928, sec. MOD Singapore 1955–7; married John Whitley 1966.

Cecil LEE; born 1911; joined Harrison and Crosfield 1934, KL; POW Siam-Burma 1942–5; returned to Malaya 1946; Sandakan, N. Borneo 1951–4; retired 1961.

Dorothy 'Tommy' LUCY (*née* Hawkings); born 1915 Shanghai; opened school Cameron Highlands 1940; VAD nurse Singapore 1941; married Peter Lucy 7 Feb. 1942; Amhurst Estate 1946–52; three children born KL; Chief Commiss. Girl Guides.

Peter LUCY, CPM; born 1908; joined Escot Estate 1928; Manager Slim River Estate 1931; General Manager Amhurst Estate 1938–52; POW

Singapore 1942–5; awarded Colonial Police Medal 1952; transferred to E. Africa 1952.

Guy MADOC, CBE, KPM, CPM; born 1911; joined FMS Police 1930; OCPD Jelebu, Kuala Kubu, Kuala Selangor, Kuantan, OSPC S. & N. Kedah; interned Singapore 1942–5; seconded First Sec. Brit. Emb., Bangkok 1947–50; CID HQ 1950, formed and commanded Special Branch 1952; Director of Intelligence 1954–7; Dep. Sec. Security and Intelligence, PM's Dept. 1957–9; retired 1959.

Nancy MADOC; born 1909; married Guy Madoc 1935; lived in Selangor, Pahang, Kedah; evacuated Singapore 1942; son born Malaya, daughter Bangkok; left Malaya 1959.

James MORICE; born 1902; joined Malayan Customs Service 1921; served in all FMS, Johore, Penang, Lumut & Singapore 1921–52; Civil Defence, Food Control 1941; interned Singapore 1942–5; State Registration Officer NS 1948–9; retired 1952.

Alan MORKILL, OBE; born 1890; joined MCS 1913; Supt. Posts and Telegraphs, 2nd Magistrate & Asst. Land Office, Kelantan 1913–6; Magistrate KL 1919; DO Kuala Pilah 1919–21, Tampin 1922–5; Upper Perak 1925–6; retired on medical grounds 1927 to run Malay Dept. Victoria League.

Robert NICHOLL; after war service in Far East joined BMA Sarawak, later Education Service; Director of Education, Principal Miri College; after twenty-four years moved to Brunei to work for Rajah of Brunei as historian.

R. B. 'Perky' PERKINS; joined Dunlops as a rubber assistant, Bahow Estate, Negri Sembilan 1925; POW Burma–Siam 1942–5; returned to planting, Kota Tingi Estate 1946; later bought own estate, Ladang Tersenium.

Anthony RICHARDS; born 1914; joined Sarawak Civil Service 1938; cadet, Kuching, Bintulu, Lower Rejang 1938–41; DO Saribas 1941; interned Kuching 1942–5; DO Kanowit, Bau, Kapit, Sarikei 1946–55; Resident, first div. 1955–7, second 1958–61; Land Committee, Resident's Native Court Magistrate 1961–4; retired 1964; pubs. incl. *Iban-English Dictionary*.

Daphne RICHARDS (*née* Oswell); born 1917; married Anthony Richards 1946; lived Upper & Lower Rejang, Kuching, Simanggang; three children born Sarawak; Red Cross voluntary work & editor children's magazine; left Sarawak 1964.

Gerald SCOTT; born 1914; joined Asiatic Petroleum Co. (Shell) 1939 as Technical Engineer, Singapore; worked part-time for Malaya Broadcasting Corp. 1941–2; escaped Singapore 1942; married Ann Kennaway 1946.

Tan Sri Dato Mubin (Mervyn) SHEPPARD, PSM, CMG, MBE; born 1905; joined MCS 1928; Temerloh, PS to Chief Sec.; Asst. Sec. Resident Perak 1928–32; Asst. Brit. Adviser, Kemaman, DO Alor Gajah, Secretariat KL 1932–41; interned Singapore 1942–5; DO Klang 1947–50; Brit. Adviser, Negri Sembilan 1952; Head Emergency Food Denial 1956; Director Public Records, Museums 1957–63; pubs. incl. *Taman Budiman* (memoirs).

Alan 'Bob' SNELUS, CMG; born 1911; joined Sarawak Civil Service 1934; cadet Sibu, ADO Lower Rejang 1934–5; DO Lawas, Kapit, Simanggang 1936–41; interned Kuching 1942–5; PS to Gov. 1946–7; DO Lower Rejang 1947–9; Resident, second div. 1949–50, third div. 1951–2; Dep. Chief Sec. 1953–63; retired 1963.

John THEOPHILUS; born 1906; joined Brit. Malay Rubber 1926; Assistant, Jindaram Estate, Nilai; transferred to Oriental Rubber 1931; Commiss. 1939, Asst. Defence Security, Singapore; POW Singapore 1942–5; Bhutan Estate, Nilai 1946; retired 1966.

Edward TOKELEY; born 1915; joined Bousteads, Penang 1935; Singapore office 1936–41; POW Siam–Burma 1942–5; rejoined Bousteads, Penang 1946; also Port Swettenham, Kota Bharu, KL, Singapore; Chairman 1966–70; retired to London office 1971.

Trevor WALKER; born 1916; joined Guthries, London 1935; KL office, plantations and mining depts. 1937–41; POW Singapore 1942–5; rejoined Guthries 1946, Director 1957; Singapore 1963, Chairman; retired to London office 1968.

Hugh WATTS; born 1897; joined Henrietta Estate 1920; Bukit Sembilan Estate 1922, then Sungei Ulat Estate, Parit Ular Estate; MSVR, Port Dickinson in slump; joined Brown Estate, Penang 1933; POW Siam–Burma 1942–5 returned Brown Estate 1945; estab. Sungei Ara Estate, Penang 1966 and still Man.-Director.

Mary WATTS (née Culleton); born 1892; joined Malayan Nursing Service 1927; nursing sister Batu Gajah hospital; resigned on medical grounds 1930; married Hugh Watts, Klang; lived in Kuala Selangor and Penang; evacuated 1942; rejoined husband Penang 1946; still runs dispensary.

Capt. Robert WILLIAMSON, OBE, DSC; born 1891; apprentice King Line 1906; able seaman sailing ships 1909–11; 2nd Mate W. Indies trader 1912; RNR 1914–9; joined Indo-China SN Co 1920; Master Upper Yangtse 1921–6; Asst. and Marine Supt. Shanghai 1927–40; war service 1941–6; retired 1955.

Brig. George WORT, CBE; born 1912; served Wilts Regt. Singapore 1933–6; seconded to Malay Regt. Port Dickson 1939; wounded Singapore POW 1942–5; seconded Malayan Govt., Col. 'A' HQ Federation Army 1956–7; Military Adviser Malayan HC, London 1957–8.

Capt. Monty WRIGHT; after war service in Far East joined Straits Steamship Co. c. 1947; Ship's Master and later Deck Superintendant; retired 1977.

GLOSSARY

In addition to words found in the text I have included a few words and terms of special relevance to the British East Indies, particularly where their origins – Portuguese, Indian or otherwise – or their usage are of unusual interest. However, for all its wealth of tongues the South-East Asian melting-pot has yet to come up with an equivalent of that feast of Anglo-Indianisms, *Hobson-Jobson,* and so I suspect that errors over derivation or exact meaning remain in this short list. I have consulted R. J. Wilkinson's romanized *Malay-English Dictionary* and Anthony Richards' *Iban-English Dictionary* (1981) but I have nevertheless stuck with the common usage of the day as regards spelling.

M – Malay; Hind. – Hindustani; Port. – Portuguese; Pers. – Persian; SS – Straits Settlements; CC – China Coast and Concessions

A

adat – customary practice or law (M)

Adviser – senior British official in UMS

angmoh kwei – red-haired spirit, devil or apparition, thus European (SS & CC)

almeirah – wardrobe (der. Port. *almario*), in M *almari*

amah – Chinese maidservant, nurse (der. Port. *ama*)

amok – violent homicidal condition defined by Fauconnier as 'self-liberation through revolt', thus 'to run amok' (M)

APC – Asiatic Petroleum Company (Shell)

atap – *nipah* palm-leaf thatch (M)

ayah – Indian or Malay maid, nurse (SS der. Port. *aia*)

B

baju – Malay open shirt with long sleeves

barang – things, thus luggage (M)

batu – rock (M), thus Batu Ferringhi ('foreigner's rock') off Penang

besar – great (M), thus *tuan besar* – great gentleman; firm *besar* – great firm (Guthries, Sime Darby, Bousteads, Barlow, APC, Harrisons, depending on loyalties); and boy *besar* – head servant.

bomoh – Malay medicine man

box-wallah – derogatory term for British businessman derived from Anglo-Indian term for door-to-door salesman (SS)

'boy' – native servant, traditionally summoned by the vocative 'boy!'; thus cook-boy; Number One boy; boy *besar*

bukit – hill (M) as in Bukit Timah

C

cash – copper coinage (pidgin der. Tamil *kasu*)

chick – split bamboo screen (Pers.)

chi-chak – small house lizard (M); not to be confused with larger *gekko*

China Coaster – European with Far Eastern experience, notably at sea (CC)

chin-chin – salutations (pidgin der. Chinese)

chit – note, signed bill (Hind.), thus *chit*-shy – one who avoids paying his round

chokra – young man, boy (Hind. SS)

chop – seal, brand (pidgin der. Hind. *chap*), thus first-*chop* – top quality goods (SS & CC)

chummery – shared household of bachelors (SS from India)

compound – enclosed area round bungalow (der. M *kampong*)

comprador – buyer, steward (Port.), thus Chinese manager of a *hong*

concession – Chinese treaty port open to foreign traders

conductor – head overseer on rubber estate, usually Tamil (Port.)

coolie – Indian or Chinese labourer paid on daily basis (der. S. India), term now regarded as offensive but normal M for daily-paid labour as *kuli*

creeper – trainee assistant on tea or rubber estate pre-WWI (orig. Ceylon)

cumshaw – tip, gift (CC & SS der. Mandarin *kan sieh* – thanks)

D

dato – title conferred by sultan meaning elder, grandfather (M), also *datuk*

dayang – honorific, madam (M – 'girl')

dhobi – washerman (Hind. SS)

DO – District Officer, known as Assistant Adviser in UMS

Dog – *see* Spotted Dog

durai – sahib, gentleman (Tamil)

Dutch wife – wickerwork bolster used to keep cool in bed (orig. Dutch E. Indies)

E

Eastern Cadet – junior civil administrator recruited to the Eastern Cadetships, comprising Ceylon, Hong Kong and Malaya

engkerumong – set of small gongs making a scale (Sarawak)

F

FMS – Federated Malay States, comprising Perak, Selangor, Negri Sembilan and Pahang

G

gaji – wages (M)

gamelan – wooden percussion instruments from Sumatra and Java

gin-sling – John Collins or gin and lime cocktail topped up with liqueurs (not to be confused with Singapore sling, made with whisky)

godown – warehouse (der. M *gudang*)

H
haji – honorific; one who has made the *haj* or pilgrimage to Mecca (Arab.)

haram – forbidden by Islamic law (Arab.)

Hari Raya Puasa – Islamic festival celebrating the breaking of the fast of Ramadan in July

hong – house of business, thus firm (Cantonese cc & ss)

I
Istana – palace, (sometimes *astana*) (poss. der. Arab.)

J
jaga – watchman, usually Sikh (m *jaga* – to watch)

jamban – commode (m) or thunderbox

jinriksha – rickshaw (Japanese)

joss – idol, luck (pidgin der. Port. *deos* – god), thus joss-house – Chinese temple; joss-stick – incense (cc & ss)

K
kampong – area of cleared land, thus village settlement (m)

kangani – foreman of estate labour (Tamil)

kapitan China – head of Chinese Community (der. Port.)

kathi – Islamic judge (Arab.)

kebaya – woman's jacket (m)

kebun – estate (m), incorrectly used by Europeans for gardener – *see tukang kebun*

kedai – shop (m)

Kempeitai Japanese Secret Police

kemudi – helmsman or Malay captain (der. m – *kemudi* – oar, rudder)

keramat – spirit, sorcerer (Arab.) thus *keramat*-tiger – tiger infested by spirit of sorcerer

kerani – clerk, usually Indian (der. Hind. *kirani*)

kling – man from Kalinga, thus term for South Indians in S.E. Asia, now regarded as offensive

koi hais – Anglo-Indian term for old India hands

kongsi – coolie lines, part. Chinese tin-mines (der. Mandarin *kong hsi* – company)

kota – fort (m), thus Kota Bharu

kris – Malay wavy-bladed dagger

kuala – river mouth (m), thus Kuala Lumpur – muddy estuary

L
lalang – coarse tropical grass (m)

lampu – lamp (Port.)

landas – rainy season, n.e. monsoon (Iban)

lascar – Indian or Malay deckhand (Port. corruption der. Persian *lascari* – soldier)

lie-off – afternoon siesta

M

makan – eat (M), thus dinner; *makan kechil* – canapes served before meal ('small eats'); *makan angin* – evening promenade ('eating the air'); *makan suap* – take a bribe ('eat a bribe')

mak yong – Malay court entertainment combining dance, opera and drama

mandor – overseer of labour (Port. *mandador* – one who commands), thus mandarin

mata-mata – police (M – *mata* – eye), also known as *orang-mata*

MCS – Malayan Civil Service

mem – honorific, European woman (der. Anglo-Indian *memsahib*)

menora – dance drama of Kelantan State

merdeka – freedom (M), thus Independence

minim the – tea money (M), thus small bribe or sweetener

missie – European girl (SS), European woman (CC)

monsoon – seasonal winds blowing n.e. across South China Sea November-February and s.w. May-September (der. Arab. *maussim* – season)

munshi – language teacher, interpreter (Arab.), also known as *guru*

N

narlikis – Tamil labour, derogatory term from *narlaki* – tomorrow

negri – state (M), thus Negri Sembilan – nine states (see FMS)

nyai – concubine (Bali M 'younger sister', Sarawak)

O

orang – people (M), thus *Orang Asli* – original people, aboriginals of Malayan peninsular; *orang mata* – eye people, policemen; *orang puteh* – white people; *orang utan* – forest people, thus ape

P

padang – open land (M), thus playing field or parade ground, also known as *medan*

padi – growing rice (M)

pahit – bitter (M), thus gin and bitters; *pahits* – cocktails

parang – machete (M)

pasar – bazaar or market (Hind.) but also used to describe township

pawang – medicine man, spirit medium (M)

penghulu – parish headman (M), leader of up-river area

peon – office messenger (Port. footman), also known as *tambi* (M)

prahu – Malay boat

pulau – island (M), thus Pulau Tioman

punkah – fan, originally suspended from ceiling and pulled by hand (Hind.)

PWD – Public Works Department, thus 'PWD tree' – kapok tree, said to have been designed and built by PWD engineer

R

Ramadan – Islamic month of fasting, known in Malaya as Pusa (fasting)

Resident – senior British administrator in FMS, Malay Settlement or Sara-

wak division; thus Residency. In Penang and Malacca known as Resident Councillor, later Resident Commissioner
ronggeng – Malay dance originating from Malacca
rattan – rotan cane or creeper (M)
rumah – house (M)

S

sampan – small boat (Chinese *san-pan* – three boards)
sapei – two-stringed guitar (Sarawak)
sarong – covering (M), thus wraparound skirt worn by Malay men and women
selamat – peace (Arab.), thus greeting
selat – Strait
Shanghai jar – water container in bathroom, also known as Siam jar, *tong* or Suchow tub
shroff – Indian or Chinese accountant (Arab.), thus shroffage – commission; also used as verb as in 'to shroff an account' (CC & SS)
siammang – large gibbon (M)
sola topee – sun helmet, trad. made from *sola* pith, often incorrectly written 'soler'
songkok – black Malay cap
Spotted Dog – Selangor Club in Kuala Lumpur, also known as the 'Dog'
squeeze – inducement, customary bribe (CC & SS)
stengah – half measure of whisky (corr. M *sa'tengah* – one half), sometimes wrongly pronounced 'stinger'; also derog. term for Eurasian
Straits Settlements – British administered colonial territories of Penang Island and Province Wellesley, Malacca and Singapore – and including at different periods the *Dindings* (protected areas) or Perah, Labuan, Christmas Island and Cocos Keeling
sudoh mati – dead, colloquial Anglo-Malay
Sumatra – sudden squall blowing across Straits of Malacca from Sumatra
sungei – river (M), thus Sungei Siput
syce – groom, thus chauffeur (Arab. from India)

T

taipan – European head of a *hong* (CC & Singapore)
tapper – rubber estate worker who taps rubber trees
tindal – foreman of labour, boatswain in charge of *lascars* (der. Malaya *tandu valli* – oarsman)
topee – hat (Hind.), see *sola topee*
tuak – rice wine, toddy (M)
tuan – honorific, sir (der. *tuanku* – prince), for men of rank, thus Europeans; *tuan besar* – great gentleman, boss of firm; *tuan kechhi* – small gentleman, European Junior; also *tuan kampani* – Malay term for Honourable East India Company, later used to denote crown rule (SS)
tukang – craftsman (M), thus *tukang ayer* – water-carrier, scullion, often written *tukan; tukang kebun* – estate craftsman, thus gardener, usually known simply as *kebun*

tutup – closed (M), thus *tutup* jacket – jacket buttoned up to the neck

typhoon – cyclonic tempest (orig. disputed, deriving either from Arab. *tufan* – wind-storm, or Chinese *tai-fong* – great wind)

U

ulu – headwaters of river (M), thus up-river region; *see penghulu*

unofficial – European other than government official

UMS – Unfederated Malay States, comprising Kelantan, Treugganu, Kedah, Perlis and Johore

V

veranda – open-pillared gallery round house (orig. disputed but probably Port. *verandas* – balcony)

W

wa-wa – small gibbon also known to Malays as *unka* (both words being onomatopoeic)

wayang – drama on stage (M), thus *wayang kulit* – shadow play with puppets